HOW THEY STARTED

How 25 ***good ideas*** *became* ***great companies***

Carol Tice & David Lester

crimson

How They Started

This first edition published by Crimson Publishing Ltd

ISBN 978 1 78059 074 5

Typeset by Mac Style, Nafferton, East Yorkshire
Printed and bound in the United States of America by Sheridan Books Inc, Michigan

Contents

Acknowledgements

We must first thank all the founders of the businesses featured who consented to give detailed, frank and insightful interviews about the very earliest days of their companies. Many revealed stories and information that have not been shared publicly before.

Many early-stage investors in these brands, founding team members, and other associates of the founders were also generous in sharing their memories and knowledge of the fledgling brands we feature in this book.

And we must also thank the companies, many of which are no longer run or owned by the original founders. These businesses, in numerous cases, provided additional supporting information and photography that they have kindly agreed to let us use here.

Finally, it is appropriate to thank those at Crimson Publishing, who have spent a considerable amount of time putting this book together.

Carol Tice, as co-author, has been instrumental in securing exclusive interviews and personally authored 11 chapters herself. Her dedication, resourcefulness and writing ability have ensured that the stories told here are unique and of the highest quality. But, as she says, "My biggest thanks go to my husband Larry ... without you, nothing gets written."

Introduction

Most of us have come across an idea we think would make an awesome business. That sixth sense, this-is-special moment when you're standing in a place that's crying out for a new restaurant/bar/whatever. Or you get that feeling of boiling frustration with a product or experience and think "this should be so much better." Truth is, most of us don't act on those would-be killer thoughts.

This book is about the people who did. It tells the remarkable stories of people who had innovative ideas and built them into some of the hottest businesses on the planet. From afar, the scorching success these companies have had makes it look easy. It's not. The stories themselves are as compelling as most novels, with more twists and turns than most founders would have anticipated. It's probably better they didn't know what lay ahead, or they might never have started at all.

We decided to write this book to look much more deeply into why and how some of America's most successful companies got started. It seems much harder to set something up from nothing than to take something that's working and grow it. And we've found it even more fascinating than we'd expected.

How we selected the companies featured

Of all the many stand-out companies, how did we come up with this list? We started with the idea that we wanted to write about companies most people knew about. That way, the stories are more real, and also more enjoyable.

We knew we wanted a variety—some of America's established corporate giants as well as plenty of more recent, fresh and disruptive startups, which will be more helpful to anyone currently starting up, or thinking about doing so. We also knew we wanted a selection of business types—for all the opportunities and great startups in technology, this nation is home to many young, game-changing companies in other sectors, too. And we wanted founders from a variety of cities and backgrounds. Finally, we wanted entertaining stories—and we weren't disappointed.

We hope that after reading this book, many of you will feel more confident about acting on an idea you might have to start or expand a small business. That's part of the job we hope this book does.

But some of you will also be struck by how hard it can be to build a business to that level. And how risky. If some of you finish this book and decide that starting up might not be for you after all, then we will still have accomplished something worthwhile.

We don't believe everyone should start a business. We are often asked what it takes to start a company and make it a success. Part of what it takes is the resilience and commitment to get through the hard times that almost every startup will face along the way. Not everyone has that.

What else does it take? The stories here give us the same answer as the hundreds of other entrepreneurs we have interviewed or gotten to know. Mainly, it takes an innovative idea, passion and commitment. With enough of that, everything else should follow. The other essential qualities include a willingness to work unbelievably hard, getting at least comfortable with simple business finances, and the ability and determination to focus.

What about luck? "Be lucky." "Good luck." We use phrases like this all the time. How important is luck to a startup? You will surely make your own mind up as you read the chapters here. Our sense is that most entrepreneurs make their own luck. As the saying goes—the harder you work, the luckier you get. There are occasions when an entrepreneur gets lucky, but so long as you work hard and do the right things, at some stage "luck" is likely to happen to you, too. The people who appear luckiest are usually the ones who have looked around and seen an opportunity, and have worked their tails off to make it happen.

One surprising theme in the book is education and money—and in some cases, the lack of both. Sure, both help, but not having a college degree or wealthy parents is no longer a barrier to starting your own business. It's the American Dream—if you work real hard, you can still come from nothing, build a business of your own, and make it successful.

For over a hundred years, this country has spawned bold and ambitious companies which have led the world in many different sectors. And arguably, this has never been more true than now, with American entrepreneurs leading the world in many fields. And that is no coincidence.

America is a truly great country for a startup. The culture is unusually open to new ventures, which means it is cooler and more acceptable to start a business here than in probably any other country. There is much better access to financing than anywhere else, too—the business angel and venture capital communities are better developed and more open to startups. There are many top-notch business schools and unrivalled support—magazines, websites and blogs, books, and so on. And right now, America offers the biggest market in the world; all-accessible with a common language and robust infrastructure. Taken together, these are huge advantages. Against that, there is probably more competition here than any place else, too.

There has probably never been a better time to start a new business—there is more affordable technology lowering the barriers to entry, new digital opportunities everywhere and more help and resources to support entrepreneurs than ever before. Today, you can set up faster and cheaper than ever before, and access national and international markets straight away.

We hope that some of you will read this book and be so inspired you go on to build a great company—and feature in a new edition a few years from now. (Contact us via our website www.howtheystarted.com if you'd like to be considered.)

But more than anything else, we hope you enjoy reading this book as much as we enjoyed creating it.

David Lester (editor) and
Carol Tice (main author)

SPANX

Sara Blakely: putting her butt on the line

Founder: **Sara Blakely**	
Age of founder: **29**	
Background: **Fax machine sales, stand-up comedy**	
Founded in: **2000**	
Headquarters: **Atlanta, Georgia**	
Business type: **Men's and women's intimate apparel**	

In 1998, Sara Blakely was a 27-year-old, bubbly blonde aspiring lawyer whose day job was selling fax machines. Then one day, she didn't like how she looked in a pair of white pants.

Her handcrafted solution would revolutionize the stodgy women's shapewear category, which hadn't changed much since Playtex introduced its first rubber girdle in 1940. Sara's comfortable support undergarments were designed for real women's figures and marketed with a sassy attitude previously unheard of in women's lingerie. Launching her product in the strangely male-dominated women's underwear category would take two years and require scores of prototypes, a brazen shared bathroom visit, and a little help from a red backpack.

Flunking and faxes

Sara would later chalk it all up to failing the Law School Admission Test (LSAT). The Florida State University graduate had always wanted to be a lawyer like her father; however, her failing LSAT scores would ultimately point her in a different direction.

The Clearwater, Florida, native drove to Disney World in hopes of getting a job playing Goofy, but learned that at 5′6″ she was too short. She was offered the role of a chipmunk, but decided to forgo the hot costume for a job selling fax machines door-to-door instead.

Seven years later, she was at a convention for top-selling fax-machine sales reps. She recalls one motivational speaker at the event giving a speech on how there are no bad products. "I'll prove it in four words—Teenage Mutant Ninja Turtles!" he shouted. She would think of this speech again a few years later, when she got a product idea of her own.

Do these pants make my butt look big?

The trouble began with an expensive pair of chic, cream-colored pants Sara bought in 1998. They sat in her closet, seldom worn, because she felt they made her rear end look a bit lumpy. She had a nice pair of open-toed shoes they would work with, but hesitated to wear the outfit. She realized she probably needed some kind of support undergarment to give the pants a smooth line, but was certainly not about to wear a girdle.

"Traditional shapers were too thick and left lines and bulges, and underwear leaves a panty line," she says. "And thongs, I'll never get—they put the underwear exactly where we have always been trying to get it out of."

In a moment of inspiration, Sara took out a pair of scissors and cut the feet off a pair of her support pantyhose. Voila! Her pants looked great, and she still had the naked-foot look she wanted for the shoes. She went to a party in Atlanta's trendy Buckhead neighborhood that night, feeling fabulous. There was one problem—the cut-off bottoms of the pantyhose kept rolling up her legs all night. Sara thought if she could find a way to keep the legs from rolling up, she'd have a great product.

"Traditional shapers were too thick and left lines and bulges, and underwear leaves a panty line," she says. "And thongs, I'll never get ..."

Little did she know it would be a two-year sojourn from that "Ah-ha!" moment to getting a finished, packaged product ready for sale.

Learning the ropes

In her quest to become a successful inventor, Sara was armed with little but an engaging smile and a passionate belief that she had created something women would find supremely useful. She'd never taken a business class in college, had no experience in fashion merchandising and certainly had zero insight into hosiery manufacturing.

Knowing she'd need a manufacturer to create a prototype of her product, she began looking up hosiery mills in the phone book. She discovered the product-sourcing platform thomasnet.com, which listed all the manufacturers in the US. From there, she learned that there were a lot of hosiery manufacturers located fairly nearby in North Carolina. Over the course of about six months, Sara cold-called all the hosiery makers and asked if they would be interested in making her prototypes. Every single one said no.

Pressing on, Sara decided to prototype her garment herself while she continued seeking a manufacturer. She stocked up on sewing supplies at Michael's and other local craft and fabric stores and started sewing. Soon, she had a design that offered the control-top support of typical pantyhose but stopped just below the knee, assuring a smooth line down a woman's thigh.

Over the course of about six months, Sara cold-called all the hosiery makers and asked if they would be interested in making her prototypes. Every single one said no.

As she worked on her prototype, she decided she needed to patent her invention. She looked up three of the top law firms in Atlanta, and made appointments. For her presentations to the lawyers, she brought her product and printed materials in a very special container—her lucky red backpack from college.

To say the lawyers were not impressed with Sara's idea would be an understatement. One kept looking around the room while she pitched her product. He later confessed he found her idea so ridiculous that he suspected he was being filmed for a *Candid Camera*-type reality TV show.

All the lawyers quoted Sara upwards of $5,000 to handle her patent paperwork. Since $5,000 was the total savings she had in her bank account, that wasn't going to work. Instead, Sara headed to Barnes & Noble, got a book on how to write a patent application, and started drafting. She researched hosiery patents at night in the Georgia Tech library.

The pantyhose tour

Sara made a list of nearby hosiery and shapewear manufacturers and embarked on a road trip, once again bringing along her lucky red backpack. For several weeks, she drove around, meeting plant managers in person. They were invariably male.

The conversation followed a similar track at each stop. The plant owner would begin by asking, "And you are ... ?"

"Sara Blakely," she would reply.

"And you're with ... ?" they'd ask.

"Sara Blakely," she'd say, smiling wider.

"And you are financially backed by ... ?" they'd return.

Smiling even wider, Sara would say, "Sara Blakely."

At each stop, after this exchange, Sara was gently shown to the door.

"So nice to meet you," the owner would say. "Best of luck with your idea."

But the road trip wasn't a total loss. On plant tours, Sara learned a lot about how women's undergarments were made. She learned how various yarns could be combined to give a garment different characteristics.

Two things she saw on the tour would shape her company's approach to the business. First, she saw that to save money, most manufacturers utilized one average-sized elastic on all their products' sizes.

Second, she discovered that the manufacturers all used hard-plastic forms of women's bodies to test their garments. Now she knew why so many women's undergarments didn't fit well: small and large sizes didn't have the right-sized waistbands, and real women never tried on the products before they hit stores.

> Sara saw how to stand out in the market: her product would be customized to fit different sizes and be tested on real women.

"They'd put the underwear on the form," Sara recalls, "and then these men would stand back with their clipboards and say, 'Yep, that's a medium.'"

Immediately, Sara saw how to stand out in the market: her product would be customized to fit different sizes and be tested on real women.

Several weeks after Sara's road tour, she got a call from one manufacturer she'd visited in Charlotte, North Carolina. He informed her that he had decided to help her make her "crazy" product.

"What made you change your mind?" Sara inquired.

He responded with: "I have two daughters."

A name with "K" appeal

From the start, Sara knew she needed a fabulous, attention-getting name for her product. But it took more than a year to come up with one.

She wanted to incorporate a "K" sound. She knew two of the most recognizable brands were Kodak and Coca-Cola, and both had a strong "K" sound. Also, from stand-up comedy, she knew it was a trade secret that the "K" sound can make people laugh. Suddenly, driving through Atlanta traffic, the name hit her: she would call her sassy new undergarment Spanks.

"The word came to me, like it was written across the windshield of my car, and I pulled over to the side of the road and wrote it down," Sara says.

At the last minute, she changed the spelling to SPANX, as she knew it was difficult to trademark real words. The "X" gave her the "K" sound she wanted while forming a unique, new word and it signaled what the product did: help women make their butts look better.

Up to this point, Sara had not told anyone but lawyers and manufacturers about her invention. She didn't want to risk hearing any negative feedback about it.

"A great idea is most vulnerable at the moment you have it," she says. "Something just told me intuitively to keep it inside. I had a year under my belt before I said, 'OK everyone, it's footless pantyhose.' And of course they all looked at me like 'Are you crazy?' But if you're a user of your product and you know it works, then just stick with it, and find the people who will help you get it made."

Making shapers from lacquer

Heartened to have a manufacturer on board, Sara moved to complete her patent application. She recruited her artistic mother to make a sketch of her wearing the product to submit on the application. The final step was to decide what legal claims the product would make in its packaging and marketing.

For this touchy area, she went back to the *Candid Camera* lawyer and asked if he would help. He still didn't understand her idea, but he told her for $700 he was willing to spend a weekend on it. The attorney asked to speak to her manufacturer to get the garment's technical specifications.

The manufacturer was Southern with a deep accent. When the attorney asked what the garment was made of, he replied, "Cotton and lacquer." The attorney duly noted this and completed the application.

That night, Sara couldn't sleep. She planned to file her patent application the next day. She kept wondering: how was there lacquer in the product? The next day, she called the manufacturer back.

"Ted, can you spell lacquer for me?" she asked.

"Shore," he drawled. "L-y-c-r-a."

With the lacquer mystery solved, the application was quicky changed and sent on its way. For $300, Sara trademarked her name on the US Patent Office's website, and for $150 incorporated her business name.

Seeing red

The next step was to design the packaging for SPANX. Sara toured hosiery departments in big stores and noticed the department was a sea of beige and gray. Every package looked identical, down to the same photo of a half-naked model. She knew she wanted her packaging to have a completely different look, so that if she could land shelf space with a big retailer, SPANX would immediately stand out. Also, she had no money for advertising, so the package essentially would *be* the ad.

"I chose red, which was extremely unconventional," she recalls. "Then, I put on three cartoon-illustrated women who were very different-looking. No one had done that, either."

The original footless SPANX packaging.

She worked on her design nights and weekends for three months on a friend's computer, while working days at her fax-sales job. Her goal was to make the package look like a present a woman would buy for herself, rather than a commodity women dread buying. To write the package copy, she bought 10 different pairs of pantyhose and read the packages. Whatever language they had in common Sara concluded must be needed for legal reasons, so she added it to her package.

Her tagline proclaimed the brand's attitude: "Don't worry, we've got your butt covered." To gauge whether her sassy approach was offensive, she tested the packaging out on her mother and her boyfriend's mother.

"They laughed hysterically," she reports.

She knew she wanted her packaging to have a completely different look, so that if she could land shelf space with a big retailer, SPANX would immediately stand out.

She sent *The Oprah Winfrey Show* a gift basket with a few prototypes of SPANX in it. A long shot, but a girl can dream.

Putting her own butt on the line

In October 2000, with a product prototype and package ready to go, Sara thought big. Her first sales call was to her local Neiman Marcus store. Once they finished laughing, they instructed her to call the buying office in Dallas. She did.

Sara told the buyer, "I invented a product that's going to change the way women wear clothes, and if you will meet with me, I will fly there."

Incredibly, the buyer agreed. Sara took a Ziploc® sandwich bag from her kitchen, put a prototype inside it, and loaded it into her lucky red backpack. As she prepped for the trip, friends begged her to take a designer handbag. Surely, they thought, she wouldn't take her ratty old backpack to a meeting at temple-of-luxury Neiman Marcus ... her friends even prompted her to buy a Prada bag and return it later. But Sara was firm: the lucky red backpack was going. She also wore her cream-colored pants.

Sara modeling SPANX under cream-colored pants.

At Neiman Marcus, Sara found herself standing before the most impeccably dressed and groomed woman she'd ever seen. Even her pen was fabulous. Sara had brought a sample and a color copy of her packaging prototype. After about five minutes of pitching, Sara felt a growing panic. This is my shot, she thought. How could she make this woman understand how unique SPANX was? Suddenly, she knew.

"You need to come to the bathroom with me," Sara told the buyer. "I'm going to show you what my product can do."

She quickly did a before-and-after for the buyer, modeling the cream-coloured pants with and without SPANX on.

"She instantly got it," Sara says. "She said, 'Sara, this is brilliant, and I'm going to try it in seven of our stores.'"

Searching for new crotches

Floating on a cloud, Sara returned home to Atlanta and quit her fax-sales job. She called her manufacturer and exultantly shared the news of her first big order. Neimans wanted SPANX in stores in three weeks, granting the product a single display "pocket" in seven stores. The manufacturer was less excited than she expected: he had only two machines for making the crotch of the pantyhose, known in the trade as the gusset. And both of his machines were already in full use by another client.

The manufacturer confessed that he hadn't reserved any plant capacity for her; he assumed she planned to give away her initial run of SPANX as Christmas gifts for a few years, and that would be the end of it. If she was going to produce a large order quickly, Sara would have to get her gussets made somewhere else.

"I was like, 'Let me get this straight. I just landed Neiman Marcus, and I have no crotches?'" Sara recalls.

A frantic search began for another company that could fill her gusset order. The savior for her crotch emergency appeared in the form of seasoned apparel-maker Gene Bobo, who was then 80 years old. His factory, just down the road from Atlanta in Norcross, Georgia, would make her gussets from then on.

Creating word of mouth

When you have a brand-new product nobody knows about and limited funds, how do you create buzz around it? This was the question Sara now pondered. For the first year, she toured stores for sales trainings and public appearances, happily pulling up her pants legs to show customers her SPANX. She also called on dozens of media outlets, garnering media coverage for SPANX in fashion magazines and on talk shows.

With SPANX in stores in seven different cities, it was hard to be everywhere at once. Sara got out her rolodex and started calling anyone she knew in a town where SPANX were stocked. She developed a pitch that went like this: "Hi! Remember me, your friend from fourth grade? Can you go to the Neiman Marcus store and tell them you're looking for SPANX, and I'll send you a check? Great."

The gambit worked: SPANX was profitable from the first month, and topped $1 million in sales the first year. Sara celebrated the milestone by buying a flat-screen TV.

> "Hi! Remember me, your friend from fourth grade? Can you go to the Neiman Marcus store and tell them you're looking for SPANX, and I'll send you a check? Great."

Just as she was running out of both friends and money, Sara got the life-changing phone call that is every inventor's dream. In the vast ocean of products Oprah's show is sent each year, SPANX got noticed. Oprah had tried SPANX and loved them. It turned out Oprah had been cutting the bottoms off support pantyhose to wear them with pants and open-toed shoes for years.

Oprah planned to do a show naming SPANX one of her favorite products of 2000, and wanted to specifically highlight both Sara and her company.

The first orders shipped from Sara's apartment.

The Oprah team asked where the company was headquarted, and Sara answered, "my apartment."

She explained it was a two-person show with her boyfriend at the time. "When someone called and asked for the shipping department," Sara says, "my boyfriend would say, 'One moment please,' and then hand me the phone." She was spending nights packaging and shipping the product from two card tables. The Oprah team loved the story, and soon a 10-person film crew descended upon Sara's tiny Atlanta apartment to shoot a video of her operation. To create the Oprah video, Sara called friends over to sit with her on the living-room floor for a "staff meeting."

Building a team

After the show aired, interest in SPANX exploded. Other major department stores including Nordstrom wanted to stock the product. Movie stars wanted to wear it under their Oscar-night gowns. SPANX lasted 18 months operating out of the apartment before growing into an office in Decatur, Georgia, in 2001 and growing its staff up.

In hiring, Sara looked for people who were enthusiastic about the brand, then trained them for their roles. A friend of a friend heard she needed an assistant and came over to help. Two weeks later, Sara asked her to be the head of product development, a job she still holds today. Likewise, Sara once walked to a bagel shop with a woman who recognized her and raved about SPANX. Sara hired her to be head of public relations. A key hire in 2002 was former Coca-Cola executive Laurie Ann Goldman, who became SPANX's CEO. The staff numbered 11 by year end.

One rule Sara made was that everyone who works at SPANX wears the products. Even the men. Most of the company's new product ideas over the years would come from feedback from customers and staffers. This period saw the company add Control-Top Fishnets (the package proclaimed "No more grid butt!"), Power Panties and Mama SPANX Maternity Pantyhose. In 2003, SPANX outgrew that first headquarters and moved to more spacious quarters in Atlanta's Buckhead neighborhood.

Shocking the BBC

As word of SPANX spread, Sara planned a trip to pitch London department stores, including Harrods and Selfridges. As part of her trip, Sara managed to secure an interview with the BBC, but it didn't go quite as planned.

A staid male news anchor asked Sara, "Tell us what SPANX can do for women in the UK."

Sara began to explain, "It smoothes and separates your fanny ... " only to see all color drain from the anchorman's face. "Fanny" is actually slang for vagina in Britain. The trip wasn't off to a great start, but SPANX did manage to enter the UK market in 2003.

The company continued adding products, expanding beyond hosiery into intimates and apparel. All of its product names have the same cheeky attitude, from Bod-a-Bing! dresses to Skinny Britches lightweight shapers.

Where are they now?

Today, more than 200 styles of SPANX are sold online, through catalogs and in apparel chains including Bloomingdale's, Dillard's, Lane Bryant, Neiman Marcus, Nordstrom, Saks Fifth Avenue and the Sports Authority. From that single pocket of space in Neiman Marcus, SPANX now enjoys ample shelf space in many chains, including its own boutique inside New York's flagship Bloomingdales store on 59th Street.

In 2006, Sara started The Sara Blakely Foundation to provide help to young women entrepreneurs. The foundation donated $1 million to The Oprah Winfrey Leadership Academy Foundation in South Africa the following year.

SPANX has continued to innovate and create new product lines, expanding into bras and swimwear. In 2008, SPANX introduced Bra-llelujah, a back-fat-concealing bra which Sara now calls her favorite product. The next year, a lower-priced line, ASSETS by Sara Blakely, was created and sold into Target stores, making SPANX shapewear more affordable to more women everywhere. Next came the high-fashion Haute Contour line, and in 2010 SPANX leveled the playing field and introduced SPANX for Men, a line of support T-shirts and cotton comfortable underwear. In the summer of 2011, SPANX also introduced its first line of active apparel. What's next for SPANX? Sara concluded, "If I can invent a comfy stiletto, then I will retire!"

Electronic Arts

Winning the game

Founder: **Trip Hawkins**	
Age of founder: **28**	
Background: **MBA and former Apple Computer executive**	
Founded in: **1982**	
Headquarters: **Redwood City, California (originally San Mateo, California)**	
Business type: **Multi-platform games**	

N**ot many entrepreneurs spend 11 years planning** their business's start. But from his first foray into business at age 17, Trip Hawkins knew he wanted to start one. He just didn't know what it would do. Then, in 1971, he got a glimpse of an early prototype microcomputer at a friend's house, and an idea began to take shape. In the future, he realized, home computers would be commonplace.

From that initial flash of insight, the biggest company in digital gaming would arise. Trip knew it would take time for home computers to catch on, but he began laying a course that would position him to profit from the coming electronic age.

He chose a date for his business launch: 1982. Just as planned, Trip did start a home-based, one-man business that year. That company became Electronic Arts, which now employs 7,600 and raked in a $677 million profit in 2010. How did it happen? Trip puts it down to a couple of personality traits: persistence and fearlessness.

"I was feeling completely sure of myself and totally confident about what my plans were, and pretty bulletproof," Trip recalls.

The very first game

Trip's interest in games began in childhood—and so did his interest in business. While still a teenage student at Harvard University, he borrowed $5,000 from his father to create a board game centered on his love of sports, AccuStat Football. The money allowed Trip to create several hundred copies of the tabletop game.

The game was loved by players but was a commercial failure, teaching Trip indelible business lessons that would shape his future plans.

"It was a thorough business experience for me, as I had to design, manufacture, have a marketing plan, and even assemble the product," Trip recalls. "It helped me realize I was going to be an entrepreneur, but I was also disappointed that I failed. It made me a lot more careful and thoughtful before I started EA."

At Harvard, Trip graduated *magna cum laude* with a self-designed major in strategy and applied game theory, then added a Stanford MBA in 1978. Trip chose his first employer, Apple Computer, deliberately. He had seen the Apple II debut at a computer fair the year before, and wanted to work for a home-computer company.

The Jobs years

In Steve Jobs, Trip found a mentor who would greatly shape his outlook. It was early days at Apple: the company based in Cupertino, California, had just 50 employees when Trip joined.

Trip's responsibilities at Apple grew over his four-year tenure, but he never lost sight of his primary goal: to acquire business savvy and watch for personal computers (PCs) to become more popular and powerful. From Jobs, he'd learned to think of himself as creative and unstoppable.

The time was growing ripe for his startup. One gaming company, Brøderbund, debuted in 1980. Trip heard from one investor who was interested in funding a game startup. He worried he was getting behind the curve.

In Steve Jobs, Trip found a mentor who would greatly shape his outlook. ... From Jobs, he'd learned to think of himself as creative and unstoppable.

His dream of starting a company had crystallized into what Trip thought of as his "big idea." Most software companies, he'd realized, treated developers like serfs instead of fostering their creativity. He wanted to start a game company that would operate like a music label.

"By this time, I had experience working with prima donna software development geniuses and realized these are really creative people," he recalls. "I began to realize I could work with them as independent artists, and treat them as artists."

Enter the crocodile

At just this time, Trip read in an airline magazine about venture capitalist Don Valentine of Capital Management (which would soon become legendary Silicon Valley firm Sequoia Capital). The article related that Valentine was so intimidating that one young entrepreneur actually fainted in his office during a pitch. His management style was likened to that of a crocodile, lying in wait and listening and then rearing up to rip everyone's ideas apart.

While this might have cued most would-be business owners to pitch someone else, the article prompted Trip to call Valentine and ask for a meeting. He admired Valentine's attitude and thought he could get frank advice from him, which was exactly what Trip wanted. He wasn't afraid of Valentine's bite.

Knowing Trip's track record at Apple, Valentine readily agreed to a meeting, and Trip arrived at the Sand Hill Road office with some trepidation. He had no written business plan yet for the company he had christened Amazin' Software, and Apple was gearing up to launch the Lisa computer. He thought Valentine would urge him to fulfill his commitments at Apple and finish his launch work. But that wasn't Valentine's opinion at all.

"He said I should quit Apple right away," Trip says. "He offered me free office space, which is like saying, 'If you pull this together, I'll want to fund it.' It was the encouragement I needed to take the final step."

Amazin' software in the hall

Trip quickly wrapped up his work and left Apple in April 1982. Before taking Valentine up on his offer of free office space, Trip spent several months working out of his house, refining the business plan. He incorporated the company in May 1982 and funded it initially with $200,000 of his own Apple stock profits.

During this time, Trip worked on learning about the music-industry business model he planned to emulate. He flew to Los Angeles after a venture contact introduced him to legendary A&M Records co-founder Jerry Moss. Trip also spoke with a music-industry lawyer and got a copy of a recording contract to learn how to structure contracts for his software "artists."

While still working from home, Trip made his first few hires. The first was experienced PR man Richard Melmon, whom Trip knew from a stint at Apple. Melmon left his job at VisiCorp, maker of early spreadsheet product VisiCalc, to join the nascent company.

"He was by far the most important and highest-ranking guy I hired that year," Trip recalls. "I hired him because I felt I should have someone older than me around to provide a little adult supervision."

Melmon and Trip would turn out to clash, and their versions of events differ—Melmon's biography suggests that he, not Trip, raised the funding money for EA, for instance. In any case, Melmon would end up departing EA after just a few years.

> The budding company quickly outgrew its one small room in the back of Valentine's office suite, with some staff camped at card tables in the hallway.

From Apple, Trip drew product manager Dave Evans, gaming fan Joe Ybarra, and one of the rare women in tech at the time, Pat Marriott. The trio would be Amazin' "producers," working with talented game designers to create products and bring them to market.

The team was rounded out by an office manager, Stephanie Barrett. In August, the small troupe took up residence in Valentine's Sand Hill Road offices. The budding company quickly outgrew its one small room in the back of Valentine's office suite, with some staff camped at card tables in the hallway.

Playing hardball

Trip kept paying the bills: for payroll, equipment, and software development in-house, as well as fees to outside software "artists." He had the resources to keep going in this fashion for another year or so but felt he needed to bring in investors to tap their business expertise and accelerate the company's growth.

Several investors were interested, but Trip zeroed in on those he wanted on board, starting with Valentine, and Ben Rosen from Sevin Rosen Funds, whom he knew from Apple. Others came knocking: Trip recalls picking up the phone at his home in the Portola Valley to find future legend John Doerr, who was then new to Silicon Valley venture capital firm Kleiner Perkins Caufield & Byers.

As he wasn't desperate for the cash, yet, Trip was feeling cocky. Thinking that Valentine wanted too rich a deal, Trip played the venture capitalists off against each other to get a better valuation for his company, lowering the percentage of Amazin' the venture capitalists' money would buy. In the end, he raised $2 million in the first round at the end of 1982, half from Valentine, with the other half split between Sevin and Kleiner.

Amazin' moved to a small office in Burlingame, California, in October 1982. During the company's short stay there, Trip continued hiring, luring Stanford pal William Bingham ("Bing") Gordon. Other early hires were Tim Mott, David Maynard, and Steve Hayes, all from Xerox PARC. Shortly, Amazin' moved to more spacious quarters in San Mateo, California, where the company would remain for more than a decade.

Becoming Electronic Arts

Around the time of the move from Valentine's office, the newly hired team began to agitate for a new company name. Some team members disliked the Amazin' moniker. In one early business plan, Trip had used the name SoftArt as an amalgam to convey both software and artistry. But both Trip and Melmon knew Dan Bricklin, founder of VisiCalc maker Software Arts, and thought it best to avoid such a similar name.

Trip wanted to include the word "Electronic," and suggested it might be called Electronic Artists, in part as a tribute to independent movie studio United Artists, whose model of artist-driven production he sought to emulate. But Hayes reportedly objected, saying that the developers were the artists rather than the staff. Finally, the team settled on Electronic Arts as the new name.

Bad timing

Despite all of Trip's years of planning for his launch, the newly renamed company's timing turned out to be a bit off. The technology needed to play truly full-featured electronic games had arrived, but had not yet been widely adopted by consumers. The dominant game system at the time was an 8-bit Atari console, which offered a puny amount of memory.

Trip knew from the start he didn't want to create games for the Atari. While waiting for the game-console industry to mature, the company would focus on creating games for PCs. This posed its own challenges as the most popular PC of the time, the Commodore 64, did not yet come with an external disk drive. One would be added in late 1983, but at an extra charge that would discourage many home users.

To counter this problem, Trip devised a workaround that ended up being used in Europe for the company's first game releases: the games were converted to audio signals on a tape cassette. With the help of an A/B adapter cord, the data could then be input to the computer to play the game.

In 1982, EA's producers had released their first games for the Apple II–*Hard Hat Mack* and *Axis Assassin*–as well as a few games for the hated Atari 800 console–*Pinball Construction Set, Archon, M.U.L.E.*, and *Worms?*. In keeping with Trip's record-artist philosophy, each game was packaged like a record album with an eye-catching, graphical cover. This immediately set EA's products apart from competitors, whose packaging was less slick-looking.

Rather than signing a distribution deal with an established company or competitor to get the games into stores, Trip and the entire team set out to meet thousands of mom-and-pop computer store owners to sell them, one by one. It was hugely time-consuming, but paid off in new relationships–and a distribution scheme in which there was no middleman distributor and EA kept more of the profits. Of the first group of games, *Archon* and *Pinball Construction Set* emerged as the big sellers.

A key game was released in 1984 that would set the course for much of EA's future success. The basketball-themed *Dr. J and Larry Bird Go One on One* took Trip's record-artist theory one step further, leveraging the name recognition of the two sports stars to sell games. Fans loved the chance to essentially *be* one of their sports idols, and the game went on to be EA's best-selling release for the Apple II.

In keeping with Trip's record-artist philosophy, each game was packaged like a record album with an eye-catching, graphical cover. This immediately set EA's products apart from competitors.

During the scramble of the first few years, Valentine fulfilled Trip's expectations, offering universally critical feedback and never making a positive comment. In July 1984, he sent Trip an EA budget with two numbers circled: burn rate and cash reserves. "Two months left!" it said. But Trip knew sales of *Dr. J* were going to avert a financial crisis.

Trip quickly learned that while he was envisioning the game designers as the prime selling point, gamers were loyal to the game, not the designer, a revelation that would shift the company's marketing focus for good. Sales that first year were $5 million–the company was off and running.

Just six months after the first venture capital round, Trip went back and raised $3 million more in investor funding, mostly from the same investors, plus A&M's Moss. For the second round, with a few products out and several of them shaping up as solid sellers, Trip was able to obtain the funds at a company valuation four times greater than on the first round.

The desert years

As the company was releasing its first games, the hope was that soon game consoles would become a viable platform for EA's games, too. But instead, the game-console industry collapsed. Atari's system was dated and the company had failed to plan ahead to release a new, more robust version. Consumers lost interest, causing retailers to stop stocking the games and suspect electronic games might be just a fad.

Trip remembers the next few years as a time of serious hunkering down. He imagined his team as the Fremen of Frank Herbert's classic sci-fi novel *Dune*, recycling their own sweat to survive the desert. The company scored successes with more celebrity-driven games, including *Jordan vs. Bird: One on One* and *Earl Weaver Baseball.*

By concentrating on games for computers and releasing popular titles, the company was able to bring in $11 million in sales in the company's fiscal year ending March 1985. EA began to turn a profit in fall 1984.

"We were profitable," he recalls, "but we had to be disciplined about how much we spent. We made sure we didn't overstep our bounds."

In 1988, Trip decided to try international expansion as a means to grow during the gaming-industry doldrums. The company acquired game-creation houses in Australia and France, opened an office in Japan, and in general overspent. Trip remembers the international foray as a "misadventure" from which the company beat a hasty retreat.

Trip remembers the next few years as a time of serious hunkering down. He imagined his team as the Fremen of Frank Herbert's classic sci-fi novel Dune, recycling their own sweat to survive the desert.

Breakout success

Fortunately, 1988 also saw the release of a game that would prove to be one of the company's biggest franchises. Originally called *John Madden Football* and later *Madden NFL*, the game would go on to release annual versions and sell 85 million copies through 2010. *Madden* would be joined in 1993 by another major sports franchise, *FIFA*. Together, the brands would drive the success of EA Sports, one of the company's biggest niche brands.

On the heels of the Madden success, EA went public in September 1989, netting $8 million for the company and more for its investors. The IPO (initial public offering) gave EA a valuation of $84 million. Sales that year were $63.5 million, and profits were $4 million.

Getting Sega on board

As EA was enjoying its successful IPO, a glimmer of hope appeared on the game-console horizon. Nintendo had a successful 8-bit game machine over the previous few years which, like the Atari before it, EA mostly ignored. But now, the more robust, 16-bit Sega Genesis console was coming to America. Trip was determined to turn it into a gold mine.

There was a major problem, though: it wasn't known exactly what machine Sega would bring to the States. EA designers obtained a Japanese Sega console, in hopes the US machine would be identical. One big fear was that for the US market, Sega might implement a security "chip" on its games, a feature Nintendo employed.

In analyzing the Sega machine, EA's software designers found it used the identical 16-bit microprocessor the team was familiar with from its Sun workstations, as well as Apple's Lisa and later models. Taking the gamble that a security chip wouldn't be introduced and torpedo the effort, EA moved forward to reverse-engineer game designs for Sega's console based on the team's knowledge of the microprocessor.

While this was in process, Trip also actively contacted other software design studios to offer EA's help in creating games without Sega's official blessing. At the same time, Sega was calling on Trip to negotiate a license agreement. But Trip didn't want to pay through the nose for the right to be an official Sega licensee. He put the word out that EA would release its games with or without a license agreement with Sega.

"I was rope-a-doping them," Trip recalls, "being really polite, pretending to show some interest–then telling them what I didn't like about their agreement."

The situation came to a head as May 1990 loomed. EA planned to unveil its Sega games at the Consumer Electronics Show that month. Sega caught wind that EA was setting itself up as an alternate channel for dozens of other Sega game producers. This idea terrified the Japanese firm, and then-chairman David Rosen was deployed to get Trip in line.

"Rosen read me the riot act and told me there'd be a big scandal and a lawsuit if we released the games without a license," Trip says. "But they were much more willing to make a deal than I realized, because they wanted this problem to go away."

On the eve of CES, a favorable licensing agreement was finally hammered out after a round-the-clock negotiation session between Trip and Sega's attorney. Instead of paying the $8 per unit Sega wanted, EA would pay just 40 cents. The deal would be a bonanza for both sides–EA's games helped bolster Sega's market share in the US, and the alliance gave EA a huge market for product at a low fee.

Whereas Nintendo didn't allow any one producer to release more than five games a year, EA was able to introduce 40 games for Sega in the next two years, skyrocketing the company's revenue. Another 23 games would come from independent studios affiliated with EA. Nintendo introduced a 16-bit machine the following year to compete with Sega, and allowed developers to adapt existing games for the new system, opening up another major revenue channel for EA. By the end of 1993, EA's market capitalization soared to $2 billion.

Where are they now?

In 1991, Trip left EA to start a new gaming company, 3DO, but the effort failed. In 2003, Trip founded another multi-platform gaming company, Digital Chocolate, where he is CEO today. The 400-employee company had more than $30 million in 2010 revenue. Its hit games include Millionaire City. *The company has had its games downloaded onto mobile devices more than 100 million times, and its online computer games have seen more than 100 million sessions.*

EA would continue to dominate its industry for two decades, the only gaming company to enjoy such an unbroken streak of success. The company would go on to introduce many more wildly popular games, including Need for Speed *in 1994, and* The Sims *in 2002, which captivated female gamers and spawned many sequels. The company also grew through many acquisitions, including the 2011 purchase of online-game hit studio PopCap Games for $750 million.*

Toward the end of 2011, EA's history of linking with well-known celebrities and brands continued with the planned launch of Star Wars: The Old Republic, *a MMOG (massively multiplayer online game) in which players engage in battles on planets featured in the Star Wars movies.*

Pixar

Doing the impossible

Founders:	**Ed Catmull, John Lasseter and Steve Jobs**
Age of founders:	**41, 29 and 30**
Background:	**Computer graphics PhD, Disney animator and Apple computer founder**
Founded in:	**1986**
Headquarters:	**Emeryville, California**
Business type:	**Computer-animated motion pictures**

At first glance, Pixar seems an almost magically successful company. It's cranked out an unprecedented, unbroken string of hit animated movies: *Toy Story, A Bug's Life, Toy Story 2, Monsters Inc., Finding Nemo, The Incredibles, Cars* and many more. It's hard to imagine, but the company that is now Hollywood's most reliable mega-hit factory faced a grueling, 10-year climb to success.

Pixar's founders faced a daunting obstacle: when the company started, their dream—to create a full-length, animated feature entirely on the computer—was simply impossible. *The technology did not yet exist.* It took a few strokes of luck, a very generous benefactor, and the combined talents of two of the founders to keep the company alive and to build the technology needed to make the first computer-animated film.

Computer graphics meet animation

Pixar grew out of a division of *Star Wars* creator George Lucas's Lucasfilm production company. An early employee of the Computer Division was Ed Catmull, a computer graphics enthusiast and 1974 PhD graduate of New York Institute of Technology, then the cutting-edge hotbed for advances in the field. Ed was excited by computer graphics' potential for use in animation.

In the early 1980s, the Division worked on solving some of the technical challenges of animating objects on the computer, such as eliminating the jagged edges of computer-mapped objects, making realistic shadows, and creating lifelike "motion blur" as objects passed across the screen. There were hardware problems, too, as computers didn't yet have the power and speed required to quickly process or "render" images. The Division developed useful tools for conquering these problems, including the software Renderman, which quickly became the industry standard.

Ed was looking for an animator who would bring the new tools to life. At the same time, a Disney animator was looking for a more visionary company where he could explore computer animation.

John Lasseter had wanted to be a Disney animator from childhood, and studied under the studio's top animators at California Institute of the Arts, where he won two student Academy Awards®. He was quickly hired by Disney and worked on films including *The Fox and the Hound*, but was frustrated in his efforts to sell the tradition-bound studio on the merits of three-dimensional computer animation. Minutes after pitching then-studio head Ron Miller his idea for a 3-D animated version of the popular children's book *The Brave Little Toaster*, John was fired.

While John was devastated, this was great news to Ed, who had seen John's short-film work at computer graphics conferences. The two ran into each other at a conference aboard the *Queen Mary* in Long Beach, California, and Ed immediately asked John to do a freelance project for Lucasfilm. By 1984 John was working full-time for the Division.

Ed was looking for an animator who would bring the new tools to life. At the same time, a Disney animator was looking for a more visionary company where he could explore computer animation.

At first, John found Lucasfilm an intimidating place. "I mean, there I was, surrounded by all these PhDs who had basically invented computer animation," John relates in *To Infinity and Beyond! The Story of Pixar Animation Studios*. "But then I realized they couldn't bring a character to life with personality and emotion through pure movement like I could."

Though the animators in the Division were considered a sideline to the main hardware and software teams and were installed in offices down a back hallway, they were kept on because their work helped demonstrate the Division's tools to other animators. At 1984's SIGGRAPH computer graphics conference, John made a splash with his first work for Lucasfilm, a one-minute computer-animated short featuring a bumblebee, *Andre and Wally B.* The work was made possible by a new high-speed computer the Division had developed that was designed for computer animation and offered more rendering speed.

With the computer's creation, the need for a name arose. In a move emblematic of the company culture Pixar would develop, the name chosen was a collaboration. Division co-head Alvy Ray Smith, who'd grown up in New Mexico and learned Spanish infinitive verbs often end in "-er," suggested "Pixer," as a cool way of saying "pixel-maker." Others countered that an "-ar" ending would sound more high-tech, and so it became the Pixar Image Computer. The name would soon serve as the company's moniker as well.

Time to go

While the Division had some small success selling the Pixar computer to customers such as movie studios and medical-imaging firms, it faced an uncertain future. Two of its best products, EditDroid and SoundDroid, which broke ground in editing film and sound had been spun off and were no longer generating income for the Division.

A tense two years followed the SIGGRAPH success, in which the Division faced repeated threats of shutdown. Ed fended off many attempts by Lucasfilm to fire key employees. He sensed it was important to keep together the brain trust he'd built.

But George Lucas was growing increasingly uninterested in overseeing a technology company where the technology was still far from commercially viable. He sensed a large capital investment would be needed for the Division's leaders to achieve their ultimate goals. He also didn't want to run a hardware company. Lucas wanted to sell.

Ed fended off many attempts by Lucasfilm to fire key employees. He sensed it was important to keep together the brain trust he'd built.

Alvy and Ed realized they needed to learn how to run the Division as a stand-alone business. The pair headed off to a local bookstore, purchased a "how to start a business" book, and wrote a business plan for Pixar, envisioning a 40-person company. Now, all they needed was an investor willing to pay Lucasfilm's asking price: $15 million plus another $15 million in funding for the new company.

Enter Steve Jobs

Time dragged on, and no buyer was materializing to buy Pixar. There was one bright spot, though: Apple Computer employee Alan Kay, who had attended the University of Utah with Ed, heard about the Division's sale. He thought his boss, tech-wunderkind Steve Jobs, might find Pixar interesting.

Steve did. Apple was known for its groundbreaking 2-D computer graphics. Initially, Steve envisioned that Apple would buy Pixar and apply the team's talents to improving computer graphics. Smith and Ed declined the offer, as they wanted to continue toward their goal of using computer graphics for animated film. Turning down an apparent savior for their financial woes was a controversial move amongst Division staff that "nearly tore us apart," Ed recalled.

As it turned out, Steve was in a power struggle with then-Apple CEO John Sculley over low sales of the first Macintosh computer—a struggle he would ultimately lose. After Steve got the ax in spring 1985, he reconsidered Pixar's goals. Seeing the animation work the team had done, Steve was converted to their mission of creating computer-animated films.

"I ended up buying into that dream both spiritually and financially," he recalled a bit ruefully in the documentary *The Pixar Story*.

He contacted Lucasfilm again, with a plan to spin Pixar out on its own. While Pixar hung by a thread at Lucasfilm, the negotiations dragged on, leaving the team to agonize over whether Pixar had a future. It took until February 1986 to hammer out the deal.

After Steve got the ax in spring 1985, he reconsidered Pixar's goals. Seeing the animation work the team had done, Steve was converted to their mission of creating computer-animated films.

With no other buyers on the horizon, Steve snapped up Pixar for a relative song: $5 million to Lucasfilm and another $5 million in guaranteed funding for the new company. At last, Pixar had won independence and fresh funding with which to drive toward its goal of creating feature films.

The long climb

Steve might have hesitated if he had known it would be nearly a decade from the day he inked the deal until Pixar would become financially self-sustaining.

If $5 million sounds like a lot of money, it went fast at the highly technology-reliant new film-production studio. Pixar needed to both hire top animators and break new technical ground to develop the ability to create a realistic-looking, feature-length film entirely on the computer. The team was soon scrambling for ways to bring in revenue.

From Lucasfilm's San Rafael, California, headquarters, Pixar moved to a complex in nearby Point Richmond. The building quickly acquired a look that was a cross between a college dorm and an acid trip. Animators each decorated their cubicles in themes to suit—one looked like a wooden clubhouse, another an opium den. Workers rode scooters and teeter-totters in the halls, and generally let creativity run free.

As at Lucasfilm, there was some success selling the Pixar computer, but the audience was limited. Pixar bundled the computer with software and sold it as CAPS: the Computer Animation Production System. Disney bought the system, which brought breakthrough effects to *Beauty and the Beast*, the first animated feature to be nominated for a regular Best Picture Academy Award®.

Pixar continued to grab attention for its breakthroughs. Its next was a computer-animated short film, *Luxo Jr.*, directed by John, in which an amazingly lifelike desk lamp and a smaller "child" lamp play with a ball. Computing power was so limited that a plain black backdrop was used for the short. Nonetheless, the film played to a standing ovation at SIGGRAPH, and playful Luxo would become the Pixar symbol.

This was great for Pixar's reputation, but still didn't pay many bills. Only 120 computers were sold by 1988, and Steve was applying pressure to make the company profitable. Budgets were repeatedly trimmed.

"He put us through a lot of pain," Alvy Ray Smith recalled. "But, at the same time, he was unwilling to let the company go bankrupt."

Going commercial

While Pixar continued to make successful short films, the company turned to a more lucrative art form to bring in more cash: TV commercials. The first ad, "Wake Up," was for Tropicana orange juice. The team became known for its skill in creating animated characters for commercials, including a boxing bottle of Listerine. John won a Clio award, the ad industry's Oscar®, for "Conga," an ad that featured gummy Life Savers candies dancing in a nightclub.

Recruited for the commercial-making effort were two animators who would later direct films for Pixar, Andrew Stanton and Pete Docter. When

Stanton arrived he had literally never touched a computer before. He was a quick study, and soon created a computer-animated Trident chewing-gum ad in which a spearmint-leaf singer sang at a cabaret piano.

Goodbye, hardware

The commercial side did well financially, but the huge cost of hardware and software development was crushing the company. The company had mushroomed to 140 employees. At the same time, the CAPS system needed ongoing support to maintain Pixar's good relations with Disney.

The studio was taking note of Pixar's progress, and after each short film John would get a call asking him to quit and come back to work for Disney. That John kept turning Disney down bolstered morale greatly at Pixar. Even though Pixar constantly teetered on the brink of financial collapse, John chose it over the security of the big studio.

When local hardware firm Vicom Systems offered to buy the Pixar Image Computer and CAPS system, Ed knew it was a major turning point. He felt strongly that the hardware-side costs would prove fatal to the company and that both sides of the business would fare better separately. The sale was made and Pixar shrank back to 50 employees, greatly lessening its overhead.

Most of Pixar's focus was on making short films and commercials. One of those shorts, *Tin Toy*, about a wind-up toy, triggered a fateful comment from Disney animator Joe Ranft, who had worked on *Beauty and the Beast*.

Seeing the film with John at a 1988 Dutch animation festival, John recalls Joe's enthusiasm for the concept: that toys could be alive. Joe thought many more stories could be told this way. And the wheels started to turn in John's head about doing just that–telling a new, bigger story about toys.

"I'll always be grateful to Joe for seeing the larger potential in *Tin Toy*," John says in *To Infinity*. "Who knows if I would have looked at it as a door to a bigger world if it hadn't been for him?"

Shortly afterward, Disney upped the ante with John. After a shareholder revolt, Disney's leadership changed and Walt Disney's nephew Roy Disney was now in charge. If the studio couldn't hire John back, Disney reasoned, they would partner with Pixar to produce a computer-animated film.

Steve served as Pixar's negotiator, hammering out a three-picture deal in 1991 with Disney chairman Jeffrey Katzenberg. Pixar would produce, while Disney would promote and distribute. The terms were less than stellar, but

Pixar had the machinery in place at last to make and distribute its first feature.

It would take four long years for that first picture to make it to the screen.

"It took us a long time to build the technical foundation," Steve told TV personality Charlie Rose in an interview shortly after the release of *Toy Story*. "We were pioneering every step of the way."

The making, and remaking, of *Toy Story*

The task facing Pixar's animation staff was a daunting one. The team estimated it would take 100 early '90s supercomputers two years to render all the animation needed for a computer-generated feature film. As it turned out, the production took so long that more powerful computers became available—but rendering the film still took a full year.

"It took us a long time to build the technical foundation," Steve told TV personality Charlie Rose in an interview shortly after the release of Toy Story. "We were pioneering every step of the way."

John soon discarded the idea of building the feature around the star of *Tin Toy*, and he developed an entirely new storyline featuring a cowboy ventriloquist dummy named Woody and a newfangled electronic toy spaceman, Buzz Lightyear. Later, Woody and Buzz both became 12-inch dolls so that they fit together better onscreen. The jealousy between old and new toys was at the heart of the film.

But as production proceeded, Disney's Katzenberg carefully watched its progress and issued copious notes. The story went through rafts of revisions as Katzenberg pushed to make the characters more "edgy," more adult. In particular, Woody became an increasingly nasty character. John knew he was going down the wrong road when actor Tom Hanks, who was voicing Woody, noted that he rarely got to play jerks.

Finally, a year into production, Pixar brought its assembled reels to Disney for a screening. The event became known at Pixar as "the black day."

The film was a disaster. It wasn't funny. It didn't have the heart that had won renown for John's short films.

Disney wanted to halt production, lay off most of the Pixar team, and move a few key Pixar animators to its own Burbank, California, headquarters to rework the film under close supervision. In John's view, this was to be avoided at all costs. John begged Disney for two weeks in which to write a new storyline and prove they could complete a winning film.

Energized by the reprieve, Pixar staffers worked around the clock to recapture the fun and joy they originally saw in the *Toy Story* idea. Woody became a far more likeable character, and the interplay between the toys crackled with jokes again.

Incredibly, within the scant two weeks granted them, Pixar completely remade the entire first third of the movie. Impressed with the new version, Disney reversed its decision: production was back on.

As the story continued to be animated, Ed's technical team faced the daunting task of fully animating 80 minutes of film. Previously, the most computer animation in a film had been 10 minutes of dinosaurs in *Jurassic Park*. Rapidly, the team constructed programs that would allow networked computers to work together to speed the rendering process.

In all, Steve would invest a staggering $55 million in Pixar prior to *Toy Story*'s release. The company would likely have faced extinction without his commitment, John recalled in a Facebook-page tribute the week of Steve's death in October 2011: "He saw the potential of what Pixar could be before the rest of us, and beyond what anyone ever imagined," John wrote. "Steve took a chance on us and believed in our crazy dream of making computer-animated films."

As Pixar readied *Toy Story* for release, there was a huge question hanging over the project: what would audiences used to 2-D animation think? Would they take to Pixar's computer-generated toys? The first preview Disney held for the movie while it was still in process got the lowest scores in the company's history. However, a later screening of the nearly completed film received high marks.

"He saw the potential of what Pixar could be before the rest of us, and beyond what anyone ever imagined," John wrote. "Steve took a chance on us and believed in our crazy dream of making computer-animated films."

The fears proved unfounded. *Toy Story* opened in November 1995 and was an instant smash. It would go on to gross more than $360 million dollars and spawn two sequels that would each gross even more. The movie won a Special Achievement Oscar® as the first-ever computer-animated film.

Unfortunately, Pixar didn't benefit much from *Toy Story*'s success. In particular, its agreement with Disney left Pixar with little participation in the lucrative merchandising associated with *Toy Story*. So the millions of Woody and Buzz toys sold did not enrich Pixar's coffers. But Steve was thinking ahead about this, and had a plan to prevent Pixar from missing out on this revenue in future.

The IPO

Confident that *Toy Story* would be a success, Steve began pushing during late production for the company to do a public offering. John thought the idea crazy, thinking it would be better to wait until Pixar had two successful films under its belt. But Steve's logic was that to better their deal with Disney, the company would have to put up half the production money for future films.

To do that would take big money. Steve was at the limit of what he could contribute. Pixar needed to go public to get more capital to finance future pictures.

In a high-risk gambit, Steve timed the IPO to debut the same week as *Toy Story*'s release. But with the film's success, Pixar's IPO was the largest of 1995, raising $140 million. With the IPO, Pixar changed its name to Pixar Animation Studios, signaling that its entire focus would be on animation going forward. With the IPO cash in hand, Pixar renegotiated its Disney deal, obtaining a 50 percent share of merchandising on future films.

Where are they now?

With each successive film, Pixar broke new ground in animation and it became known for developing moving, unique storylines that enthralled audiences. From animating hundreds of insects in huge crowd scenes for A Bug's Life *to creating animated fur in* Monsters Inc., *and realistic fabric and human hair for* The Incredibles, *Pixar's team kept advancing the standard. Pixar films have won six Best Animated Feature Oscars®.*

Pixar's deal with Disney had been extended through the years but was coming to an end in 1995, prompting a re-evaluation of whether the studio was the right partner going forward. A rift had emerged between the two: Disney wasn't willing to accept Toy Story 3 *as one of the movies Pixar owed under their contract, preferring an original feature rather than a sequel. Disney also announced it would make sequels of all Pixar films, with or without Pixar's participation. In 2004, the two broke off renegotiation talks.*

The impasse played a role in another management upheaval at Disney. Then-CEO Michael Eisner was ousted in favor of Bob Iger. Iger wanted Pixar back in the fold, and made a new offer: to buy Pixar outright.

In 2006, Disney acquired Pixar for $7.5 billion in stock. The move returned John to Disney at last as chief creative officer for both Walt Disney and Pixar Animation Studios, and Ed now serves as president of both Walt Disney and Pixar Animation Studios.

Since uniting with its former production partner, Pixar has continued cranking out the hits, including Ratatouille, Wall-E *and* Up. *Ironically, when* Toy Story 3 *finally came out in 2010, it became the highest-grossing animated film by any studio to that date, earning over $1 billion.*

Zipcar

Motoring to a billion

Founders: **Robin Chase (shown) and Antje Danielson**	
Age of founders: **Both 42**	
Background: **MBA business executive, and PhD researcher and instructor in environmental studies**	
Founded in: **2000**	
Headquarters: **Cambridge, Massachusetts**	
Business type: **Car sharing service**	

Americans love their cars. So when two women friends started a business offering by-the-hour car rentals as an alternative to car ownership, skeptics thought the concept would never shift out of "Park." Twelve years later, Zipcar is the world's largest car sharing service, with over 650,000 members using more than 9,000 cars. When the company went public in 2011, it was valued at $1 billion.

The road to the top of this niche market was a bumpy one, however. First, the pair had to sell investors on a business model that was untried in the US. Then, they had to sell those venture investors—who rarely invest in women-owned businesses—on the idea that two women with no previous start-up experience should run it.

Getting schooled

Environmental issues were always a passion for German native Antje Danielson, but her first few jobs didn't reflect that. She worked for a couple of years in car sales and repairs, then for three years as a research assistant on a semiconductor project at Hahn-Meitner Institute in Berlin. She returned to school and earned her PhD in geology at Freie Universität Berlin. Afterward, she came to Boston to teach at Harvard on a NATO fellowship, while her husband finished up his PhD at MIT.

At Wellesley College, Robin Chase triple-majored in English, French, and philosophy while holding down several positions on the college newspaper and serving as president of the philosophy club. One of her first jobs after graduation was for Boston-based healthcare consultancy John Snow Inc. In 1986, she earned her MBA in applied economics and finance from MIT's Sloan School of Management. She then became the finance and operations director at a school that provides international environmental programs to high school and college students.

For 13 years after getting her MBA, Robin alternated work with time off as her three children were born. At one point she returned to JSI, while in another stint she was managing editor of the government scientific journal *Public Health Reports*. At the end of one of her stay-at-home stints, Robin decided she wanted to return to work as an entrepreneur, with greater autonomy and flexibility, rather than work for someone else.

More than a playdate

As a new stay-at-home mom in Cambridge, Robin got more involved in her children's activities. She made new friends, including Antje, whose son was in the same kindergarten class as Robin's daughter. The two kept running into each other on the playground, Antje recalls.

Antje was leading a research project on how to reduce carbon emissions from cars, which produce roughly one-third of global carbon emissions. For a Harvard energy-research project, she looked into how other countries reduced car trips.

She soon discovered car sharing. The concept began in Switzerland in 1987 with two small cooperatives, which rented out cars by the hour to members. Car sharing quickly spread to Germany, Austria, the Netherlands, France, Italy, Norway and the UK. In 1999, approximately 200 car sharing organizations operated in 450 cities, Antje's research showed. Together, the companies had an estimated $200 million in sales. Notably, the car sharing sector was growing 30 percent annually. Antje learned that every car sharing vehicle eliminated the need for about 7.5 individually owned cars.

At that time, there were only two small car sharing services in the US, both on the West Coast: Car-Sharing Inc. in Portland and Flexcar in Seattle. Sensing a business opportunity, Antje says, "I ran a few simple, back-of-the-envelope calculations and came out saying this could work out financially."

On a family visit back to Berlin in late spring 1999, Antje did a little field research on car sharing companies there. Where did the companies park the cars? How did they secure the keys?

Antje learned that every car sharing vehicle eliminated the need for about 7.5 individually owned cars.

Though excited by car sharing, Antje felt uncertain about launching the business herself. Her background was environmental science, not business. Antje's husband suggested she approach Robin, and the two met at a local café, where Antje explained her idea.

"She said, 'Here's what I saw in Berlin—what do you think?'" Robin recalls. "Really, the light bulb went on over my head. This is what the Internet is made for: sharing a resource easily with people."

"You're too slow"

In fall 1999, Robin began work on a business plan for a proposed startup to offer a car sharing service in Cambridge. Meanwhile, Antje investigated the technology they would need and tapped contacts from her car sales days. Their research showed car sharing was projected to grow to a $50 billion market by 2007.

> "Really, the light bulb went on over my head. This is what the Internet is made for: sharing a resource easily with people."

Flexcar had applied for federal funding, which meant their application—complete with budget figures—was a public document. Antje studied it, but disliked the government-subsidy model Flexcar used, which kept hourly rental rates too low at $3.50 per hour. While setting fees higher, the plan kept the average rental below the typical $45-a-day rate charged by traditional car rental companies.

By December, Robin and Antje were ready for some feedback. Robin approached her former mentor, Sloan School of Management dean Glenn Urban. Antje and Robin went to Urban's office for a meeting.

The pair expected Urban to poke holes in their model, or to say Americans wouldn't take to car sharing. Instead, he told the women their idea was too big for Cambridge. Car sharing had huge US potential.

Robin recalls, "He said, 'Your business plan is way too slow. You've got to scale it up by a factor of three.' We were really shaken by it."

Apparently, the car sharing business wouldn't fulfill Robin's dream of launching a small startup she could fit around family responsibilities. For several days she "moped and mulled" around the house, wondering what to do.

The answer came from her 12-year-old daughter, who noticed Mom's quiet mood and cornered her in the kitchen one night. Robin explained how successful the company could be, and how car sharing might positively impact the planet, but that it would likely mean round-the-clock work hours for a while. Her daughter knew the family donated some of what it made to children's causes.

"And she said, 'Are you kidding? You could make more money and save so many children's lives if this succeeded. You should absolutely do it,'" Robin recounts.

Testing, testing ...

Finding the right name for the business involved considering dozens of potential names. But the website URLs for many early favorites were already taken.

Eventually the list narrowed to five, three of which were notable: Wheelshare, U.S. Carshare and Zipcar. Robin wrote the names on 3x5 cards and started taking consumer polls. Wherever she was–in coffee shops, in the bank line, at her children's swim meets–she would get out her cards. Then, saying nothing about the planned business idea, she'd ask people what thoughts each name evoked.

She learned fast. Wheelshare made people think of "wheelchair." U.S. Carshare tested poorly, too: some 40 percent of consumers disliked the word "sharing." Also, that URL was taken, with the site owner willing to sell only if he could receive a 10 percent stake in the company.

Zipcar tested best. Robin also tested another small pack of 3x5 cards with five slogans. The winning tagline was: "Wheels when you want them."

Finding seeds

It was time to build the reservation and car security technology and to lease the initial cars, which meant time to raise money. Robin began talking up Zipcar to alumni, businesses, environmental groups, and her local networks. In February, she had one Sloan classmate and her husband over for dinner, hoping for a little advice.

Instead, the woman turned to her husband and said, "What do you think, honey? Should we invest $50,000 in Robin's company?" They became Zipcar's first funders. The funding was structured as a loan convertible to Zipcar equity once the company's valuation was established in its first venture capital fundraising round.

In all, Zipcar would raise $75,000 pre-launch, a figure Robin looks back on as laughably low. Technology costs were substantial and quickly consumed almost the entire amount. Their first engineer had to be persuaded to work for equity. As quick as money came in, it disappeared. As launch time neared, Robin found the company with just $68 in the bank.

There was an unpleasant surprise when it came to negotiating the car leases. After financing the first car with Robin's home as collateral, the car leasing companies wanted a $7,000-per-car deposit for each additional vehicle, as this was a business startup that could fail. Worse, American insurers were uninterested in covering the start-up's vehicles. Robin was beginning to doubt the company could launch on time when she had a breakthrough.

Their first engineer had to be persuaded to work for equity. As quick as money came in, it disappeared. As launch time neared, Robin found the company with just #68 in the bank.

"I was at a cocktail party in Boston for the opening of Salesforce.com and ran into an angel investor I had been talking to," Robin recalls. "He said, 'How're things going?' and I said, 'I really need $25,000, and I need it by tomorrow.'"

By 10 a.m., the angel sent Robin a check for $25,000. She was now able to lease the three additional cars Zipcar needed for its launch.

Tech headaches

Antje and Robin knew technology would be key for a US car sharing company. The European companies stashed keys in small lockboxes near the cars and gave members the combinations. Members called a phone line to make car reservations, and filled out handwritten mileage logs when they used a car for a trip. American drivers would expect a more streamlined solution.

They envisioned using wireless technology—then in its infancy with respect to consumer applications to connect the cars to a computer system. Members would reserve cars online, with the system electronically transmitting the reservation information to the member's chosen car. Each member would receive an electronic card they could hold over a proximity card-reader inside the vehicles to gain keyless entry. The system would track how long a member drove the car and the miles driven, transmitting that information back to the billing department.

Building this technology would be costly and difficult.

"Zipcar turned out to be consumer good number two—after cellphones—that figured out what to do with wireless," Robin says. "We had to build everything from scratch."

Antje's difficult task was to figure out the technology, even though she wasn't an electrical engineer. She researched what was available, working with new hire Paul Covell, an undergrad MIT engineer. Together, they concluded that RFID (radio frequency identification) technology was Zipcar's best bet. To this day, the company uses RFID, a technology that came into widespread use with retailers.

Early in the process, Robin and Antje discussed the delicate issue of who would be CEO. They decided that Robin, with her formal business education and deeper networks for fundraising, would be best suited to the role.

A pregnant pitch

The seed money was quickly exhausted, and Robin began raising more money. At pitch meeting after pitch meeting, she heard the same thing: the company needed to "professionalize" its management. (Translation: Hire an experienced businessman to run the company.) The dot-com boom had just busted, and investors were wary. Zipcar was an unproven concept in the US, and the women didn't have start-up experience.

Desperate for more funding, the women hired a former hotel industry executive CEO, Keefer Welch, to serve as Zipcar's president. Welch solved the insurance puzzle, locating one US insurer willing to offer Zipcar a policy.

Despite this success, Robin describes Welch as "a wrong-phase hire." Welch's experience was running much larger operations, with pre-established performance goals. He had no start-up experience, and the women found many of his ideas unproductive. After a few months, they severed the relationship.

> At pitch meeting after pitch meeting, she heard the same thing: the company needed to "professionalize" its management. (Translation: hire a man to run the company.)

Meanwhile, Robin was talking to investors anywhere she could find them. Late one afternoon, she took a phone call from a prospective new Zipcar member. It soon became clear to the caller that he was talking to the company CEO.

"Are you looking for money?" he asked. When Robin answered "Yes," the caller got Robin a meeting with MIT-based angel investor group Hub Angels.

Robin usually did these presentations rather than Antje, which at this point helped downplay the fact that Antje was pregnant. After the meeting, members of Hub Angels Investment Group planned an office tour. The group arrived a few minutes early, and before Robin had arrived, so Antje, now eight months pregnant, started chatting to them in the reception area. When Robin arrived a minute or two later, Antje introduced her as "my partner."

Robin saw a look go around the room. The investors thought that she and Antje were lesbian partners and that they were having a baby together! Quickly, Robin spelled out that the pair were *business* partners. Hub Angels went on to provide $500,000 in funding, part of the company's $1.3 million Series A funding round which closed in November 2000.

The tech-less launch

Though their technology was far from perfected, Robin and Antje knew they needed experience with customers and real revenue in order to move forward. So in mid-June 2000 they launched, despite a bank balance that was near zero.

For the first six months, the online reservation system couldn't communicate with the cars. Members—known as Zipsters—had to fill out mileage logs by hand. Most members never knew, but any member could wave their Zipcard at any vehicle and drive away. Occasionally, a member would accidentally take the wrong car, and Robin would get a call from another member who had found an empty parking space at their reserved time.

They started by leaving car keys hidden in glove boxes, out of view of potential thieves. With so few cars on the street, several times drivers had walked away with the key. Retrieving these keys took time and prevented the vehicle from being rented in the meanwhile. So Zipcar switched to leaving keys tethered to the steering column, in full view of potential car thieves. But with so few cars on the street, it was a risk they were willing to take. Thankfully, no vehicles were stolen before the new technology was ready that would prevent vehicle access by anyone other than the reserving member.

Marketing smart

Robin presents Zipcar in action.

Robin and Antje expected word of mouth to be their primary marketing method, but knew they'd need to do some work to generate media coverage and spread the word further. Robin chose an "urban hip" look for Zipcar with a simple green logo. Members were also issued bumper stickers with slogans such as "My other car is a Zipcar" to put on their own cars.

The mainstay of Zipcar's marketing campaign was a simple postcard that cost just 7 cents apiece. Clear plexiglass mailboxes were installed at Zipcar's parking spots with postcards customers could take, and the two women and hourly helpers handed them out everywhere, at community meetings about environmental issues and at subway stops.

Antje got a midnight call from a member whose reserved Zipcar had a dead battery. So Antje bundled her infant son into a car seat, drove across town, and gave the member a jump start.

In a canny marketing move, the first few Zipcars were all green Volkswagen Beetles, a fit with the urban-hip positioning. The distinctive cars had just been redesigned and reintroduced by VW. This meant the cars were visibly different from traditional rental cars, immediately signaling that Zipcar was something new. The marketing strategy worked, and customers began signing up. As they used the service and liked it, they told others, and membership started to grow.

Riding the emotional rollercoaster

Through 2000, the women juggled their home responsibilities with the demands of Zipcar's members. One rainy night just a few months after giving birth, Antje got a midnight call from a member whose reserved Zipcar had a dead battery. So Antje bundled her infant son into a car seat, drove across town, and gave the member a jump start.

"As a founder, you really do everything," Antje says. "It's an emotional rollercoaster. It would probably kill you if you did it your whole life, but the initial stages are exciting."

The first year was a rocket ride, with the company expanding to 35 cars and 700 members in just over six months of operation, growing as much as 20 percent a month. By the end of the first year of operations, says Robin, the Boston market was operating at breakeven.

When Antje returned from maternity leave as 2000 drew to a close, it became apparent to Antje that Robin wanted to helm the company solo. With Robin's business experience, she had the expertise to run the company, whereas Antje didn't. The two had agreed at the outset to a 50-50 division of equity and Antje couldn't force Robin out. Antje left Zipcar in January of 2001.

The competition heats up

With Boston taking to Zipcar, Robin turned her attention to the first expansion market, Washington, DC. It turned out to be a tough market to crack. Timing was bad: the launch came two weeks before the 9/11 attacks, which sent the capitol into a media maelstrom and a psychological depression. Three months later, rival Flexcar entered the market, making DC the first US city with competing car sharing companies.

Worse, Flexcar won key car sharing parking spots in an open-bid contract with the Washington Metropolitan Area Transit Authority. Robin recalls it as "the first bad thing that ever happened" to Zipcar. While DC had ample parking and Zipcar easily found spaces, the Washington Metro also gave Flexcar valuable free marketing on the subway in addition to the parking spaces. The two competitors would duke it out in DC and other markets for years.

Robin continued to run Zipcar as it expanded into its third market, New York, in early 2002 and began to pilot relationships with universities in towns outside major cities. In September, after having spent grueling months setting up a $7 million funding round, Robin saw the deal fall apart at the final hour. She spent that fall regrouping in order to successfully raise $4 million. By the end of it, Robin was "100 percent wrecked. I didn't have an ounce of energy left." The board wanted fresh blood, and named former Boeing executive Scott Griffith the company's new CEO.

When she departed in February 2003, Robin recalls, the company's run rate was $2.5 million, and it had grown into the largest car sharing company in North America. Under Griffith's leadership, Zipcar would continue its rapid expansion, forgoing profits in order to reinvest in the business to reach more markets ahead of its competitors. Sales shot from nearly $31 million in 2006 to more than $186 million in 2010.

"The interesting thing to me is that Zipcar is an idea someone else had," Robin says, reflecting on the company's success. "We just executed it better. My goal was to be the dominant nationwide and global player and to transform transportation and urban life. In fact, we did."

A Zipcar car pictured against the NYC skyline.

Where are they now?

In 2007, Zipcar acquired archrival Flexcar for an undisclosed sum.

Today, Zipcar is the car sharing industry leader. The company went public in April 2011 in a $200 million IPO, of which Zipcar netted $117 million. By early 2012, it operated more than 9,000 cars and had over 650,000 members. The company has programs that help large corporations and governments meet energy reduction goals by using Zipcar. In all, the company raised over $61 million in private funding prior to its IPO.

The company continues to be unprofitable on a full-year basis, though it had a profitable third quarter in 2011. In 2010 Zipcar acquired London car sharing firm Streetcar Limited and in 2011 exercised rights to buy Spain's Avancar.

After leaving Zipcar at the end of 2000, Antje became a principal in the environmental consulting business Ecochange. She is the administrative director of Tufts Institute of the Environment (TIE). She also serves on the sustainability advisory board of GreenerU, a Massachusetts company that helps college campuses use less energy.

Since leaving Zipcar, Robin has founded two other companies (GoLoco and Buzzcar) and serves on several advisory boards for the US government, the International Transport Forum and the World Resources Institute.

eBay

Buying power

Founder: **Pierre Omidyar**	
Age of founder: **28**	
Background: **Software engineer**	
Founded in: **1995**	
Headquarters: **San Jose, California**	
Business type: **Online auction site**	

Fifteen dollars might seem an insignificant amount, but it was the sum of money that sparked the business known today as eBay, the global auction site with $11.7 billion in revenue.

Founder Pierre Omidyar, a software engineer, was experimenting with online auctions as a hobby and advertised a broken laser pointer for sale. He was amazed that someone would consider paying just under $15 ($14.83 to be precise) for an item that didn't work, and it convinced him that there was potential in a business that catered to people's passion for collecting.

The laser pointer was duly sold and shipped and has gone down in history as eBay's first transaction. Today eBay is the world's largest online marketplace and one of the most successful companies of the dot-com era—and is still making headlines around the world.

Technology guru

Born in Paris, Pierre moved with his family to Washington, DC, in 1973 when he was six years old, and he was fascinated by computers and technology from an early age. While other kids were out playing sports, he was more likely to be found indoors tinkering with hardware and learning how to program computers. He taught himself to program in BASIC and used his technology skills to get his first job, computerizing his school library's card catalog for $6 an hour.

Unsurprisingly, Pierre later decided to major in computer science at Tufts University, where he nurtured a passion for Apple software. It was an early sign of his entrepreneurial flair and desire to do something different. At the time, Apple was seen as a trendy, non-traditional technology company, a minnow challenging established giants such as IBM. With a beard, sunglasses and his long hair tied back in a ponytail, Pierre sported a look that was well suited to his love of Apple.

In the late 1980s and early 1990s, he worked as a Macintosh programmer, securing a number of jobs at software companies in Silicon Valley before deciding to venture out on his own. Together with friends he founded Ink Development Corporation, which aimed to produce software for pen-based computers, forerunners of the Palm Pilot. This part of the business, however, did not take off as rapidly as he had hoped, and a year later Pierre decided to focus on another offshoot of the business—online commerce. The company was subsequently renamed eShop, and it operated as an electronic retailing company. While the concept of the Internet was gathering momentum around the world, the pace of technology was still too slow for Pierre's liking, and he quit eShop in 1994 in order to pursue a business that would propel him one step closer to the Internet. Pierre retained a stake in eShop, however, and in hindsight this proved to be a wise move. Barely two years later, eShop caught the attention of software giant Microsoft, which acquired the company and made Pierre a millionaire before his 30th birthday.

All things Internet

By this point, Pierre had caught the Internet bug. Luckily, he was in the right place at the right time, as a host of other online businesses were now starting to emerge. Pierre cultivated his interest in the Internet by joining mobile communications startup General Magic. It was during his time here that the idea for AuctionWeb, which would eventually become eBay, took shape. Like many great business ideas, Pierre's creation stemmed from a bad personal experience. A few years prior, he had placed an order online for shares in a company that looked promising, but he soon discovered that the stock had soared by 50 percent before his order had been fulfilled.

He thought it unfair that some buyers were favored with one price, while others had to settle for another. Pierre believed an online auction was a better way of arriving at a fairer price for all concerned, and with the development of the Internet such a concept could become a reality. "I've got a passion for solving a problem that I think I can solve in a new way," he said at the time. Pierre wanted to test the Web's ability to connect people around the world and offer a platform where buyers and sellers could share information about prices and products.

"Instead of posting a classified ad saying I have this object for sale, give me $100, you post it and say, 'Here's a minimum price,'" he once said, recalling his early strategy in an interview. "If there's more than one person interested, let them fight it out."

The bigger picture

It was going to take time and patience to develop his business idea, but Pierre relished such a challenge and worked around the clock, holding down his day job during the week and working on AuctionWeb in his spare time in the evenings and on weekends. In fact, he wrote the initial code for eBay in one weekend. It was a labor of love and an all consuming hobby. With his concept for an online auction, Pierre wanted, above all, to promote the idea of a community on the Web, one that was built on fairness and trust.

"I've got a passion for solving a problem that I think I can solve in a new way."

Once the code was complete, Pierre launched the site; however, he had no idea what types of things people might want to buy and sell. As an experiment, he advertised his broken laser pointer for sale, and to his surprise, he found a buyer who was interested in broken ones. Pierre created a handful of categories–including computer hardware and software, antiques, and books and comics–in which users were soon listing, viewing and bidding on items.

Because he intended to offer the service for free, it was imperative that he keep overhead as low as possible. To this end, Pierre ran the site from home, paying $30 a month to his Internet service provider (ISP). He also decided to register the business and picked the name Echo Bay Technology, which he thought "sounded cool." But when he tried to register it, he found that it was already registered to a Canadian mining company, so instead he shortened the moniker to eBay.

To boost traffic, Pierre eschewed advertising and PR and deals with other sites in favor of generating awareness by word of mouth. He posted announcements about the site in online newsgroups to attract attention, and this had the desired effect: computer geeks and bargain hunters emailed one another with details of the site. Despite the lack of paid advertising, eBay soon gathered momentum, and healthy numbers of visitors began listing and buying all manner of goods. Toward the end of 1995, Pierre's ISP began to charge him $250 a month, suspecting that the growing volume of traffic was putting a strain on its system. This marked a turning point for Pierre and signaled the moment when he decided to turn what was until now just a hobby into a full-fledged business.

Pierre wanted, above all, to promote the idea of a community on the Web, one that was built on fairness and trust.

eBay's headquarters in San Jose, California.

"That's when I said, 'You know, this is kind of a fun hobby, but $250 a month is a lot of money,'" he has since recalled. Pierre had designed the site to be able to collect a small fee based on each sale. Implementing this charge now would provide him with the necessary money to fund overheads and expand the business. He decided to charge 5 percent of the sale price for items below $25 and 2.5 percent for items above this threshold. Later he would add a charge for listing items.

Going for growth

With the new fee structure, the fees collected began to surpass his salary at the time, which made it an easy decision to quit his job and devote his full attention and time to eBay. In June 1996, with the site recording more than $10,000 in revenues for that month and 41,000 registered users, Pierre hired his first employee, Jeff Skoll, who had previously been involved in two high-tech startups. Pierre also set up feedback capabilities on the site to enhance the buying and selling process and reinforce his original mission of creating a trusted community. A year later, eBay was attracting more consumers than any other online site.

"By building a simple system, with just a few guiding principles, eBay was open to organic growth–it could achieve a certain degree of self-organization," Pierre said in one interview.

In 1997, with the business growing at a phenomenal rate, Pierre invested substantially in advertising for the first time and helped design what has now become the business's iconic logo. The year marked another milestone as the one millionth item was sold on eBay: a toy version of *Sesame Street*'s Big Bird. By 1998, the site was making a name for itself as the best place to trade for Beanie Babies, tiny stuffed animals that were fast becoming a collector's item.

Fortune continued to favor Pierre's sense of timing. Toward the end of 1997 and throughout 1998, business communities around the world were experiencing the dot-com boom, and seemingly everything online at the time became attractive to investors and consumers alike. Pierre recognized that the business was becoming too big for him to handle alone and that the time was right to seek outside help and expertise. He had already filled several roles, among them chief financial officer, president and CEO, as well as chairman of the board.

Pierre decided to seek outside funding and sold a 22 percent stake in the business to venture capital firm Benchmark Capital in return for an injection of $6.7 million, which some reports have suggested was the most lucrative investment ever made in Silicon Valley. Benchmark began the search for an experienced management team, and the new recruits included Margaret (Meg) Whitman, a Harvard Business School graduate who had previously worked for Disney. She took the role of president and CEO, while Pierre remained as chairman. Meg poached senior executives from the likes of PepsiCo and Disney who helped to take the company public in 1998 and presided over a big investment in advertising.

The IPO, too, was a phenomenal success and provided funds for further expansion. Pierre and Meg watched the share price jump from $18 to $50 in a matter of minutes, and within two months of listing, the price had reached $100. By early 1999, Benchmark's stake was worth $2.5 billion, equating to a staggering return of 50,000 percent. After a secondary offering, eBay's valuation peaked at $26 billion.

Teething troubles

Rapid growth came at a price, however. In June 1999, following a site redesign, eBay suffered a number of breaks in service, with one lasting 22 hours. This had a severe impact on consumer interaction with the site and knocked more than $8 off the price of its shares. Further outages occurred, and company revenues took a severe hit. According to reports at the time, the service interruptions cost eBay $3.9 million of its second-quarter revenues after it refunded listing fees and granted extensions on auctions.

At the time, the 22-hour outage was one of the worst Internet crashes in history, and a backlash quickly ensued as users wasted no time registering their complaints on an Internet newsgroup dedicated to the site. Others raised questions about the robustness of the technology.

Keeping the customer foremost in mind had always been Pierre's aim, and he set about reassuring customers about the quality of eBay's service. Staff worked around the clock to address technical problems, and eBay made some 10,000 phone calls to the site's top users, alerting them to the problems, apologizing for the inconvenience and assuring them that everything possible was being done to get the site back up and running.

A few users however, began turning to other sites that were giving eBay a run for its money with their own versions of online auctions, most notably search engine Yahoo! and online retailer Amazon. The latter had launched online auctions in March 1999 with a model similar to eBay's, including a commission on sales and a rating and feedback system. New competition, however, appeared to be a good thing, as eBay beefed up its services in response. It expanded the range of products on offer, streamlined the buying and selling processes—and set its sights on global growth.

Worldwide expansion

In 1999, eBay launched sites in the UK, Australia, Germany and Canada, and Pierre and Meg also implemented a strategy that involved selling more expensive goods on the site. This entailed launching a series of regional sites, which they believed would facilitate the sale of larger items that would be cumbersome and expensive to shift, such as vehicles. eBay also began to focus on making targeted acquisitions, and a year later the company bought online retailer Half.com, which allowed users to buy goods directly without going through an auction process.

eBay's well-known bright signage.

By 2001, eBay had added Ireland, Italy, Korea, New Zealand, Singapore, Japan and Switzerland to its portfolio of international sites, and its user numbers had swelled to 42 million. Such rapid expansion was an impressive feat in itself, more impressive for having been achieved against a backdrop of doom and gloom in the dot-com community. Many Internet businesses had sought a public listing and seen their shares and valuations soar in the same vein as eBay's. But by 2001 the landscape had changed, and one online business after another went bust.

Such rapid expansion was an impressive feat in itself, more impressive for having been achieved against a backdrop of doom and gloom in the dot-com community.

As for eBay, it suffered through its own travails. The Asian market, for instance, proved very difficult to crack. By 2002, just two years after its launch, the company had pulled the plug on its operations in Japan, admitting that it was struggling to make inroads in a market where competitors such as Yahoo! already had a well-established auction model. According to reports, eBay was able to offer only 25,000 items on its Japanese site, while Yahoo! Japan offered close to 3.5 million. But as one door closed, another one opened. eBay's entrepreneurial spirit and appetite for global challenges persisted, and the management team set its sights instead on China, buying a third of Eachnet.com, the country's leading online auction site.

eBay also looked at ways of improving its services, and in 2002 it bought electronic payment system PayPal in a deal valued at $1.5 billion. PayPal was the leading player in the online payment market, and eBay's own payment system, Billpoint, had failed to dent PayPal's market share. It seemed to make sense to team up with PayPal's winning formula, and Meg hoped the acquisition would help speed up eBay's existing payment processes.

In 2004, eBay introduced the "Buy it now" function, enabling sellers to bypass the auction process and sell immediately to consumers. A year later, it launched a business and industrial category, offering items from the industrial surplus market. Its most surprising move came a year later, however, with the acquisition of Internet telephony provider Skype in October 2005, at a cost of around $2.6 billion. At the time, eBay said it planned to integrate Skype with its auction website to smooth the sales process in those categories that called for better channels of communication, such as used cars and high-end collectibles. The deal also enabled eBay to extend its global reach by accessing an audience in Europe and Asia, areas in which it had so far failed to gain a strong foothold.

Survival of the fittest

While some analysts questioned the logic behind the eBay-Skype deal, and others said eBay paid too much, one thing was clear: by the time it celebrated its 10th anniversary in 2005, eBay had proved itself many times over as an Internet business that was here to stay. It had peaked during the dot-com boom and survived while other high-profile, venture capital-backed brands such as Boo.com, eToys and Webvan had disappeared altogether.

Today, more than seven million new items are listed on eBay each day and more than 112 million items are available at any given time.

Although eBay's foray into online auctions in China ultimately proved unsuccessful (it closed the website at the end of 2006 and instead entered into a joint venture with a Chinese company), eBay had more success with Skype. In 2007 Meg Whitman said that Skype had more customers in China than in the United States, and the growth rate in China was higher than anywhere else.

Fittingly for an Internet business, eBay has not been slow to capitalize on other technology opportunities, as it now offers a site enabled for mobile devices, text-message alerts and blogs. It has also further diversified its services to offer "Best of eBay," a site dedicated to finding the most unusual items advertised, and "eBay Pulse," which provides information on popular search terms and most-watched items.

More recently the company has branched out into other international markets and expanded its auctions business into event ticketing and comparison shopping, while navigating its fair share of challenges. The company has seen the overall growth of its core auction business slow down, and it has had to deal with numerous incidents of fraud carried out on the site. What's more, eBay has faced intense competition from search engine giant Google, which in 2006 launched Checkout, its own online payment system. Amazon, too, has begun to attract independent sellers, the core of eBay's business.

The company's success has been credited in part to its ability to innovate as well as to adapt.

The inside of eBay's headquarters.

Where are they now?

As of 2011, eBay had around 100 million active users globally. Its three biggest markets are the US, the UK and Germany. In Forbes's *2010 list of the world's billionaires, Pierre Omidyar was listed at number 148 with personal wealth of around $5.2 billion. He remains chairman of eBay but has kept himself busy with other ventures, such as Omidyar Network, a philanthropic investment firm.*

In April 2008, Meg Whitman stepped down as CEO (and in 2010 ran unsuccessfully for governor of California). She was succeeded by John Donahoe, president of eBay's Marketplaces division, who remains CEO today.

In 2009, eBay sold 70 percent of its share of Skype for $2 billion (having paid $2.6 billion for the online communications company in 2006). But in 2011 Microsoft acquired Skype for a massive $8.5 billion, valuing eBay's 30 percent share at $2.8 billion.

The full-year 2011 revenues showed an increase of 27 percent on 2010 levels to $11.7 billion. The company generated net income of $3.2 billion. PayPal also saw significant rise in revenue, with a 28 percent year-on-year revenue increase to $4.4 billion, with the payments provider adding a million new accounts every month in 2011.

The company's success has been credited in part to its ability to innovate as well as to adapt, a vision that has been with the company since the very beginning, and that continues to hold true today. The site introduced new measures to make its auctions and fixed-price listings easier to use, revamped its feedback mechanisms and strengthened its anti-fraud provisions in a bid to make eBay a safer place in which to trade. As Pierre explained in an interview in 2000:

"What eBay did was create a new market, one that wasn't really there before. We've had to evolve our strategies and policies from what I built in the beginning, which was a self-policing community of people, to one where we take a more active role in trying to help identify the bad actors", he said.

Etsy

Etsy

A handcrafted success

Founders: **Rob Kalin (shown), Chris Maguire, Haim Schoppik and Jared Tarbell**	
Age of founders: **All early to mid 20s**	
Background: **New York University (Rob, Chris and Haim), New Mexico State University (Jared)**	
Founded in: **2005**	
Headquarters: **Brooklyn, New York**	
Business type: **Online marketplace for independent creative businesses**	

In 2005, **Rob Kalin was a 25-year-old college student**, carpenter, photographer and painter looking for a good way to sell his wares. He would join with two other friends at New York University to create exactly that: an online marketplace for handcrafted goods. He gave it a short, nonsensical name: Etsy.

From a website cobbled together in just a few months in Rob's Brooklyn apartment, Etsy would grow in five years to move more than $300 million in merchandise, be valued at more than $300 million by investors, and employ more than 250 people.

The ironic secret of Etsy's success? Rob put more energy into helping the crafter community and promoting the lifestyle of buying handmade goods than he did into making Etsy a viable business. That philosophy would cause much conflict and turmoil at the company, but would also draw an enthusiastic user base and enable Etsy to succeed.

"Profit isn't a focus," he said flatly in a 2010 video interview with the influential technology blog *TechCrunch*. "To me, the most important part of commerce is the social aspect. This is a huge opportunity to reinvent what e-commerce means. That's our goal."

A little client project leads to a big idea

In 2005, Rob and his friend Chris Maguire were hungry New York University students doing freelance Web-development work to try to cover their tuition. Chris was just 21. The pair formed a design company, iospace, but quickly tired of client work and wanted to create their own online business. The question was what it would do.

Rob's time at NYU overlapped only briefly with Haim Schoppik's, but the two had something in common besides NYU: both were high school dropouts. Boyish, redheaded Rob had basically flunked out of high school—he had a 1.7 grade point average—and then bounced through six different colleges before landing at NYU. He only made it into the school through subterfuge, faking a student ID at MIT and then using a recommendation letter from an MIT professor he'd met to gain admission.

For his part, Haim dropped out of high school at 16 to pursue his first love, computer programming. After a couple of years in the workforce, including stints as a site administrator for Goldman Sachs and Reuters, Haim went back to school. All three were students at NYU's Gallatin School of Individualized Study, where students create their own majors.

Entrepreneurial ideas seemed to grow in Rob's head like weeds, Haim recalls, though many were of dubious value, such as opening a photo-scanning store. One early idea of Rob's was to create an online community productivity software application. He even wangled $10,000 in financing to develop the idea, from a local realtor for whom Rob had built a home bar, Spencer Ain.

"Rob's hidden ability is talking rich people out of their money," Chris says. "That's what he's best at."

Unfortunately, the concept floundered shortly after Rob got the money. The pair needed another website idea that could justify the investment money they were quickly spending.

"To me, the most important part of commerce is the social aspect. This is a huge opportunity to reinvent what e-commerce means."

The turning point proved to be the duo's pro bono revamp of a crafters' chat-forum site, GetCrafty.com, which was owned by an NYU professor's wife, Jean Railla. The project gave Chris and Rob the chance to work on community forum software. More importantly, they had a chance to chat with many of the site's members online.

"People kept saying they wished they had a better place online to sell their stuff," Chris says. "eBay was too big, too expensive, and too ugly for what they wanted. And we were like, 'There's an idea. We could build that.'"

Three months with three men and three cats

The idea of a crafters' e-commerce website caught Haim's interest. At 25, Haim was the most seasoned worker of the group, bringing needed site administration and design experience to the project. The trio soon converged on Rob's Brooklyn apartment, which became the designated launchpad for the site.

"eBay was too big, too expensive, and too ugly for what they wanted. And we were like, 'There's an idea. We could build that.'"

The apartment had several bedrooms, but Rob's roommates had departed, leaving just Rob and his three pet cats. Chris and Haim would rarely make it back to their own homes over the next few months as they worked frantically to build the as-yet-unnamed website.

"We literally lived there," recalls Haim. "There are unflattering pictures of me asleep with my mouth open, drooling. We'd wake up and go to work and work until we crashed."

As the team built frantically and ran through its capital, the question quickly became how much site to build before launch. Rob was taking counsel from his grandfather, who had worked at both IBM and GE. He advised the trio to wait until they had a full-featured website and a solid business plan.

Haim working away in their first "office," Rob's apartment.

But Rob was also talking to a friend from his Brooklyn neighborhood, restaurateur Sean Meenan, who had created several successful eateries including popular Café Habana. The two had cemented their relationship when Rob built Sean a cool computer made of orange plexiglass for an Internet café. He liked Rob's hustle: before the site's launch, he noticed Rob out distributing flyers about the site at a Brooklyn craft fair.

Sean had the opposite opinion from Rob's grandpa: launch as soon as you possibly can, and add more features later. This latter theory won out, and a fairly bare-bones version of the site would launch after nearly three months of work, in June 2005.

During this frenetic period, Rob was also out raising more money. He returned to realtor Ain for more funding, who also brought in his brother, Judson Ain. Sean was the third investor in the startup's $315,000 seed-funding round.

Why would Sean write a 25-year-old, first-time entrepreneur a six-figure check for an as-yet-unlaunched e-commerce website?

"I was a big believer in Rob," he says. "He has a unique perspective and he's really smart. And there was something really sincere, innocent and hopeful about this project."

Origin of a made-up name

As the site neared launch, Rob hunted for a name for the new business. He knew he wanted it to be something short—short website addresses are easier to remember—and he wanted a made-up word around which he could build a brand.

Watching the Italian director Federico Fellini's classic film *8½*, Rob kept hearing the actors say "etsi," Italian for "oh yes." He also noted that in Latin it meant "and if." Americanized with a "y" ending, the company was christened Etsy.

The free launch

In June 2005, Etsy launched as a free e-commerce site for crafters. Why? The billing system wasn't built yet. Etsy had no way to assess, track or collect payments.

Sean had the opposite opinion from Rob's grandpa: launch as soon as you possibly can, and add more features later.

It would be several more months before Etsy would be able to institute its initial fees: 10 cents per listing and a 3.5 percent fee on items sold. For now, crafters could get onto the site, put up listings and pictures of their wares, and sell them. Search tools for customers were rudimentary. Still, Etsy was up and going, and crafters took notice immediately.

"The biggest landmark is after we launched, we actually saw someone list something," Haim recalls. "Holy shit, somebody actually used us! And later on, somebody actually bought something. That was a real moment for me. From there, it just grew and grew."

As crafters signed on and began to use the site, the team continued to work madly on fixing problems and adding features. For instance, sellers of vintage items wanted more categories for their wares.

The breakthrough addition was chat forums. The team had seen the power of forums on the GetCrafty site, but never imagined how crafters longed to share their problems and ideas. By the year's end the team would be moderating 100 forum posts a day. (By 2008, it would be 15,000 posts.) Of course, managing all this took work, work, and more work for the small team.

"Our work arguably never stopped," says Haim. "There were always improvements to make and bugs to fix. We were literally always building it."

Quickly, it became clear that more robust search tools would be needed to sift through the growing piles of merchandise—jewelry and sock puppets, paintings and hand-sewn pillows. Rob knew a visual artist in New Mexico, Jared Tarbell, who was adept at working in the graphics program Adobe Flash. Jared had been hesitant to join before the launch, but once the site was up, he began working remotely from New Mexico on new search features.

His first search tool allowed users to search for items by color, a useful feature for decorators. Etsy ended up patenting the technology, which is used by many retailers today. Other features added later were more whimsical, such as one that would select Etsy sellers who were celebrating their birthday. A geolocator was also added so shoppers could view goods from a particular country or city.

Rob, Chris, Haim and Jared in California, circa 2006.

"Our work arguably never stopped," says Haim. "There were always improvements to make and bugs to fix. We were literally always building it."

While the tech team had their heads down, Rob had his eye on the big picture. He considered Etsy's marketplace nothing short of revolutionary. He wanted it to be a tool to enable consumers to abandon mass-produced, cheap goods in favor of getting to know small merchants and purchasing their wares. On the seller side, more people would be empowered to make an independent living.

"Etsy is about offering viable alternatives to mass-produced objects in the world marketplace," he told the *Financial Times*.

While it wasn't done intentionally, launching as a free site had its advantages in attracting crafters. Once the pay model was introduced several months later, many users would accept the fees and continue to be Etsy sellers.

By the end of 2005, several thousand crafters had sold $170,000 of goods on Etsy. Of course, there was little profit in it for the team, since the site was free for about half of its six months of operation.

It wasn't clear in these early days if Etsy would grow large enough to become profitable. Most of the products were low-priced, so Etsy's commissions were small. But crafters loved the site, and shoppers were buying.

Rob, Chris and Haim's California adventure

Now that the site was up and enjoying modest success, the budding company grappled with growing pains. As more users came on, the site developed problems and sometimes crashed. When it was down or a feature didn't work, users would see a cartoon of a flaming Haim known as "Haim on Fire" with the caption, "Don't worry–Haim's working on it!" After one major 2007 outage, Etsy crafters expressed gratitude for Haim's round-the-clock efforts to restore the site by making crafts incorporating the Haim on Fire image.

The cartoon Etsy put up when their website crashed.

Etsy needed more powerful computer servers, more staff–and more money. Fortunately, word had spread rapidly about the little startup. The tech press loved Jared's innovative Flash features, while crafting magazines printed glowing tales of crafters who'd seen success on Etsy and been able to turn crafting into a full-time business.

To connect with Silicon Valley venture capitalists, Rob laid plans to visit California. Rob's Brooklyn pal and investor Sean Meenan came along as Rob's wingman.

Rob had contacted Flickr co-founder Stewart Butterfield via email, expressing his admiration for Flickr and asking him to take a look at Etsy. He did, and liked what he saw. Flickr had recently sold to Yahoo! for a reported $30 million, putting Stewart and his co-founder/spouse Caterina Fake in the investing business. Both were enthusiastic about Etsy and would take the lead in helping secure Etsy's first round of venture funding.

Through Fake and Delicious founder Joshua Schachter, whom Rob had met at a New York party, Rob met a couple of heavy-hitting venture capitalists at Union Square Ventures: Fred Wilson and Albert Wenger (who had briefly been president of Delicious).

Together, these investors committed $1 million in November 2006 to Etsy in its "Series A" venture funding round. Union Square would invest over $3 million more the following year. The negotiation was a triumph for Rob, who was nervous pitching Union Square as he'd heard the firm wanted at least a 20 percent stake to invest in a startup. Rob didn't want to give up that much ownership.

He boldly offered Union just 1 percent of the company, take it or leave it. Wilson immediately agreed, and Union Square was in. Albert says investing in Etsy was a no-brainer.

"They didn't have to pitch," he says. "I could go on the site and see people were genuinely excited to have a marketplace just for them. The existing venues—craft fairs and consignment shops—were incredibly inefficient. I thought, 'This is what the Internet is for—connecting people and enabling this kind of commerce that has a personal component to it.' Plus, they had youthful enthusiasm aplenty."

The money was raised to fund "Etsy 2.0," a major upgrade of the site. To stay close to their new funders, the Etsy trio rented a house in San Francisco's Noe Valley area and set to work coding the new version.

One bright spot in the frantic money raising and site-rebuilding of 2006 was that Etsy doubled its listing rate to 20 cents. Haim says there was some griping from sellers, but as the fees on Etsy were still substantially lower than eBay's—and far simpler to understand—most accepted it.

During this time, Etsy picked up a marketing manager, former rock-band member Matt Stinchcomb. To this point, Etsy had put almost no money into marketing. Matt created "street teams," bringing together Etsy sellers by market area or interest group. The groups offered support for crafters and put on local craft fairs and how-to events. This promotional method got the word out about Etsy and built crafters' loyalty to the brand.

Etsy closed out the year having handled $3.8 million in sales for its merchants. But the Brooklynites didn't take to California, and returned home after just a month in the Noe Valley house. Soon Chris and Haim would be coding at Haim's house, with Chris crashing on the uncomfortable couch they dubbed "the spine crusher."

The team continued on in this way until Etsy got its first Brooklyn office in 2007. It was a heady time: the company had just seen its millionth sale, and two million items would be sold before the end of the year. With its first real office, Rob started Etsy Labs, installing silk-screening machines and other craft supplies and holding events where crafters would create goods on site.

The company also added a new revenue stream to its business model, offering sellers the chance to pay a $7 fee to have their product featured prominently in Etsy's "Showcase."

In Rob's view, Etsy sellers were like the tiny fish that band together to repel scary big fish in the children's story *Swimmy*, by Leo Lionni. Bringing crafters together on the site, he hoped, would enable them to better compete with big-box stores.

Some crafters found a dark side to being an Etsy seller, though. Crafters reported toiling 14-hour days at what amounted to less than minimum wage to create their wares. On the flip side, success could get you banned from Etsy. The site's rule was that all goods must be handmade. If sellers became popular and wanted to make more goods than they could personally handcraft, they had to leave the site.

Doubting Thomas

Sales volume skyrocketed in the next few years, hitting $26 million in 2007 and $87.5 million in 2008. With growth, though, came chaos. The company staff mushroomed to 60 without a planned structure for how they would interact. Silos developed. Teams lost focus. The site struggled to keep up with crafters' demands for more features.

At the same time, the site's explosive growth drew more interest from funders. Etsy was able to raise a much larger funding round in 2007: $27 million from Accel Partners, Acton Capital Partners, Hubert Burda Media, and Union Square.

With investors looking on and increasingly anxious for the site to turn a profit, Etsy needed someone more seasoned to create a stronger corporate structure. Former Amazon and NPR Digital Media manager Maria Thomas was hired as chief operating officer. Maria was quickly elevated to CEO, with Rob stepping away from day-to-day responsibilities to focus on creating a charity that would help empower crafters.

The leadership change was a breaking point for Chris and Haim, who were burned out from the years of long hours. In particular, Haim had been working in the company's rented New Jersey data center under hellish conditions, locked alone inside a security cage in a noisy, cold, poorly lit, windowless cavern he dubbed "a raver's prison." The two identified pressing problems and told Maria about their proposals to solve them, and were rebuffed. They asked to do research-and-development work for new Etsy projects. Again, the answer was no.

"She said, 'I have no interest in any of this—I'm bringing in all my own people,'" Haim recalls. "It was time for us to go, because this was never going to work. If you don't have board seats, you don't have power—that's the most valuable lesson we learned."

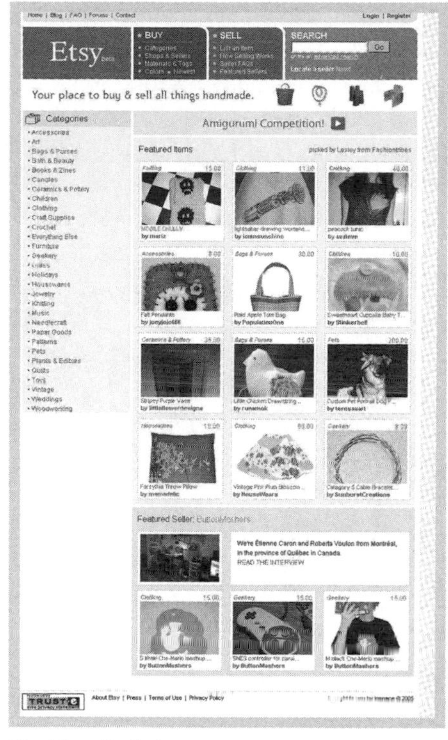

The Etsy site today.

In 2009, Etsy moved to larger, art-filled offices on the fifth floor of a former printing company in Brooklyn's artsy DUMBO neighborhood (the acronym stands for "down under the Manhattan Bridge overpass"). The new space would allow Etsy to add employees and offered more room for Etsy Labs activities.

The return of Rob

Maria accomplished some critical milestones during her time at Etsy. Most importantly, the company turned profitable in 2009 and saw over $180 million in sales transacted by its merchants. Revenue increased sevenfold during her tenure. The company laid plans to open its first foreign office, in Berlin, and made its first acquisition, buying online-advertising startup Adtuitive for an undisclosed sum.

But there was a feeling amongst both staff and crafters that the company had lost its way on the creative side. A community council was formed to try to involve crafters and respond to concerns, but the discontent persisted.

Ultimately, Rob was drawn back to the helm. In December 2009, Rob returned as CEO of Etsy, and Maria left the company.

Where are they now?

In 2010, Etsy had seven million registered members and 400,000 sellers. Ten million items were listed for sale, and the site received 940 million page views. The company saw revenue of $40 million on over $300 million in merchandise transactions. By September 2011, Etsy had already exceeded the previous year's sales, with nearly $358 million in revenue.

In August 2010, Etsy raised an additional $20 million from Accel, Hubert Burda, Acton, and Index Ventures. In all, the company has raised more than $51 million. Etsy is the subject of regular rumors of a public offering, but as of fall 2011, no plans had been announced.

Post-Etsy, Chris and Haim work together at the startup Postling, which makes social media management tools.

In July 2011, just eight months after his return, Rob announced he would depart Etsy again. Chief Technology Officer Chad Dickerson, who had joined Etsy at the same time as Maria, assumed the CEO mantle. Union Square's Fred Wilson said this second departure felt like goodbye.

"Rob is so very much that founder who cares intensely," Wilson wrote on his blog, A VC. "He has given so much to the company over the years, and he just completed a product road map that provides a guidepost for what Etsy will become in the coming years. Etsy is his creation and will always be."

Groupon

Turning coupons into cash

Founders: **Eric Lefkofsky, Andrew Mason and Brad Keywell (shown, left to right)**	
Age of founders: **42, 30 and 42**	
Background: **Serial entrepreneurs and law students (Brad and Eric) and entrepreneur and public policy student (Andrew)**	
Founded in: **2008**	
Headquarters: **Chicago**	
Business type: **E-commerce**	

Coupons have been around since the late 1800s, when Coca-Cola began mailing out free Coke offers. More than 100 years later, a new company would put an Internet spin on coupons—and create one of the fastest-growing companies ever seen. Sales exploded from $5,000 in 2008 to top $1 billion in 2011.

Groupon offered a new marketing avenue for small merchants: the online daily deal. The wild popularity of Groupon's deals attracted over $1 billion in venture capital, spawned legions of competitors, and led to an IPO that valued the startup at a staggering $12.7 billion. The most improbable thing about Groupon's success, though, is that the shopping-deals site was launched as an afterthought, by founders whose initial goal was to make the world a better place.

Start up early and often

Eric Lefkofsky started his first business while studying law at the University of Michigan. Apex Industries sold carpets to incoming students and grew to $100,000 in annual sales. Next came a T-shirt company, Mascot Sportswear, which he built and sold off.

Next, Eric teamed with law-school pal Brad Keywell to buy Wisconsin apparel firm Brandon Apparel Group. The two borrowed heavily to grow the company to $20 million in sales. But then fashion trends changed, sales crashed, and Brandon went out of business. In the aftermath, the pair faced multiple lawsuits.

On his blog, Eric called Brandon "a huge failure. We over-leveraged the company and it eventually crumbled under the weight of that debt when the industry began to consolidate against us."

While the Brandon legal mess dragged on, Brad and Eric started their first e-commerce venture in 1999. Starbelly.com sold corporate promotional items. At the height of the dot-com boom, Starbelly raised $9.5 million in venture capital, and quickly sold to retail chain Ha-Lo Industries for $240 million. When Ha-Lo failed shortly afterwards, shareholders filed class-action and civil lawsuits against Eric and Brad. Discouraged, Brad took a job with famed business magnate Sam Zell.

Eric pressed on, though. "I never thought of stopping," he wrote on his blog. "I just put my head down and kept moving forward, kept working toward success."

Eric's next company, InnerWorkings, developed proprietary software to enable printing companies to bid for jobs online. A key funder for InnerWorkings was found when Eric went to a college reunion. There, a classmate introduced him to venture investor Peter Barris of New Enterprise Associates (NEA). Eric would later meet NEA investor Harry Weller as well, and NEA invested in the company. InnerWorkings went public in 2006 and today is a $400 million business.

In 2005 Eric teamed with Brad again, spinning out the supply-chain and logistics division of InnerWorkings to found Echo Global Logistics. The following year, they co-founded MediaBank, a technology-enabled media-buying software company. In 2012 MediaBank announced a merger with competitor Donovan Data Systems to create a $1 billion company, MediaOcean.

For its part, Echo grew rapidly, received over $17 million in funding from NEA, and went public in 2009. But perhaps Echo's most notable achievement was hiring a certain idealistic young Web developer: Andrew Mason.

Raised in Mount Lebanon, Pennsylvania, Andrew also had the entrepreneurial itch. At 15, he started a food delivery service, Bagel Express. After high school, he moved to Chicago to attend Northwestern, majoring in music. He played in punk bands and had a wacky side—for a long time, one of his social media profiles featured a shot of him in his underwear. But his true passion was social justice, and Andrew planned to get a master's degree in public policy.

Getting to The Point

To earn extra money, the grad student placed a Craigslist ad for web-development work, and was hired on at Echo. He caught Eric's eye by pulling a round-the-clock work stint.

"He took it on himself to rewrite a program in six or eight weeks," Eric remembers. "He was pretty young and he was sleeping at the office. I just thought he was super-talented."

Soon after, Andrew departed to return to school. Several months later, though, Andrew reconnected with Eric. Andrew had an idea for a website that would help citizens come together to work on social-action projects. He called it The Point.

On the site, individuals could start campaigns—to raise money for a new park, for instance, or to pressure a corporation to recycle. People would pledge to help by taking action or donating. When a critical mass of people signed on, a "tipping point" was reached whereby the campaign moved forward.

Intrigued, Eric offered Andrew a $1 million investment if he would quit school and begin work on The Point immediately. So in January 2007, Andrew left campus life behind and started building the site.

In the original business plan, three potential revenue models were identified for The Point: advertising; taking a percentage of the money raised in fundraising campaigns; or charging a fee for helping groups of people buy items in bulk at a discount. But the initial goal was simply to build the site, draw big traffic, and focus on the social-change mission. Monetization would come later. In the meanwhile, Andrew kept his burn rate low by hiring just a few developers to work on The Point's launch.

"We had the ability to iterate and experiment without spending a lot of money," Andrew says.

He paid rent for a small suite in Echo's vast offices inside a remodeled former Montgomery Ward warehouse in downtown Chicago. In November 2007, The Point went live, and over the next year drew only a small following. This made it unlikely that either advertising or fundraising commissions would generate substantial revenue.

> The initial goal was simply to build the site, draw big traffic, and focus on the social-change mission. Monetization would come later.

To raise more money for The Point, Eric reconnected with his longtime funders at NEA, Harry Weller and Peter Barris, who invested $4.8 million in January 2008. Weller remembered Andrew from InnerWorkings and says he jumped at the chance, even though The Point's business model was as yet unformed.

"This was a bet on the team," Weller says. "We knew the idea would transform over time. We really thought highly of Andrew—he was a sort of inspirational, visionary guy paired with two strong operator/entrepreneurs."

Under increasing pressure to generate revenue, Andrew began investigating the idea of group buying through the Internet. To start, Andrew studied companies that had tried group buying and failed.

"The process of coming up with the idea," Andrew says, "was a process of eliminating the reasons that the previous attempts at the concept failed."

One Seattle startup Andrew looked at, Mercata, had raised nearly $90 million before going bust in early 2001. Mercata let consumers band together to bid down prices on goods and services they wanted. Mercata's "auctions" took too long, though, and customers lost interest. Merchants didn't want to participate either, as they made less margin. Mercata also focused on selling items such as consumer electronics, for which bigger competitors such as Amazon could offer lower pricing.

Get your Groupon

One day during this time, Andrew was inspired after taking an architectural tour around Chicago. He realized local discount deals would work well for group buying. Theaters had empty seats, restaurants empty tables, museums could use more members. The merchants could make a discount offer to fill some of that unused capacity, and the extra revenue would be found money.

Each deal would last only one day, so customers could buy quickly. He'd sell only one deal a day, which would allow for a focused marketing effort. There would be a tipping point for each deal that the merchant could set. If enough customers didn't buy the deal, nobody got it.

It wasn't hard to come up with a name. The product was a "group coupon," or Groupon for short. At first the name was "Get Your Groupon."

The local-deal idea offered a revolutionary new way small merchants could affordably advertise online. Groupon also used the Internet in a novel way that NEA's Weller says grabbed his interest: instead of encouraging people to stay home and online, it encouraged them to go out and experience new things in their community. It wasn't world peace, but it was a positive goal.

"We could make life better for small-business owners and increase buying power significantly for consumers," Andrew says. "Somebody who makes $30,000 a year can live like they make $60,000. That translates into freedom and experiencing more life—and that's something we could all get very excited about."

To sign up his first merchant, Andrew simply went downstairs. The owners of Motel Bar, a restaurant and bar on the ground floor of Echo's Montgomery Ward building, readily agreed to do a deal offer. In October 2008, Andrew put together the first Groupon, a two-for-one on Motel Bar pizzas. Customers would pay The Point and receive a voucher through the site, which they would redeem later at the restaurant. The Point would send Motel Bar its share of the proceeds.

"We could make life better for small-business owners and increase buying power significantly for consumers. Somebody who makes $30,000 a year can live like they make $60,000."

"We went from idea to launched product in just over a month," Andrew says. "And it was a success—25 people had to buy in, and it tipped."

Encouraged, Andrew tried more deals. But in 2008, Groupons were still a sideline to The Point. Revenue for the year was just $5,000.

For Andrew, a couple of key deals that came shortly afterward demonstrated the potential of Groupons. One was for a stay in a sensory deprivation tank, an offbeat service Andrew was unsure would sell—but it did. Another notable offer was for a $180 tooth-whitening treatment, a much higher price than Andrew had yet tried. When hundreds of people signed up, the team knew Groupons could be a real revenue stream for The Point.

"We realized we'd tapped into this insane demand," says Eric. "People wanted to go skydiving, try that massage parlor, become a member of the Art Institute, or go on an adventure trip—but they needed something to push them. Groupon was that thing."

In January 2009, Chief Technology Officer Ken Pelletier threw a late holiday party at his small apartment for the entire The Point staff, their spouses and friends. It would be the last time the company would fit in such a small space.

"People wanted to go skydiving, try that massage parlor, become a member of the Art Institute, or go on an adventure trip—but they needed something to push them. Groupon was that thing."

It was clear Groupon wasn't a revenue model for The Point—Groupon *was* the point. The company was reorganized and renamed that month, with Brad serving as a director. One year later, Groupon would have 300 employees. The year after that, Groupon would have a staff of 5,000.

A bumpy ride on a hockey stick

Chicago clearly loved Groupon, snapping up $100,000 worth of deals in the first quarter of 2009. It was time to test Groupon deals in another market to see if Groupon would work beyond the founders' home turf. The second Groupon market, Boston, opened in March.

Any doubts about the business model were quickly laid to rest. Boston took off just as Chicago had. Everyone realized Groupon wasn't just a good local money-making idea—it was a huge, global idea.

As it happened, Groupon's timing was perfect—the economy had just gone into the tank, and bargains were hot. Bloggers raved, the mainstream media took note, and a media honeymoon began that would boost the company's early expansion efforts.

Corporate missives were often playful, as in a blog post noting that the black background of the Groupon logo "symbolizes the constant darkness that would plague a world bereft of daily deals."

After Boston's success, board members urged Groupon to expand as fast as possible, fundraising aggressively to pay for staff and online advertising. Groupon needed to build brand recognition and acquire scale to operate efficiently. Also, the barrier to entry for daily deals was fairly low. Competitors would be coming soon, NEA's Weller forecast—and in fact one of Groupon's most successful competitors, Living Social, launched that year.

Groupon quickly added New York, San Francisco and Washington, DC, and second-quarter revenue shot to $1.2 million. Another dozen markets were opened in the third quarter, the subscriber base grew to 600,000, and sales leapt to $4 million. The pace continued in the fourth quarter, with another

13 markets opening. Groupon would close out the year with a total of $14.5 million in revenue.

The company was a venture capitalist's dream: an almost endlessly replicable model that promised good profit margins once each market was established. At year-end, the company raised nearly $30 million from Accel Partners and NEA to fuel yet more growth.

As it grew, Groupon asserted a fun, wacky corporate personality. The company hired squadrons of copywriters to create amusing ad copy for the deals. Corporate missives were often playful, as in a blog post noting that the black background of the Groupon logo "symbolizes the constant darkness that would plague a world bereft of daily deals."

Beneath the levity, growing like a weed taxed the limits of Groupon's executive team. Ostensibly an investor, Eric found himself sucked into the day-to-day operations, reporting on his blog that he served as de facto chief financial officer for nearly a year until Jason Child was hired at the end of 2010.

One big problem was employee pay. The sales staff was on a commission program initially premised on modest sales. Instead, some Groupon offers sold in the thousands, and salespeople could earn as much as $300,000 a year. This enraged some salaried support staff, many of whom were working long hours as well. After one staffer sued for equitable pay, some raises were given.

On the tech side, the company was constantly scrambling to bring on enough talent. Andrew says his biggest mistake was not opening a branch office in Silicon Valley until 2010. Chicago was not a tech hub, and it was hard to lure Californians to the Midwest.

Merchant backlash

By 2010, more than 2,500 merchants had participated in Groupon deals. As each market could only do 365 offers a year, most cities had long waiting lists. While the majority of merchants were happy and often signed up again, a distinct minority were displeased.

Reports surfaced of merchants who lost money after offering a Groupon. In a widely circulated blog post, Posies Café owner Jessie Burke in Portland, Oregon, said she had to pay $8,000 in payroll out of savings after throngs of customers bought her half-price Groupon deal, which was a money-loser.

In a Rice University study, 40 percent of Groupon merchants said they wouldn't do another offer. Groupon countered that the vast majority of merchants were happy, and the number of participating merchants continued to climb. It became clear that offers needed to be carefully structured, though, to avoid burning the merchant.

International explosion

In 2010, Groupon continued its stiff pace of entering new US markets, adding 13 more in the first quarter alone. The company began acquiring small competitors to add more markets quickly, along with tech companies to build out the platform. But the year's defining event was the acquisition of CityDeal, for a reported $100 million.

Forbes magazine would proclaim Groupon "the fastest-growing company ... ever."

Overnight, Groupon was a global brand, adding major European markets including London and Berlin. Groupon was able to scale these markets at a breathtaking pace, taking the London market from $1.7 million to $27 million in revenue just over a year later, for example. Masterminding much of the overseas expansion were CityDeal's owners, brothers Marc, Oliver and Alexander Samwer, savvy Germans with a history of creating acquisition-worthy European clones of US companies.

A screenshot of Groupon's website today.

In all, Groupon entered 45 new countries in 16 months flat, a boggling feat. Eighty markets were added in the second quarter alone, taking Groupon from zero to more than $100 million in overseas business in 2010. Investors liked what they saw. In April, Groupon raised $135 million, from Accel, NEA, Battery Ventures, and Russian tech mogul Yuri Milner's Digital Sky Technologies. In August, *Forbes* magazine would proclaim Groupon "the fastest-growing company ... ever."

Besides its overseas expansion, Groupon broke new ground by offering its first national deal. An offer for $50 worth of clothes for $25 from apparel chain Gap sold 433,000 Groupons for $10.8 million. The Gap deal generated tons of press, and better yet, 200,000 new subscribers.

With small imitators springing up in many cities, Groupon differentiated itself by introducing a "Preferences" feature, enabling subscribers to receive offers in categories of interest only. The company also introduced a Groupon Rewards program, in which customers earn more discounts by shopping a merchant more frequently.

No sale

By now, Groupon had grown successful enough to attract not just media attention, imitators, and investors, but also buyout offers. But the team wasn't keen to sell, preferring to continue growing the company themselves.

In mid-2010, Yahoo! made an offer rumored to be between $3 billion and $4 billion, only to be quickly rebuffed. The struggling search engine had its own problems, and the Groupon team wasn't interested in an alliance.

The next offer was harder to turn down. It was from Google, for a whopping $5.75 billion. But reports were that antitrust concerns shot the deal down. Instead, Groupon turned to private-equity investors again, raising $450 million at the end of the year, which dwarfed 2010's $313 million in revenue.

The funds kept flowing in, with Groupon raising another $492.5 million in early 2011. Interest from funders grew as the inevitable next step for the fast-growing phenomenon neared: a public offering.

IPO or "disaster"?

As the company prepped its IPO in early 2011, the executive team seemed to crack under the strain. First, President and Chief Operating Officer Robert

Solomon quit in March after one year, followed by founding CTO Pelletier, who cited exhaustion. His replacement, former Google executive Margo Georgiadis, lasted only a few months. One communications head, Bradford Williams, lasted just two months. The C-suite turnover foreshadowed the rough waters ahead.

After Groupon filed its IPO papers in June 2011, the company was criticized for both the form and content of its filing. It used unconventional financial-reporting methods, prompting restatement requests from the SEC. Eric and Andrew made statements that leaked to the media and were viewed as potential violations of SEC "quiet period" rules. An aura of suspicion enveloped the company.

Groupon's restated figures showed $1.1 billion in revenue for the first three quarters of 2011 and a $214.5 million loss—a surprise, as Andrew had said Groupon was profitable the prior year. Also news: over $940 million of the $1.2 billion in venture capital Groupon raised had been paid out already to its founders and a few early backers, rather than being used as working capital at Groupon. As a result, the company had more payables due than cash in hand. The filing also revealed that the number of US merchants placing Groupon deals had begun to decline in the second quarter, although the international merchant base continued to grow.

Critics charged that Groupon's daily-deal model was too easily replicated and would be outdone by competitors such as Google Offers, which launched in April 2011. Others opined that group coupons were a fading fad.

"Groupon is a disaster," proclaimed Forrester Research analyst Sucharita Mulpuru in one widely circulated article. Meanwhile, the US stock markets tanked in summer 2011 after Standard & Poor's downgraded the nation's credit rating, putting the IPO on hold.

In the end, investors turned a deaf ear to the media din, as did Groupon subscribers, who continued to buy. Groupon's IPO effort survived all the travails, and the company went public in November 2011. The IPO priced at $20 a share, above its planned $16–18 range, raising $700 million in the highest-valuation IPO since Google in 2004.

Where are they now?

At the time of its IPO, Groupon offered more than 33 million deals in a single quarter, to nearly 143 million subscribers in 175 cities across 45 countries. Sixty percent of Groupon's business is now international.

In early 2010, Eric and Brad co-founded the venture fund LightBank, which focuses on disruptive technology startups. Eric also serves on the boards of several nonprofits. Brad serves on several company and nonprofit boards, and he and Eric teach at the University of Chicago's Booth School of Business. Andrew continues as CEO of Groupon.

In May 2011, the company introduced Groupon NOW, which enables merchants to implement short-term flash sales. In early 2012, the company reported it was nearing its break-even point.

LinkedIn

Connections are key

Founder: **Reid Hoffman**	
Age of founder: **35**	
Background: **Technology and product development**	
Founded in: **2003**	
Headquarters: **Mountain View, California**	
Business type: **Professional networking site**	

There's an old saying in business: it's not *what* you know but *who* you know. LinkedIn set out to make this a reality in the online world, creating a site aimed at helping professionals connect with each other. Set up in 2003 in the wake of the dot-com crash, the business survived a harsh economic climate and became profitable four years after launch. Today the company has more than 51 million members in over 200 countries and says that someone joins LinkedIn every second.

Technology guru

Reid Hoffman grew up in Berkeley, California, and it seems ironic now that during his childhood his father never let him have a computer, thinking it was irrelevant. It wasn't until Reid went to college, where he studied artificial intelligence and cognitive science, that he got one. In the early 1990s, he won a scholarship to study philosophy at Oxford University, but after a year he realized that the world of academia was not for him. Instead, he had a few ideas for technology-based businesses, one of which was a personal information manager for a hand-held device. Convinced his idea had potential, he networked his way to meeting two venture capitalists. They didn't turn him down flat but advised him to get some experience producing and selling products, and then come back.

Following their advice, Reid sought a job at a high-profile technology company. He landed his first job at Apple in 1994, again using his networking skills (he heard about an opening in software development through the roommate of a college friend and applied to the company directly). Nearly two years later, he left Apple for a job at Fujitsu, this time in product management and business development.

During this time, Reid always planned to work for himself one day. His aim was to build up experience, skills and confidence and prove to the venture capitalists that he was taking them at their word. At both companies, he set himself a strict timeline and mapped out the areas he needed to master before he could strike out on his own, including design and product management, building a team, and producing and selling products successfully.

Reid always planned to work for himself one day. His aim was to build up experience, skills and confidence and prove to the venture capitalists that he was taking them at their word.

In July 1997, Reid quit his job at Fujitsu to set up Socialnet, one of the earliest versions of a social networking site. He'd thought up the concept of social networking long before most people had started using the Internet at all. The aim of Socialnet was to build on the kinds of relationships that people have, as a way to identify potential dates, roommates or even tennis partners. The idea was to put users "near" the people they'd be interested in, but online. The right person for you could be in the next building, but you'd never know it: everyone would be connected online, so physical locations did not matter.

Reid realized that the only way he would get the business off the ground was to bite the bullet and go for it. He looked at financing opportunities and went back to the original venture capitalists he had contacted years before. This time, they were impressed by his background and his ambitions for Socialnet, and he raised $5 million at the end of 1997.

PayPal and beyond

Just over two years later, however, Reid resigned from Socialnet because he wasn't convinced that the company was going in the right direction. The business's strategy had been to partner with newspapers and magazines to encourage subscriptions to the site, but it soon became clear that this was not viable and would not give them the user numbers they needed. Reid had a difference of opinion with the board and left soon after. He had learned a valuable lesson: you can have a brilliant product but unless you know how to reach tens of millions of people, the product will count for nothing.

"There are three words people use for retail: location, location, location. For the Internet, it's distribution, distribution, distribution," Reid said. "If you don't get this, the value of your site is zero. I hadn't realized this when working at Apple and Fujitsu as they worked with big channels of established customers."

He told a friend, Peter Thiel, who had studied with him at Stanford, of his intentions to start another company. Peter was one of the founders of Internet payment system PayPal, and at the time was its chief executive. Reid had been one of its board members since its launch in 1998, and Peter persuaded him to join the company as executive vice president in charge of business development instead of starting another business.

At PayPal, Reid was responsible for external relations including corporate development, banking, and international development. All the while, he continued to be fascinated by how the Internet (then in the early stages of its commercialization) accelerated the rate at which people did business. He was particularly interested in how individuals could use the Internet to promote their business profile and skills and what influence this would have on their careers.

"There are three words people use for retail: location, location, location. For the Internet, it's distribution, distribution, distribution."

It wasn't until a few years later that Reid capitalized on his online networking ideas, since he believed that it wasn't possible to perfect his business plan while still in another job. In 2002, PayPal was acquired by Internet auction site eBay for $1.5 billion, and Reid received $10 million for his share in the business. He planned to take a year's sabbatical, but just three months later was back on the business trail, too tempted by his desire to start another online business. Even after the dot-com bubble burst, Reid was adamant that there was still potential for online success.

Thriving in a harsh climate

Reid saw nothing but advantages in the harsh economic climate of the early 2000s. He wanted to create a business that would only be possible via the Internet and that would change people's lives. He reasoned that in the current climate there would be less competition and therefore a greater chance that his venture would succeed. Reid had several ideas, including a worldwide online computer game, but rejected them in favor of revisiting his passion for how people could be brought together online. He wanted to start a business that would let professional people establish profiles online so that other people could find them, effectively creating a network to enhance and further their careers.

Even after the dot-com bubble burst, Reid was adamant that there was still potential for online success.

In these years, it was harder than before to raise money for an Internet venture. Not wishing to waste any time before launching his idea—after all, it had effectively been brewing for several years—he decided to use the money from the sale of PayPal to start the business.

For Reid, having enough capital wasn't the big issue at the start—his main concern was making sure that he had the right team. He gathered a team of people he had previously worked with and known from his college days, whose experience and opinions he valued. The group included Allen Blue, Jean-Luc Vaillant, Eric Ly, and Konstantin Guericke. Konstantin had been a fellow classmate at Stanford; Jean-Luc had worked for Matchnet, an online dating business that had acquired Socialnet; Allen and Eric had worked at PayPal. Over several months they met in Reid's living room and hatched the plan that was to become LinkedIn.

Preparing for launch

As the US officially entered a recession, the founders worked on the business plan for LinkedIn for several months before launch. Having witnessed the collapse of the dot-com bubble, they knew they needed to prove that the business could grow at a low cost, make money and be sustainable.

In the face of a gloomy economy, Reid continued to believe that starting in a time of recession gave LinkedIn a competitive advantage. Even as consumer Internet ventures were no longer the next best thing, LinkedIn now had the opportunity to stand out with a fantastic idea. Investors were interested only in startups that could offer a solid, long-term business strategy, something that LinkedIn was determined to prove it possessed. The team wanted to show it had a sustainable business model based on a number of revenue streams, such as subscriptions, and at its core, a valuable proposition for prospective members.

Reid continued to believe that starting in a time of recession gave LinkedIn a competitive advantage. Even as consumer Internet ventures were no longer the next best thing, LinkedIn now had the opportunity to stand out with a fantastic idea.

The business continued to be funded by the proceeds of Reid's PayPal shares, as the founders held off seeking additional funding until they were sure they could prove the value of LinkedIn's business model. By early May 2003, the founders felt confident enough to launch the site. But it was to take several months of hard work for the idea to catch on.

Word of mouth

Reid set himself the challenge of getting a million people to register for the site. LinkedIn's premise—that people could search for other members and share information—meant the site had to have enough people signed up in order for it to be valuable. Right from the start, Reid planned to grow LinkedIn organically by word of mouth—it seemed the most cost-effective and efficient way to attract members. The speed of uptake would also help to demonstrate the site's value to potential investors.

The founders planned to look for a first round of funding to support the business's growth plans once they had recruited a sizeable number of members. The LinkedIn founders began by inviting 350 of their most important, well-connected and trusted contacts to join, encouraging them to get their friends and contacts to join, too.

This worked well. At the end of its first month in operation, LinkedIn had a total of 4,500 members in the network, and the business (using more of Reid's money) set up offices in Mountain View, California, not far from Google's company headquarters. Reid also recruited new staff members to work on the technical side, bringing the total number of employees to 13.

The site wanted to emphasize the strength of the connections between members, so it dissuaded members from adding people to their network randomly. Instead, LinkedIn encouraged members to connect with colleagues, clients and people they had worked with in the past. Connections were therefore based on the trust and experience of those individuals. Reid believed that this increased the value of people's networks by focusing on existing connections in the real world, as opposed to the random connections that are common in some social networks.

On the up

Member numbers were increasing, and timing now seemed to be on LinkedIn's side. When it launched, there were no similar businesses in operation, enabling LinkedIn to develop its concept of online professional networking without worrying about competitors. It didn't take long, however, for other professional networks to spring up, including Tribe

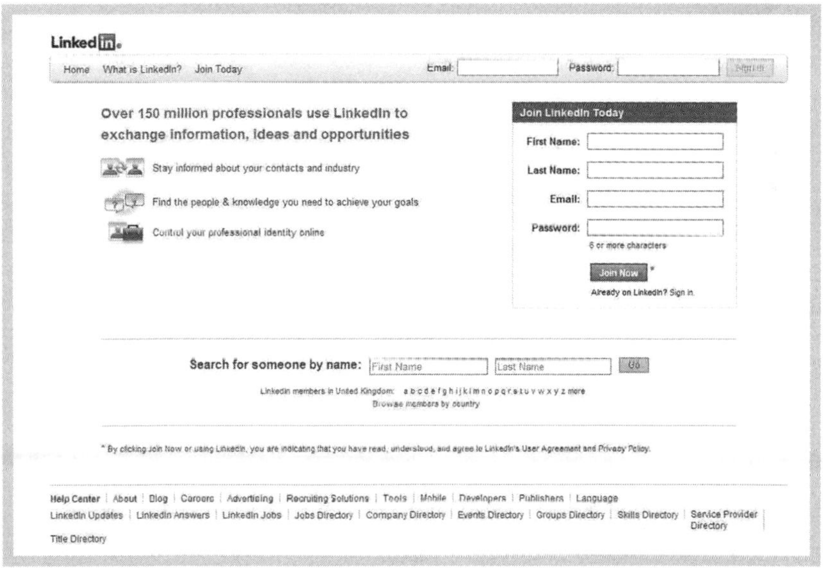

The current LinkedIn homepage.

and Friendster. With a growing interest in the sector, it was not surprising that investor appetite was waking up to the potential of social networking sites, particularly since the US economy was showing signs of a recovery. In December 2003, the stock markets were up for the first time since the Internet bubble had burst back in early 2000.

LinkedIn was now ready to seek venture capital funds. Reid recalls how he was besieged by at least a dozen unsolicited visits from venture capitalists. At the end of October 2003, he signed a deal for $4.7 million from Sequoia Capital, a leading venture capital firm whose support he'd targeted in the first place. By this time, the site was doubling in size every six weeks and had gained users in more than 80 countries and 120 industries. Several months later, Reid says, he was still hearing from venture capitalists he'd never met, begging to be allowed to buy a piece of his company even though they'd heard about it second or third-hand.

Although it was common for online businesses to use advertising as their main revenue stream, LinkedIn was determined to be different, having learned lessons from the dot-com fallout. In 2005, two years after launch, LinkedIn introduced two income streams: paid job listings and a subscription-based service, which offered users an enhanced search service allowing them to connect to people they didn't already know.

Reid decided that advertising, while not part of the original business plan, would become the site's third revenue stream, as it had built up a demographic base that appealed strongly to advertisers. The self-selecting nature of LinkedIn's membership (it targeted successful and ambitious professionals) would provide an opportunity for certain brands to reach their target audience in an efficient way. Just a year later LinkedIn turned a profit, the majority of the income coming from its premium services, such as job listings.

LinkedIn became one of the few companies that thrived in the recession that hit during the late 2000s, benefiting from the increased number of people on the hunt for jobs. In March 2008, the site saw its traffic double to just under seven million users, up from 3.3 million a year earlier. Furthermore, the site continued to develop features to increase the value of its services for users.

In September 2008, LinkedIn struck a partnership with financial news channel CNBC, enabling users to share and discuss news with their professional contacts. Community-generated content such as surveys and polls from LinkedIn are broadcast on CNBC, and in return the broadcaster provides the site with its programming, articles and blogs. The networking site sealed similar partnerships with other media owners, including *The New York Times*. Then in 2008, original investor Sequoia Capital, together with Greylock Partners and other venture capital firms, acquired a 5 percent stake in the company for $53 million, giving the company a valuation of nearly $1 billion, a remarkable achievement for a business that was just 5 years old.

Where are they now?

In 2010 the company's value rose to new levels, with hedge fund Tiger Global Management purchasing a 1 percent stake for $20 million, doubling LinkedIn's estimated value to $2 billion.

Now LinkedIn can count itself as one of the largest presences on the Web, with more than 135 million members across 200 countries and territories. In June 2011 the number of unique visitors to the site reached 33.9 million, up 63 percent from the previous year and surpassing that of early social media giant MySpace for the first time. The company went public in May that year and saw its share price more than double in just a few months, making it the most successful tech IPO of the year. But for founder Reid, who is often dubbed "the most connected man in Silicon Valley," LinkedIn's success to date may only be the beginning.

Match.com

Love online

Founder: **Gary Kremen**	
Age of founder: **30**	
Background: **MBA, founder of Full Source Software and Los Altos Technologies**	
Founded in: **1993**	
Headquarters: **Dallas, Texas (originally San Francisco, California)**	
Business type: **Online dating**	

Some say that the best business ideas come from trying to solve a problem that you understand. That's certainly a view shared by Gary Kremen, founder and ex-CEO of Match.com, the world's first major dating site and one that set the standard for much of the Web as it developed.

"I actually started Match.com trying to find love for myself," Gary admits. "I had this idea that if I could put all the women in the world on a database, and I could sort it, then I'd just marry number one."

It is not every day, of course, that a yearning for companionship gives rise to a multi-billion dollar global industry, but Gary is not an everyday person. Already a successful digital entrepreneur before he started Match.com, Gary's tale is one of sharp business acumen combined with an understanding of what makes people tick.

Early forays

Gary was born in Skokie, Illinois, in 1963 to two teachers. From an early age it was clear that he had a formidable intellect. As a child he spent hours looking through his telescope and was one of the first among his peers to purchase a home computer (when he was just 12 years old). However, early disciplinary problems at school held him back. He describes himself as a "behaviorally challenged student" and was frequently in trouble for minor vandalism and computer hacking.

Despite not having the best grades, Gary used his entrepreneurial instinct to "pitch" his qualities to Northwestern University, a strategy that worked. Graduating with a combined major in business and computer science in 1985, Gary worked as an engineer at the Aerospace Corporation for two years. It was while working here that he was first introduced to ARPANET, the Department of Defense's early precursor to the World Wide Web. Although it was a secure job, it was dull, and Gary's mind soon drifted to grander things. After taking night classes in accounting, he decided the time was right to go to Silicon Valley to earn his millions in the technology industry, and he turned down a prestigious scholarship at the University of Chicago to seek an MBA in California at Stanford Graduate School of Business.

At Stanford, Gary was part of a gifted generation of digital entrepreneurs, with classmates going on to become driving forces in household-name companies such as Microsoft and Sun Microsystems. After graduating, he found a job in a biotechnology company—nothing too exciting, but the company's CEO allowed him to sit in on board meetings, something Gary says gave him the confidence to start his own venture.

When the time came for Gary to start his own business, there was one area in which he boasted almost unparalleled expertise—the online world. "I was a nerd, okay!" says Gary. "I was online as early as 1985. How many people can say that?"

This proficiency, combined with the skills he learned while completing his degrees, gave him an advantage over the many would-be digital entrepreneurs in Silicon Valley in the early 1990s.

Gary's first venture was Full Source Software, co-founded in 1991 with partner Ben Dubin. Full Source would download software from Usenet (an early Internet community that preceded today's commercial Internet), putting it onto physical media for sale in bulk to large companies. The company was a moderate success, eventually making up to $2,000 a day, but it gave Gary an early glimpse of the enormous commercial potential the World Wide Web had to offer.

A female genesis

In 1989, Gary co-founded his second venture, Los Altos Technologies (LAT), a company that cleaned sensitive data off hard drives for the military and other businesses. (The company was sold to an employee in late 1992 and is still going strong.) While working at LAT, Gary noticed something important: large purchasers were beginning to use systems like IBM's Lotus Notes, enabling administrative staff to send electronic purchase orders without the help of IT staff. It may sound insignificant now, but Gary saw what it meant: an increasing number of women were using these tools to go online for the first time.

"It was the first time I noticed women using the Internet," Gary explains. He was an avid user of what were known as "900 number" services: telephone-based dating agencies that enabled people to meet potential partners in exchange for a fee. He realized that the crux of these services' success was their network of users, and he saw similar potential in the small but growing presence of women online. "It got me thinking, 'I wonder if I could do what they do—and charge access to these women?'" he says.

"I was a nerd, okay!" says Gary. "I was online as early as 1985. How many people can say that?"

The relatively tiny female population online at the time (around 10 percent of users) did little to faze Gary—in fact, it encouraged him. "Because there were so few women, I realized that this was the key," he says. "If you control the few women, you can charge a lot of money to the men."

Gary saw the huge revenues that print media made from classified advertising—and from dating ads in particular. At the time, papers such as the *Los Angeles Times* and *Chicago Tribune* made 10 percent of their total earnings from personal dating services and 40 percent overall from classifieds. But he also saw that the industry was slow to react to change and had some key flaws, such as slow turnaround time, lack of anonymity and potential for embarrassment. These were all problems that could potentially be solved by a secure, anonymous and instant online classifieds business. Out of these insights came the idea that would change Gary's life and set him on the path to becoming one of Silicon Valley's best-known entrepreneurs.

First steps

In 1993 Gary set out to realize his vision and founded Electric Classifieds, Inc. (ECI), under which Match.com was developed. The original name of the company was a reflection of the wider vision Gary had for the business: ECI was to be a billion-dollar online classifieds empire with dating being a headline-grabbing way of getting people to look at the Internet in a new way.

Gary took out a $2,500 advance on his credit card to pay for the domain name Match.com, as well as a host of others, including Autos.com, Housing.com, Jobs.com, and (famously) Sex.com. The bill racked up higher as he bought a $10,000 SUN workstation to host the site and hired Kevin Kunzelmann as his first employee, finding him on Usenet. Early on, Gary was also assisted by experienced software engineer Peng Tsin Ong, who helped with the construction of the site, provided 10 percent of the initial startup funding and acted as Gary's brainstorming partner. Gary also hired Scott Fraize, a software developer.

ECI started operating out of a small room located in the San Francisco neighborhood known as the "Panhandle." Gary recalls it as a "horrible" place: "I was the starving entrepreneur, living on two meals a day," he recalls. "But it was really exciting having this small team working out of a little room, watching the business grow so fast—now it's a cliché, but back then it was so powerful."

At this point, Match.com was barely more than a proof of concept; the site would not be built until 1994. Users would send a picture and personal details to ECI's email address, which would then send profiles of other local users in reply (in exchange for a fee). Despite this rather clunky system, the enormous potential of online dating was soon becoming apparent, with the company seeing explosive growth almost from launch.

"It was insanely fast," Gary recalls. "We were growing 2–3 percent a day just from new sign-ups and traffic was growing even faster than that." What made this growth even more impressive was that initially there was no money set aside for advertising, with the nascent service relying on word of mouth.

"I was the starving entrepreneur, living on two meals a day," he recalls. "But it was really exciting having this small team working out of a little room, watching the business grow so fast—now it's a cliché but back then it was so powerful."

It wasn't long before this growth attracted the attention of angel investors such as serial Silicon Valley entrepreneur Ron Posner, and just a few months after launch Electric Classifieds had raised $200,000 in funding, giving the project a much-needed cash injection after Gary maxed out his credit card.

Selling the concept

Although online personals were an attractive concept for consumers and investors alike, the problem remained of marketing the business to the wider world, and early on, ECI made a bold decision: to focus the marketing entirely on women who were already online. In the mid-1990s, as the Internet was growing in popularity, women made up a large proportion of chat room users, through the likes of AOL and Compuserve.

"I had the vision that one well-connected woman could get 50 other women—who could get 5,000 guys," Gary explains. The company began to

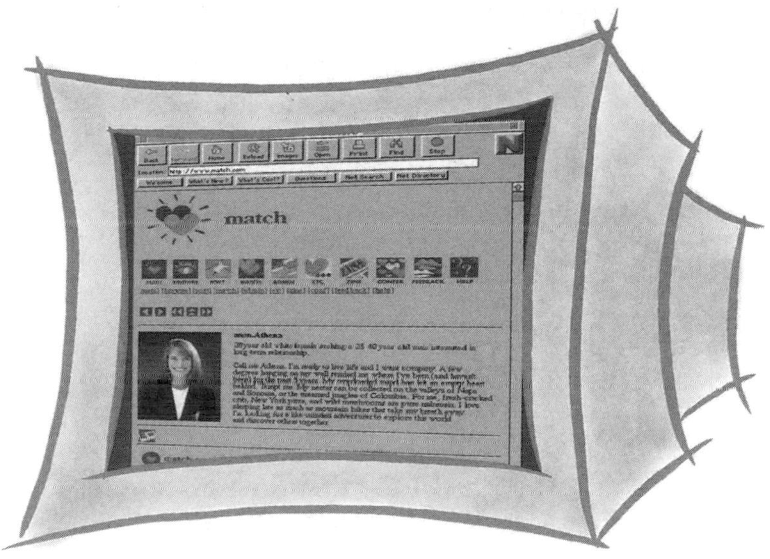

An early version of Match.com.

target the small proportion of women who were already online, advertising on female-focused chat sites such as Compuserve's Women's Wire. The marketing emphasized the safety and anonymity of the Match.com model; online security was still a concern for many women and ECI promised a risk-free service where phone numbers and home addresses were not needed. Initially, Match.com was a free service, but ECI began charging users a monthly fee shortly before the site was finished.

> Early on, ECI made a bold decision: to focus the marketing entirely on women who were already online.

Later on, the company widened its reach and began a multifaceted campaign through traditional print and television media, targeting the 25 million Americans who already used dating services but did not have a compelling enough reason to go online.

Growth, growth, and more growth

It was not long before the company's continued growth attracted the attention of more outside investors, and in 1994 Electric Classifieds received its second round of funding from venture capitalists, raising $1.7 million led by Silicon Valley venture capital firm Canaan Partners.

"It was pretty easy to raise funding because it was pretty novel—there was some skepticism at first, but once we became the market for new relationships, that disappeared." Gary says.

In 1995, just after the first round of venture capital, the early pace of expansion forced Gary to buy one of the largest servers offered by Sun Microsystems, costing $300,000. The problem was, the venture capital money had already been tied up in other parts of the expansion, leaving the company with no money to pay for the server.

"I told the sales guy that it was great, the machine looked good, but we had one problem—I had no money to pay for it!" he says. "He told me I was going to put him out of business—so I gave him my new venture guy's home phone number and told him to call him up and get the money from him. I made it his problem!" Needless to say, Gary recalls that particular venture capitalist being less than impressed. Despite these early hurdles, the Match.com

Gary shows how Match.com sorts ads according to the user's location and preferences.

website finally went live in April 1995, marking the birth of the site as we know it today.

The combination of Electric Classified's innovative business plan and its huge growth soon proved irresistible to the mass media and Match.com was catapulted out of obscurity to become the darling of the business world. It was the subject of articles in *Wired* and *Forbes*, with Gary being named #36 on a list of the 100 most influential people on the Internet. His quirky persona as CEO also proved appealing, with a notable example being an early television interview in 1995 in which he proclaimed that Match.com would "bring more love to the planet than anything since Jesus Christ."

Electric Classifieds also saw Match.com's appeal spread to some unexpected sectors. The site quickly proved popular among older women, for example. Gary had thought that this group would be the most resistant to an online dating service, but their troubles finding men in real life led them to embrace the connectivity and global appeal that Match.com offered.

Investor troubles

Despite this success, troubles were beginning to grow between Gary and his investors. The board had doubts about Gary's ability as CEO, aggravated by what he admits was his early immaturity. A major flashpoint developed when investors found out that Match.com was beginning to target the gay and lesbian sector. Gary saw this group as a loyal market that deserved to be served—but certain investors perceived it differently. "They went ballistic," says Gary. "We had some towering arguments about it."

Another fundamental disagreement soon arose between Gary and the board over the wider direction that ECI was to take. The board was increasingly at odds with Gary over strategy: they wanted to use ECI as a vehicle to sell classifieds technology to newspapers, a process that Gary fundamentally disagreed with.

"[Newspapers] were slow moving and I could see how long it took them to do anything at all. Even though some of them were a hundred thousand times bigger than us, I always knew we could take them on ourselves. I always knew working with the newspapers would turn out to be a dumb idea."

These incidents and disagreements over strategy led to Gary leaving his post as Match.com CEO in mid-1995. "We had a big fight. I left," says Gary, simply. "It was a great time to be starting other things, so I moved on to new ventures."

"It's the exception rather than the rule that the founder is a good CEO," Gary says. "The guy that has the idea is not normally the guy with the skills to manage 300 people."

Gary remained on the ECI board as the chairman, helping with the overall strategy and vision until the Match.com business was sold off to Connecticut firm Cendant in 1998 for $7 million. Again, it was a decision that Gary strongly resisted, believing the brand to be vastly undervalued. From the investors' point of view at the time, it was a canny piece of business, selling a brand for over three times what they bought it for just a few years after investing. But Gary's estimation of the true worth of the business proved to be much closer to the mark, as Cendant sold the site on to US giant Ticketmaster for the eye-watering sum of $50 million just one year later. Gary resigned from the ECI board after the sale to Cendant, pocketing just $50,000—as well as a lifetime account on Match.com.

Despite the acrimonious split, Gary believes his experience at Match.com was an instructive one. He learned that despite having a knack for good ideas and keen business insight, he was not born to be a CEO—a lesson he says can serve as a cautionary tale for other would-be entrepreneurs.

"It's the exception rather than the rule that the founder is a good CEO," Gary says. "These cases of Amazon, with Jeff Bezos being the founder and CEO, or Mark Zuckerberg—these aren't normal. The guy that has the idea is not normally the guy with the skills to manage 300 people."

Gary also learned to take a more inclusive approach with investors rather than the combative style he adopted while at the company. He advises: "When the process begins of building and getting a CEO in, you may as well be part of the process as opposed to fighting it." He adds that you have to "kiss lots of frogs" to get the "right" investors and only regrets his choice in hindsight, if not the investment itself.

Electric Classified's sale of the Match.com brand proved to be the beginning of the end for the business. Changing its name to Instant Objects, the company persisted with the doomed goal of selling backend technology to newspapers, and, despite raising an additional $25 million in venture capital, finally shut its doors in 2001.

However, this wasn't quite the end of the ECI saga. In 2004, the defunct company's outstanding debt was bought by none other than Gary himself, who then sold off some patents he had filed while at the company for a handsome profit. "I bought the debts for maybe $300,000 and made a couple of million dollars from the sale," he says. "It's a nice story."

Where are they now?

Today, Match.com competes with PlentyOfFish.com as the world's leading dating site and established the template for many other imitations, fulfilling the potential that Gary always knew it had.

It claims to have over 20 million members (1.3 million of whom are paying subscribers) with a 49:51 male:female ratio. It's also a truly global affair, with sites in 25 different countries in eight languages. The company is still under the control of IAC (InterActive Corp.) and would comfortably be valued in a multiple of hundreds of millions of dollars.

"I'm happy it's done so well," Gary says. "I knew as soon as I had the idea it was going to be huge—I've got my vision wrong many times but I got this one right."

And Gary's life after Match.com has proved just as eventful. After leaving the company, he started NetAngels, a venture that offered early collaborative filtering technology that was merged with another company, Firefly, and was eventually sold to Microsoft.

In the late 1990s, Gary became embroiled in one of the longest running and most notorious disputes in Internet history when fraudster Stephen Cohen stole the Sex.com domain—which Gary had registered for free when starting Electric Classifieds—and used it to form the basis of a multi-million-dollar pornography empire. This battle to save what was rightfully his would take Gary many painful years, with Cohen's evasiveness almost leading to his ruin. Eventually, Gary obtained some of what was owed to him, receiving a $65 million judgment that included Cohen's mansion in the prestigious San Diego neighborhood of Rancho Santa Fe. Gary now lives in the mansion, and Cohen bought himself a lengthy prison sentence.

Today, Gary devotes his time to investing in ethical and sustainable businesses and estimates he is an investor in 15 such ventures. A notable recent investment success has been Clean Power Finance, founded in 2007 as an online service that enables solar buyers and sellers to connect with financial products. Kleiner Perkins and Google were some of the other investors, and the company reportedly channels $1 million into the solar industry every day.

But did Gary ever achieve his original goal of finding love? "I finally got married about four years ago—but it wasn't through Match.com!"

Gary explains. "It was a hybrid model—I offered a reward on the Internet of a trip to Hawaii for two if you set me up with my future wife. This guy I know set me up with my wife, and he got his holiday, so everyone was happy."

Twitter

How 140 characters changed the world

Founders:	**Jack Dorsey, Christopher Isaac "Biz" Stone and Evan Williams**
Age of founders:	**29, 31, 33**
Background:	**Software developers/Google employees/serial entrepreneurs**
Founded in:	**2006**
Headquarters:	**San Francisco, California**
Business type:	**Social media/microblogging**

In five short years, Twitter grew—and *grew*—into a tool that revolutionized global communications. It became so ubiquitous that using it became a verb: to tweet. The brief status updates of Twitter would change the way news is reported, governments are toppled, and charitable donations are solicited.

But Twitter is almost as famous for what it hasn't done: turn a profit. Despite attracting a huge audience and raising over $1 billion in venture capital, Twitter continues to struggle to find a business model that will let it cash in on its popularity.

Three geek dropouts and how they grew

As a teenager growing up in St. Louis, Missouri, Jack Dorsey created software that helped taxi and ambulance dispatchers locate their vehicles. Jack attended Missouri University of Science and Technology, then transferred to New York University before dropping out in 1999.

He moved west, taking up residence inside the former Sunshine Biscuit Factory in Oakland, California, and he began working on a Web-based dispatch start-up idea. In July 2000, inspired by the Web-posting service LiveJournal, he got an idea for a simple, real-time update service—a more "live" LiveJournal.

He sketched the idea on a sheet of wide-ruled notebook paper. There would be a small box for writing what you were doing, room for a bit of contact information, and a search bar for finding others on the service.

That was it. Jack wanted to call it Stat.us.

Evan Williams grew up on a farm in Clarks, Nebraska. He lasted a year and a half at the University of Nebraska before dropping out in favor of a string of tech jobs. In 1996 he moved to Sebastopol, California, to work for technology publisher Tim O'Reilly and his O'Reilly Media. He began in marketing but floundered as a staffer and switched to writing code as an independent contractor. "I was bad at working for people," Evan would later say.

In 1999 he co-founded Pyra Labs with ex-girlfriend Meg Hourihan. Pyra's hit product was a simple, early Web-logging platform called Blogger, a term Evan coined.

Blogger lacked a business model—the platform was free. Evan wanted to focus on improving the user experience and building the audience first, then figure out how to make money.

Unsurprisingly, funds soon ran out. The small staff continued without pay for weeks but eventually staged a mass walkout that included Hourihan. Evan ran the company solo until securing an investment from VisiCalc creator Dan Bricklin in April 2001, after Bricklin learned of Blogger's woes from a post on Evan's blog, *Evhead*. The staff was rehired, and Blogger's software was rewritten so that it could be licensed to other companies.

In 2002, Evan's next-door neighbor Noah Glass introduced himself after spotting the Blogger logo on Evan's computer monitor. Noah's startup, Listen Lab, was working on a way to post audio recordings on Blogger, a feature Evan added as Audioblogger.

Google acquired Blogger for an undisclosed sum in 2003. Evan spent about a year overseeing Blogger at Google before leaving in 2004 to create a new startup with Noah.

Biz Stone studied writing at Northeastern University and the arts at the University of Massachusetts Boston, near his hometown of Wellesley, but he lasted just a year at each institution before dropping out. He worked as a designer for publisher Little, Brown and Company for three years before getting the entrepreneurial urge.

He launched the free journaling service Xanga in 1999. When Blogger's paid version came out, Xanga licensed it and Evan and Biz formed a long-distance friendship. In 2001, Biz left Xanga (which continues to operate today), and when Google purchased Blogger, he was recruited by Evan.

Hello, Odeo, goodbye

Evan and Noah saw how difficult it was to find and organize podcasts. In early 2005, they launched a startup designed to solve this problem. They called it Odeo.

Evan's Blogger success made it easy to find investors. Odeo quickly raised $5 million from Charles River Ventures and an A-list of angel investors including Evan's former boss Tim O'Reilly and Google investor Ron Conway.

Two early Odeo hires were Biz and Jack. Unfortunately, there was soon a rather large fly in Odeo's ointment: in March 2006, Apple's iTunes podcasting service launched and appeared certain to dominate the market. Moreover, Odeo's technology proved difficult to execute. The 14-member team became demoralized.

Meetings were needed to discuss Odeo's next move. Since software developers tend to work remotely and keep odd hours, getting together wasn't always easy. Staffers were constantly being messaged or emailed to ask: "What are you doing?"

This problem rang a bell with Jack. He dug out his old sketch of Stat.us.

The birth of twttr

At a playground near Odeo's offices in San Francisco's South Park neighborhood, Jack pitched the Odeo execs. They debated the merits of a Web-based communication platform that would bring together email, instant messaging, and mobile-phone texting.

"He came to us with this idea: 'What if you could share your status with your friends really easily, so that they know what you're doing?'" Biz later recalled.

Giving himself the handle @jack, Jack created the first post on March 21, 2006: "just setting up my twttr."

The first-ever tweet.

A team of four got the go-ahead to work on Jack's idea. Jack, Noah, Biz and Florian Weber—a Berlin-based expert in the emerging, open source Web-development framework Ruby on Rails—worked for two weeks to create a prototype. To enable the service to work with text messaging's 160-character limit, they set a 140-character update limit. At first, it ran on Noah's IBM Thinkpad laptop.

The team brainstormed for a name, as Stat.us was taken. "Jitter" and "Twitch" were nominees. Noah finally came up with the name Twitter, which was originally written "twttr." Giving himself the handle @jack, Jack created the first post on March 21, 2006: "just setting up my twttr."

Odeo's meeting-schedule problem was solved. More significantly, everyone found twttr fascinating and couldn't resist sharing it with friends. By the end of the first day, there were 20 users.

Shortly afterward, Biz got an insight about twttr's value after a hot August day spent ripping up carpeting in his stuffy apartment with his wife, Livia. Exhausted, Biz took a break and checked his twttr feed. He found Evan had posted a link to a photo of himself.

"Sipping pinot noir after a massage in Napa Valley," was Evan's tweet.

The sharp contrast between their weekend activities gave Biz a laugh—and he realized twttr offered a uniquely engaging way to communicate.

In short order, everyone at Odeo spent more time working on and using twttr than they spent on Odeo. A change was clearly in order. But Odeo had raised money for a podcasting product, and twttr was a text-based service. Also, twttr was an unknown quantity: "It's too early to tell what's there," Evan wrote on his blog.

Evan took a highly unusual step: he gave all of the Odeo investors their money back in late 2006.

After the buyout, Evan and Biz founded a new company, Obvious Corp., which would develop twttr and find a buyer for Odeo. A key hire was former Blogger product manager Jason Goldman, who would become Twitter's product vice president. (Odeo was purchased by startup SonicMountain for over $1 million in mid-2007.)

One of the first things Evan did after buying out the investors was to fire Noah Glass. It was the Golden Rule of business in action—Evan had the Blogger gold, and though Noah had played a key role in Twitter's creation, the two clashed, and Evan made the rules.

Being a punchline

Two months after launch, Twitter had just 5,000 monthly users. While a few techies were instantly hooked, others didn't understand how it worked, or chafed at the 140-character limit. It was difficult to describe: was it microblogging? a device-agnostic message-routing system?

"For the first nine months, everyone thought we were fools," Biz later told Terry Gross, on her national radio show *Fresh Air*. "People would say, 'That's the most ridiculous thing we've ever heard of.' The criticism at the time was Twitter is not useful. To which Ev would say, 'Neither is ice cream—should we ban ice cream and all joy?' We were having fun building it."

Besides the fun factor, what kept the team going? "From the very beginning, Ev described it as a communications platform that had revolutionary potential," says early employee Jason Stirman, who was Twitter's engineering manager. "It was this simple little website that kept breaking, and people were posting what they had for breakfast, but he had a vision for this thing, even in its infancy."

The original twttr site—which boasted a green-and-white color scheme—was replaced in the fall with a blue color scheme and revamped name: Twitter. A year after it was created, in March 2007, Twitter had 20,000 users.

"For the first nine months, everyone thought we were fools. People would say, 'That's the most ridiculous thing we've ever heard of.'"

Twitter's iconic bird logo.

Following Evan's Blogger model, Twitter was free for users. The company philosophy: build value before seeking profit. All energy went to keeping the site running and users happy. The company supported two important features created by Twitter users: the hashtag (#), enabling users to track popular or "trending" topics, and the forwarding "retweet" button.

Rocking Austin, Texas

To grow its subscriber base, the Twitter team made plans to attend the Austin music and technology conference South by Southwest (better known as SXSW). The previous year, a competing mobile-texting service—Google-owned Dodgeball—had won Best Product of SXSW. In a risky move, Evan and Biz would face down their better-funded competitor before SXSW's tech-savvy audience of more than 100,000.

Twitter's marketing plan was to install two large, high-definition plasma-screen monitors in the Austin Convention Center hallways and display attendees' Twitter updates. There would also be T-shirts emblazoned with the faux status update "wearing my twitter shirt."

Initially, the monitors didn't work, and Biz and Evan sweated through much of Friday night fixing them. Saturday morning, Twitter's server in San Francisco crashed. Then, finally, the screens worked. Attendees stopped to gawk at the message scroll—then chose which sessions to attend based on what they read. Many presenters began their sessions by announcing their Twitter handles. Attendees live-tweeted about what they heard.

In a risky move, Evan and Biz would face down their better-funded competitor before SXSW's tech-savvy audience of more than 100,000.

But Twitter made its biggest impact at night. Crowds turned like a flock of birds in the Austin streets as mobile-phone users read tweets directing them to the hottest venues and away from dull events.

Twitter was doing exactly what Evan envisioned. "It was the first time people were able to coordinate in real time," Biz recalled later. "This was spine-tingling stuff for us."

Stirman recalls, "SXSW was fertile ground for this product. You had all these tech people in the city without good ways to communicate with each other, especially at night. They had this 'aha' moment—Twitter *is* useful."

Twitter won Best New Product of SXSW 2007 and users tripled to 60,000. The team returned home to spin Twitter out of Obvious and incorporate it as Twitter Inc. By year-end, Twitter had 200,000 users. Twitter also captured the attention of the media and influential tech bloggers. It quickly permeated pop culture: in the fall, the forensic techs of *CSI* would solve a crime after following a tweeted clue.

Investors took note. In July 2007, Twitter landed $5 million in venture-capital funding led by former Odeo investor Charles River Ventures. Other funders included Union Square Ventures, Netscape co-founder Marc Andreessen, Ron Conway, and Feedburner creator Dick Costolo, who'd worked at Google with Evan.

A whale is born

After SXSW, Twitter would experience the hockey-stick-shaped, straight-up growth curve that is the dream of every start-up entrepreneur. In March 2008, when Twitter hit 400,000 users, the company set out to completely rebuild Twitter's technology to support the skyrocketing user base.

It didn't work. Twitter would be down, sometimes for three days straight. The company still had only two dozen employees. Any big pop-culture or technology event—say, Apple's Steve Jobs speaking at a conference—could cause a huge traffic spike and crash the system. Jack, Twitter's first CEO, ceded the post to Evan.

"We weren't ready for the number of people around the globe who would find Twitter so useful and so relevant to their daily lives," Biz recalled in a PBS interview.

Why couldn't Twitter fix its technical problems? It had money to hire more staff, but few engineers had both the needed expertise in Ruby on Rails and a willingness to work in Twitter's frantic start-up environment, Stirman recalls. To top it off, the founders were picky about whom they hired. As a result, Twitter's hiring lagged far behind its staffing needs. And by June 2008, QuantCast estimated Twitter had 700,000 monthly users.

At first, visitors attempting to access Twitter during outages saw the Twitter bird gazing sadly at a damaged robot. Biz wanted something more reassuring and purchased a graphic by Shanghai artist Yiying Lu of a whale being lifted out of the water by many birds, each pulling a rope.

Quickly dubbed the "fail whale," the image became both an object of derision and a cult hit. The fail whale inspired a fan club, T-shirts, and at least one tattoo. The chronic technical breakdowns did not discourage potential investors, either.

"When your product is so popular your servers are crashing every day," Stirman says, "that's the sort of thing venture capitalists salivate over."

In May 2008, Twitter would raise another $15 million from Union Square, Amazon founder Jeff Bezos's Bezos Expeditions, Spark Capital, Digg founder Kevin Rose, and social media author Timothy Ferriss.

Businesses@Twitter

Twitter's lack of a business plan made it the butt of jokes around Silicon Valley. Entrepreneurs created and compared lists of possible Twitter monetization schemes.

An April 2008 TechCrunch story on the sacking of two developers held responsible for the persistent outages mocked, "Mighdoll Out—Business Plan Still MIA."

Despite this, the founders resisted the idea of simply slapping ads on the site and searched for less-obnoxious revenue ideas. Meanwhile, big companies began experimenting with Twitter. In 2008, Dell reported it had made $1 million selling reconditioned computers from its outlet store by offering discount coupons on Twitter. Cable giant Comcast overhauled its poor customer-service reputation with its Twitter account @ComcastCares, which responded quickly to customer complaints.

At the same time, other entrepreneurs were building businesses on Twitter's back. The company's open source platform let developers use Twitter's code to create related services. Hundreds of thousands of Twitter apps would be built, including the Twitter scheduler Tweetdeck, which became so popular that Twitter would later acquire it for $40 million.

Some users tried out new personas on Twitter. A few were so amusing, they ended up with publishing and public-speaking deals. Two standouts were Fake Steve Jobs and Fake AP Stylebook.

Cable giant Comcast overhauled its poor reputation with its Twitter account @ComcastCares, which responded quickly to customer complaints.

Rise of the Twitterati

Aside from the obvious fakery of Fake Steve Jobs, however, Twitter had a big problem with covert imitators. As celebrities and prominent politicians began to show an interest in Twitter, other users were setting up accounts, pretending to be a popular film actor or rock musician, and sending out messages that embarrassed the star. To encourage celebrity participation and eliminate these spoofers, Twitter created a Verified Accounts program.

One late-2007 adopter was then-presidential hopeful Barack Obama, who cannily used social media to rally voters. In 2009, Oprah, Lady Gaga and Ashton Kutcher joined, with Kutcher becoming the first person to gain a million Twitter followers. The celebrities were a promotional bonanza for Twitter—each drawing press coverage and masses of followers, many of whom joined to connect with their idol. Oprah created a 43 percent traffic spike when she joined live on her talk show in April 2009.

The celebrity sparkle helped skyrocket Twitter's audience to five million users by the end of 2008, and to over 71 million in 2009. With just 50 employees in 2008, Twitter struggled to keep up.

"It's like we're on a rocket ship that we're just painting and suddenly it took off and we're holding on to the ship with our fingernails," Biz told the *New York Times*.

Institutional investors including T. Rowe Price and Morgan Stanley put another $135 million into the company in 2009, at a reported valuation of $1 billion. The financial support bought Twitter more time to explore non-intrusive ways of earning revenue from its mushrooming audience.

The new emergency broadcast system

Users delighted in announcing their trivial activities on Twitter. But the founders always imagined Twitter would have a higher purpose of connecting people around the world to promote good causes.

In April 2008, Twitter fulfilled that purpose. When University of California at Berkeley student James Buckley was arrested while photographing protests in Egypt, his call for help was a single-word tweet: "Arrested." His 48 followers quickly contacted the US Embassy and the press. Buckley was soon able to tweet, "Free."

In natural disasters, too, Twitter proved invaluable. When an earthquake hit China in May 2008, Twitter became the go-to news source for early disaster reports, as users on the scene tweeted information from cellphones. Reporters used the tweets in their stories, and charities joined in with Twitter-based fundraising appeals.

Twitter became an essential tool for political activists. This was brought home during Iranian protests in June 2009, when the US State Department asked Twitter to postpone scheduled maintenance that might take the service offline.

In late 2010, the Middle East began to erupt in anti-government protests that became known as "Arab Spring," and as oppressive regimes in Tunisia and Egypt toppled, political observers credited Twitter with playing a supporting role. In perhaps the ultimate demonstration of Twitter's importance, Egypt shut down Internet access in January 2011 to prevent protesters from using Twitter.

A screenshot of a Twitter news feed.

A business model is born

As Twitter struggled to find a way to earn revenue, its leadership changed repeatedly. Evan had taken the reins from Jack in 2008, while Jack left to found the mobile-payments startup Square.

In fall 2009 Evan brought on investor and friend Dick Costolo as chief operating officer. When Evan stepped down as CEO in October 2010, Costolo became the new CEO. In January 2010, Kleiner Perkins Caufield & Byers added a $200 million investment to Twitter's pot.

After some testing in late 2009 with half a dozen corporate advertisers, several revenue-generating programs officially debuted in summer 2010. Companies could buy "promoted" tweets—at $100,000 a day—and hashtagged "trending" topics. (If a promoted tweet isn't clicked on, a "resonance algorithm" detects this and removes it from view.) Local ads were announced as a coming option, but at the end of 2011 had yet to materialize.

Twitter reports that its promoted tweets get click rates of 3–5 percent, which is roughly 100 times better than typical click-through rates for online ads. In 2011, promoted tweets began appearing at the top of users' search results.

Where are they now?

In early 2011, Jack returned to Twitter as executive chairman while continuing as CEO at Square. Evan left Twitter, and Biz would follow Evan out the door to the re-formed Obvious Corp. For his part, Noah Glass's Twitter bio reads, "i started this."

In November 2011, Twitter had more than 100 million monthly users and 250 million tweets were posted daily. The company's valuation was estimated at up to $10 billion. Hiring finally sped up in 2011, with 500 new hires added for 800 employees total (100 of them in ad sales). Most notably, 2,400 companies were advertising on Twitter. One success story: Paramount Pictures estimated that in a couple of hours on Twitter it sold $1.5 million in tickets for the opening day of its film Super 8.

Internet-research firm eMarketer estimated Twitter would see $50 million in 2011 revenue and $250 million in 2012—substantial income *to be sure, but not yet a figure that justifies the level of investment funding Twitter has accepted. Is there more potential ahead?*

"We've only achieved 1 percent of what Twitter can be," Costolo says.

Will Twitter go public or be sold? The huge amount of venture capital invested—including a mammoth $800 million funding round in 2011—means a cash-generating event will likely come soon. Both Facebook and Google are rumored to have made offers.

tripadvisor®

TripAdvisor

Discovering treasure on its travels

Founder:	**Stephen Kaufer**
Age of founder:	**38**
Background:	**Degree in computer science from Harvard University**
Founded in:	**2000**
Headquarters:	**Newton, Massachusetts**
Business type:	**Travel reviews website**

TripAdvisor's 60 million-plus user reviews are some of the most widely read hotel and restaurant assessments in the world. The site draws more than 50 million unique visitors each month and ranks among the world's most trafficked websites. Just over a decade ago, however, TripAdvisor was on the verge of going bust.

A true innovator, the company rode out the storm and led where others tried and failed, building a "movement"—a thriving community that has nearly eclipsed the company itself. Waving the banner of "citizen tourism," the company attracts millions daily to its more than 50 million travel reviews. It boasts eight million photos from its members' travels, and a staggering 98 percent of new topics in its lively forums are replied to within 24 hours. People cannot stay away.

Going on vacation

In 1999, Stephen Kaufer just wanted to take a vacation. He and his wife were trying to plan a trip to Mexico, and, on the recommendation of a local travel agency, they went online to check out a few resorts. It was easy enough to find the glossy brochures and guidebooks, he says, but what he really wanted were first-hand opinions from those who had been there. Instead, at every website they visited, they found that the photos and descriptions of each resort were the same.

Stephen was frustrated. It was the height of the dot-com boom, but the principles of Web 2.0 had yet to take hold. Stephen just wanted an honest opinion of each resort, but all he could find in his fruitless Web searching was an endless loop of the same recycled promotional material. Eventually he found someone's personal home page that featured a few candid photos from one of the resorts and a paragraph about its facilities. He then realized that if the reality of this resort was quite different from its brochure, then it was probably the same for many more.

"Each time we were recommended a destination and hotel, I'd go online and search high and low to find more information, and each time, we'd find a problem—the hotel wasn't up to par, the destination was unsafe, etc," he says. "It took an enormous amount of time to research these places properly, and it was through these endless searches that the TripAdvisor concept was born—I wanted a single place where I could get the real scoop on a hotel, not just the official blurb from the property or a travel agent."

Stephen has always been an entrepreneur at heart. He co-founded his first business, a software development tool company, in 1984 while pursuing his computer science degree at Harvard. That company was eventually sold off in 1998, but, just a year later, Stephen's experience trying to book a hotel had him again thinking entrepreneurially. He said to himself that there had to be a better way to plan a vacation online. Soon after, in February 2000, TripAdvisor appeared.

"I was employed at the time, so I put the idea on hold for about a year and then started gathering a group of people who I thought would be interested in creating what would become TripAdvisor," Stephen says. "In 2000 we were up and running, albeit in a different way than we do now."

Life, and near-death, as a search engine

The company actually began life as a search engine. These were the days when sites like Lycos, Go and Excite were the most visited pages on the Web, and an upstart Google was making a fast name for itself with its authoritative search results. These were Stephen's models, but approached from the opposite angle. Rather than trying to rank results based on their perceived worth, TripAdvisor simply provided unfiltered links to any travel reviews on the Web. Stephen's aim was to unearth the raw, candid opinions of services and popular destinations in the travel industry—the opinions that lurked on personal Web pages in the furthest reaches of the Internet. Except it didn't work.

> "I wanted a single place where I could get the real scoop on a hotel, not just the official blurb from the property or a travel agent."

Stephen says he had a site he liked, but he wasn't able to figure out how it could make money. "When we first started out, our business model was entirely different to what it is today," he says. "We'd planned to sell TripAdvisor as a rich database to travel portals, online travel businesses, etc. We'd hoped to offer such high quality content that simply being in the travel business necessitated access to the TripAdvisor database, which we would then license out and/or get a share of the revenue generated on the page views from that. All the major players would have it, and no one would try to build it themselves because we'd be so far ahead of the game—that was our planned business model."

But after a year, he had only one licensing deal, and Stephen says he often joked that the quarterly revenue check he received from this wouldn't even cover the weekly free lunch he offered to his employees. "We found ourselves in the midst of a pretty fundamental problem—we wanted to be paid to have our content featured, but everyone else wanted *us* to pay *them* to have our content featured," Stephen says.

"We came across more trouble when 9/11 hit," he adds. "It was a hugely traumatic time, particularly for the travel industry. Everything we had in the pipeline was stalled and we were struggling to move ahead and looking at going out of business within the year."

In the post-9/11 days, TripAdvisor wasn't making any money at all, and Stephen was running through cash quickly. To avoid going bust, he slimmed down the team, took a pay cut, and carried on as best he could in the difficult conditions.

"Getting further investment was a tough sell—we were asking for more money, but couldn't show how we'd ever make any," Stephen explains. "We did manage to get a bit more funding, and it was about this time that we took on Expedia as a client and changed our game plan—we started targeting our content at the end user, rather than travel businesses, and making money through cost-per-click (CPC) advertising."

Voyage of discovery

Discovering a new business model was quite serendipitous for him, as Stephen admits that by fall 2001 the company was just months away from folding. Luckily, around this time Stephen noticed something interesting in his traffic figures: when TripAdvisor placed more relevant ads next to its search results, click rates on the ads soared to 15 percent—way more than the industry average of 0.2 percent. As this trend continued, Stephen found his elusive money-making potential and adopted a strategy of providing other companies within the travel industry access to its growing number of members via these targeted ads.

When users searched for localized travel information, TripAdvisor began selling keyword-based text ads for companies that offered services within those markets. In essence, the company used the gravitas of its user-generated reviews as a lead through which it fed readers on to other industry sites to complete their transactions.

"It proved very effective—we abandoned some of our original ideas and saw great success starting with Expedia, and then moving on to other big players and maintaining our growth to become what we are today," he says. "Finding a way to make this content profitable wasn't the easiest ride, though, and our business model underwent a few changes, with our biggest early success coming when we discovered TripAdvisor's unique capabilities in CPC advertising."

When he first started out, Stephen never intended to appeal to the end user, but instead planned on selling TripAdvisor's content to travel companies. When he realized the test site was getting 5,000 hits a day without any effort, he started looking for ways to monetize this traffic. When banner ads didn't prove too successful, he focused on sending extremely qualified traffic to hotels and online travel agents, and then charging them for this traffic.

With users searching for specific destinations on the website, they qualified themselves as interested in those specific destinations, and subsequently hotels in those places. Stephen saw there was huge potential here—if a user was looking at a hotel in Paris, and TripAdvisor surfaced a deep link that took that user straight into an online tour agent's booking pages for that hotel, the company could make some money.

"We approached Expedia and told them we'd like to advertise their hotels on our website in front of a highly targeted audience," Stephen recalls. "We'd only charge them for the traffic we sent them, and we explained how highly qualified our traffic was. At the time, Expedia had no idea who we were, but we'd piqued their interest and they granted us a trial period.

"After the first month they were sold—10 percent of the people who saw the Expedia links advertised were clicking through, when at the time click-through rates averaged about a quarter of a percent to half a percent. They started off paying us $10,000 a month, then $20,000, and soon enough we were into hundreds of thousands each month. We'd found ourselves a profitable business model and went from no revenue to breakeven within four months."

> "When we first started out, we'd never intended to appeal to the end user, but instead planned on selling our content to travel companies. When we realized our test site was getting 5,000 hits a day without any effort on our part, we started looking into ways we could monetize this traffic."

It was perfect. But as even Stephen admits, while the company was now on the right course, it didn't yet appreciate how valuable its user reviews really were. "People told us that they loved the information they found on TripAdvisor and that they'd like to post their own comments. So we added a 'write a review' button," he says.

As this functionality was introduced, the number of reviews grew tenfold. But in what he now admits was an error, Stephen didn't foresee the full potential of these "user reviews" and buried its user-generated content at the bottom of its pages, beneath links to reviews by outside organizations.

Banking on users

Luckily someone noticed the traffic patterns among the site's visitors, and the trend was clear: the majority were ignoring the outside links and going straight to the database of user reviews.

In March 2002, TripAdvisor turned a $70,000 profit, and from that point Stephen began thinking about the company with a view toward global expansion, he says. TripAdvisor began expanding its existing content into Spanish, German and Italian to find new audiences–and today it offers content for users in 15 different languages.

But as TripAdvisor grew into a top online destination for honest user reviews, it also experienced the first significant challenges to its commercial growth. As greater numbers of disappointed travelers felt free to post their comments, a number of hotel and restaurant owners became annoyed by the open forum TripAdvisor was providing.

"We'd found ourselves a profitable business model and went from no revenue to breakeven within four months."

Again, this was still in the pre-Web 2.0 days of the early 2000s, and the blogs and social media we now take for granted weren't yet around. A site like TripAdvisor, which was one of the first truly global forums for sharing opinions, was liberating for its users, but a cold shower for those in the hospitality industry.

Stephen's belief in sharing honest opinions works both ways, however: "Our policy is, the customer stayed there, so they get a chance to voice their opinion. But that's why we have always offered the management a response capability, so they can tell their side of the story."

What's more, the company claims that reviews are systematically screened by TripAdvisor's proprietary site tools, which are regularly upgraded. And the site's community of (now) more than 60 million monthly visitors also helps report any suspicious content, while a team of quality assurance specialists investigates suspicious reviews.

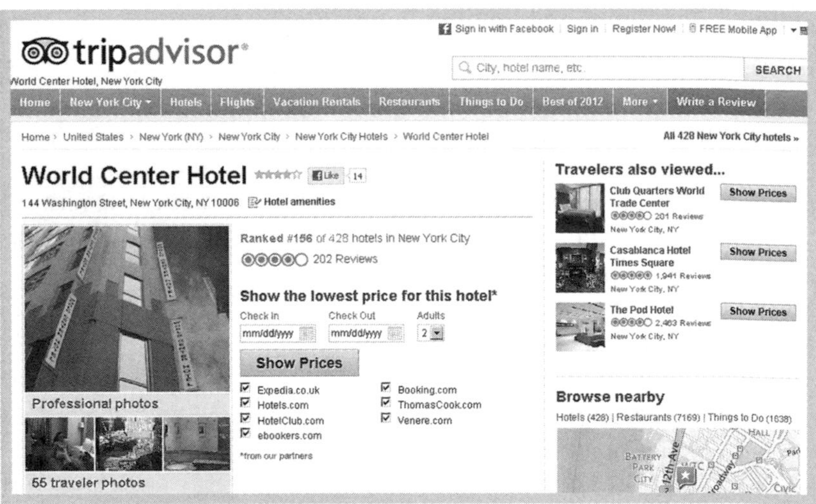

A screenshot of TripAdvisor's website today.

What's happened, Stephen says, is that the growth of TripAdvisor's user reviews and online visibility has motivated the travel industry to up its game. Hotels, restaurants and other services have increased their quality, and in a Darwinian sense, the best businesses in the hospitality industry have thrived.

"I still meet hotel owners who don't like to shake hands with me because I've hurt their business, but far more often I get people thanking me for helping their brand shine," Stephen has said.

Though he knew he had an innovative idea, Stephen admits the timing of TripAdvisor's launch proved to be another significant obstacle. By the time TripAdvisor arrived in 2000, the dot-com bubble was bursting and plenty of free-spending Internet firms had either gone bust or were well on their way. What's more, investors were growing cautious of handing money over to yet another startup.

"In our early days, we cut costs wherever we could—my wife owned a small software company that gave TripAdvisor free rent, equipment and supplies in our first year," Stephen says. "Our office was little more than an attic over a pizza shop, but it was free and it worked. We eventually got too big for this space—it comfortably fit eight people and we moved out when we hit 15—but even then we were careful to keep our overhead low. This was in the dot-com days, and even though it was commonplace to spend freely, we never did anything lavish."

Making friends the world over

"The company I started out of university was originally self-funded, and although this worked out well, I only briefly considered replicating that strategy with TripAdvisor," he adds. "By this time I had more responsibilities and a family to support, so we chose to raise money rather than self-fund. We went through three rounds of investment, raising $1.2 million in February 2000, another $2 million that summer, and a final round toward the end of 2001, which was around the same time the business really started to take off."

And when the company took off, it soared into uncharted territory for its time. There has always been a wealth of travel information out there, but before TripAdvisor it was difficult to find the most relevant information for one's needs. What Stephen had done was set a successful model for many other industries beyond travel and hospitality.

> "I still meet hotel owners who don't like to shake hands with me because I've hurt their business, but far more often I get people thanking me for helping their brand shine."

"We looked at all kinds of published travel information in newspapers, guidebooks and magazines," Stephen recalls. "We had staff members who read every single one of these articles, then tagged and indexed them in a way that was easily searchable, providing an incredibly relevant and thorough database that allowed users to search for, and immediately find, only what they were looking for.

"Over time, the focus of our content changed—eventually our travel editorial content was dwarfed by our user review content and users discovered how useful the 'wisdom of the crowds' could be in their holiday planning. Instead of listening to one source—a guidebook or an article that may be two years old—they could read 20 reviews, all posted in the last three weeks. It's fresher information that tends to be more detailed and, for many people, more reliable."

It's this combination of fresh content and targeted advertising that has given the company its incredible run over the past 10 years. TripAdvisor's traffic grew steadily and the company expanded its client set beyond Expedia.com to Hotels.com, Travelocity.com, Orbitz.com and many others.

What's more, as TripAdvisor expanded into new markets, the company that was once just weeks from going bust was suddenly attractive to potential buyers. In 2004, InterActive Corporation acquired the company and made it a unit of Seattle-based Expedia, which was TripAdvisor's first client. Under terms of the deal, TripAdvisor was allowed to operate almost autonomously, with Stephen still at the helm.

Where are they now?

TripAdvisor grew from a tiny startup in a cramped office with a test site that saw 5,000 visitors a day, into what is now the world's largest travel website in over 30 countries with over 50 million visitors a month reading reviews in 21 languages. What's more, its founder still guides the ship as CEO, which is something of a rarity in these days when CEOs leave a year or two after a company has been acquired.

As the 2000s advanced, TripAdvisor itself embarked on an ambitious plan of acquisition. In May 2007 it acquired Smarter Travel Media, operator of SmarterTravel.com, as well as BookingBuddy.com, SeatGuru.com, TravelPod.com, Travel-Library.com and The Independent Traveler Inc., publisher of Cruise Critic and IndependentTraveler.com. The next year TripAdvisor acquired UK-based user-generated travel site Holiday Watchdog.com, along with Virtualtourist.com, travel comparison site OneTime.com and a majority stake in vacation rental site FlipKey.com.

In 2009, the company purchased Kuxun.cn, China's second-largest consumer travel site and hotel and flight search engine. Finally, in 2010, TripAdvisor acquired the UK's largest independent vacation rental website, Holidaylettings.co.uk.

In recent years, Stephen says, the company has expanded its focus to providing new mobile products, and travelers can now access TripAdvisor's more than 60 million reviews and opinions via smartphones and tablets. The company's apps now have over 10 million downloads and are available in 20 languages, and its iPad app has reached number one among Apple's free travel apps in 85 countries.

In April 2011, it was announced that TripAdvisor would be spun off from Expedia as an independent company operating its brand of travel sites. Finally, later in 2011, it was revealed that TripAdvisor would go public, with the IPO valued at approximately $4 billion. On December 21, 2011, the company officially went public and became an independent company listed on the NASDAQ and a member of the S&P 500.

These days the company boasts 530 employees, around 300 of whom are based in Newton, Massachusetts, where the company was founded, with 70 more employees based in its London office, its second largest, and others in scattered locations. Its portfolio of websites contains listings and reviews of 400,000 hotels and 500,000 restaurants across 70,000 cities worldwide, and in the travel sector its Web traffic is rivaled only by Expedia.

At the time of writing, more than 250 companies have entered into an agreement to feature TripAdvisor content, says Stephen, including destination-marketing organizations, airlines, hotel chains and online travel agencies. More than 150 million people view TripAdvisor ratings, reviews and opinions on sites other than TripAdvisor each month.

Zynga

Creating Internet treasure

Founder:	**Mark Pincus (shown) (founding team: Eric Schiermeyer, Justin Waldron, Michael Luxton, Steve Schoettler and Andrew Trader)**
Age of founder:	**41**
Background:	**Three previous startups: FreeLoader, Support.com and Tribe.net**
Founded in:	**2007**
Headquarters:	**San Francisco, California**
Business type:	**Online social gaming**

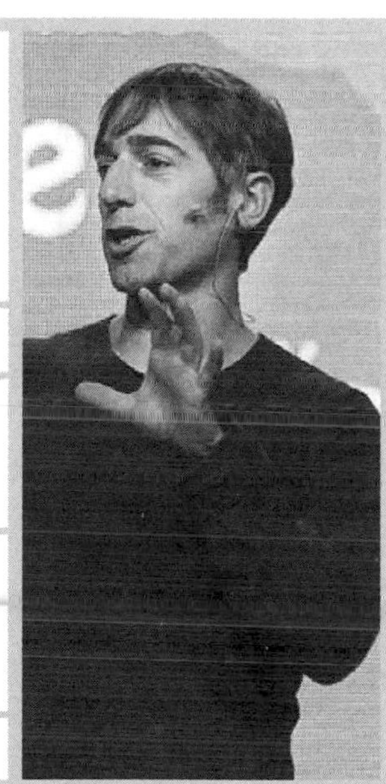

Few startups are valued at $3 billion two years after they open the doors. But that's what happened at social gaming company Zynga. The company's seeming overnight success was possible in part because its founder made his mistakes at earlier startups, before coming up with an idea that would transform the gaming industry.

Portrait of a serial entrepreneur

From early on, Mark Pincus set his sights on business success. The Chicago native graduated in 1988 from the University of Pennsylvania's Wharton business school, and followed this with a Harvard MBA in 1993. In between, he had a fitful career in finance, going through four jobs in five years.

Employers included investment firm Lazard Freres, consultancy Bain & Company, and Tele-Communications Inc. (now AT&T Capital), where he worked under telecom legend John Malone. Mark recalls he was asked to leave his Bain internship midway through the summer.

"I realized I didn't have a career working in anyone else's company," Mark recalled at the entrepreneur event VatorSplash in 2009.

In 1995, he started FreeLoader, a push-technology news service that delivered customer-selected feeds. His co-founder was Sunil Paul, a technology developer who left $1 million in unvested stock options on the table at his former employer, America Online. Thanks in part to a media blitz Mark orchestrated, FreeLoader quickly became well known.

Sunil's gamble paid off: in less than a year, the company was acquired for $38 million. Buyer Individual Inc. had initially offered $25 million, but Mark had turned it down.

While the financial windfall was incredible, Mark regretted that his short FreeLoader ownership didn't let him figure out the company's true goals. He also had the unhappy experience of working briefly for Individual after the sale. The new owner quickly lost interest and shut down FreeLoader in 1997.

"I realized I didn't have a career working in anyone else's company," Mark recalled at the entrepreneur event VatorSplash in 2009.

Later the same year, together with Stanford grads Cadir Lee and Scott Dale, Mark founded Support.com, which offered computer tech support. Support.com went public at the height of the dot-com boom in 2000 and was renamed SupportSoft Inc.

The problem? Mark wasn't interested in tech support. And once again, he had lost control, retaining just 15 percent ownership after the IPO. At VatorSplash, he described Support.com's founding as almost accidental: "Before I knew it, I was the CEO of a large, boring tech-support company."

Breaking away in early 2003, Mark co-founded Tribe Networks Inc., one of the first social media platforms. Tribe was enabled by a key patent for social network technology, purchased for $700,000 jointly by Mark and Reid Hoffman, founder of LinkedIn. But the platform didn't catch on. In March 2007, Tribe was sold to an unlikely partner: telecom/networking giant Cisco Systems Inc. Mark and co-founder Paul Martino ended up getting fired from their own startup, recalls Paul, who later became managing partner at investment firm Bullpen Capital.

After Tribe, Mark later recalled, "I stepped back and was more thoughtful. I was around 40. I realized I wanted to start a consumer Internet service that would be around for a long time, and that really mattered. I set my goals high and really wanted to start a company that would be profitable early and not controlled by investors."

Ironically, both those goals would prove challenging in his next venture. Though Mark had publicly derided other companies that took too much money from investors, his next startup would raise more venture capital than almost any other—a cool $1 billion.

Game on

Searching for the next big consumer Internet idea, Mark was drawn to the world of online gaming. People were playing games online in 2006, especially casino games such as poker. But they could play only against the computer or unidentified individuals.

At the time, Facebook had 50 million members. Mark observed that the most common activity on Facebook was viewing friends' photos. Beyond that and writing updates, there wasn't much to *do*. To address the problem, Facebook opened up its site to outside developers in 2007, so that new programs could be designed for the platform.

Mark saw his opportunity. His new startup's software would let users play against their Facebook friends. While most social networks aimed to help people make new connections online, his would offer a new way to connect with *people you already knew*.

The initial goal was to create and launch one social game. Mark decided it would be easier and faster to create a socialized version of a poker game than to create a new game from scratch. It would also be easier to get Facebook users to try a variation on a familiar game. This would turn out to be a canny move; while competitors slaved to create custom games, Mark's startup would be early out of the gate.

A non-techie himself, Mark began tapping his extensive professional network to find experienced programmers who could create and operate the game. Paul recalls Mark asking him and another Tribe co-founder, Chris Law, to meet him for lunch at a San Francisco coffee shop to discuss his start-up plans.

While Paul and Chris awaited Mark's arrival, a horrific car crash took place outside. Paul rushed out to find Mark emerging from a totaled BMW he'd been test-driving. The salesman screamed at the other vehicle's driver, who had run a red light. But Mark strolled into the restaurant clad in his usual work attire—a hoodie and jeans—and sat down as if nothing had happened.

"He was literally almost killed," Paul recalls. "I say, 'Do you want to go to the hospital?' and he says, 'No, I want to tell you about this start-up idea I have. Could you hire me a dude to write a poker app?'"

Paul and Chris loved Mark's social game idea. Chris had done research at Tribe on Korean social network sites that sold virtual "gifts" users could give to friends. Mark's social games would offer a platform for selling such virtual goods.

Another new wrinkle: unlike traditional online and console games, where players paid to purchase a game, these games would be free. Only players who chose to purchase upgrades or virtual items would pay.

The initial goal was to create and launch one social game. Mark decided it would be easier and faster to create a socialized version of a poker game than create a new game from scratch. This would turn out to be a canny move.

At first, Mark funded the new venture himself. The founding team consisted of Eric Schiermeyer, Michael Luxton, Steve Schoettler, Andrew Trader, and Justin Waldron. Nineteen-year-old Justin was a computer science student at the University of Connecticut, whom Eric recruited to serve as lead engineer.

Michael and Eric came from eUniverse (now Intermix Media). Andrew had been the CEO of Utah Street Networks, which operated Tribe.net. Server engineer Steve had worked with Mark on a short-lived project after Tribe sold. Other key early hires were Mark's co-founders from Support.com, Scott Dale and Cadir Lee, as well as Kyle Stewart, another Support.com veteran.

On Skype ... and in a garage

In June 2007, work began on *Texas HoldEm Poker* (later known as *Zynga Poker*). The team worked remotely for several months, staying in touch via Skype and AOL Instant Messenger. Justin was on summer vacation from college and living in Connecticut, while Mark and the rest of the team were scattered in various California locales. Steve was working out of a converted-garage home office in Menlo Park, and sometimes Michael—who lived in nearby Sunnyvale—would join him there. But for the most part, it was a virtual team.

Zynga's *Texas HoldEm* was launched on Facebook that fall. Facebook users took to the game quickly. Paul recalls that within a few months Mark told him Zynga was pulling in $1 million monthly. A key innovative feature of the game platform was a "social bar" that showed users what other games their friends played.

Seeing encouraging initial results, the team took an office at the Chip Factory, an office building Mark owned in San Francisco's Potrero Hill neighborhood. The staff grew quickly to 27, as Zynga hired more game developers and introduced socialized versions of other games, including blackjack, and its own versions of popular tabletop games Risk, Boggle, and Battleship.

"For me it wasn't the initial numbers that convinced me [to move to San Francisco]," Justin later wrote, "but the feeling that what we had created was fundamentally different than what gaming had been, and would therefore be completely disruptive. It felt like the first time you used Facebook or any other product that you now can't imagine living without."

Going to the dog

As Mark sought investors for the growing business, there was a problem: the startup had yet to be incorporated and was operating informally as Presidio Media. It was time to solidify the business structure and pick a name to brand the business.

Mark looked no farther than his beloved pet American bulldog, Zinga, who accompanied Mark nearly everywhere. The name comes from an African word for a beautiful female warrior. The domain name Zinga.com was already taken, so with a spelling change, the name became Zynga in February 2008. Zinga's profile would also become the company logo.

Zynga's logo features the profile of Mark's beloved pet American bulldog, Zinga.

Ka-ching + a light bulb

The combination of Mark's previous start-up track record and the poker game's early success made pitching investors easy. In February 2008, Zynga raised $10 million in Series A financing, with the round led by Union Square Ventures. Participants included Paul Martino, LinkedIn's Hoffman, MTV founder Bob Pittman, Facebook investor Peter Thiel, and Foundry Group.

One possible funder that didn't get on board was gaming industry leader Electronic Arts. Paul says Mark was nearly laughed out of the building. The games were all *free*?

"A lot of people didn't believe it—that you could build a company with that as a revenue model," recalls Steve, who's now founder of education startup Junyo. "But we knew we were on to something."

There was an upside to the EA meeting—Mark met EA executive William "Bing" Gordon, who immediately grasped how social gaming would shake up the industry. Gordon told Mark his goal should be to create an Internet treasure—the sort of company that provides something so useful, customers can hardly remember life without it. A Google. A Blackberry. A Facebook. Mark realized that was exactly what he wanted to do with Zynga.

Doubling down on revenue

In these early days, Steve recalls, "We weren't concerned with revenue. We were still working on trying to reach more users and find out ways to make the game fun, so they'd stay and keep playing."

One possible funder that didn't get on board was gaming industry leader Electronic Arts. ... The games were all free?

To bring in some income during this initial ramp-up, Mark essentially sold *Texas HoldEm*'s traffic to other developers, who placed ads on the pages where Zynga's Facebook games ran.

If players clicked on the ads, Zynga received a commission. The company collected just under $700,000 in revenue in 2007 this way. As Zynga's traffic grew, this income stream became a rushing river.

By early 2008, Zynga reported its audience was clicking the ads 50,000 times a day, with Zynga pocketing 50 cents each time. Then, in March 2008, Zynga introduced the ability to buy virtual poker chips. To Mark's surprise, some players spent $20 at a time.

Though fewer than 5 percent of players would spend real dollars to purchase virtual goods, the small purchases added up. Sales in 2008 leapt to $19.4 million. The company lost more than $22 million for the year, though, as it invested in more staff and Facebook ads to lure new players.

In July 2008, Zynga would raise $29 million more in venture capital and add $15.8 million more in November. The funding would help Zynga make a key purchase: YoVille, a game studio whose eponymous game would prove a major franchise for Zynga.

From the mafia to a farm

That fall, Zynga had its first big success with an original game. In *Mafia Wars*, players fought others as they built a mafia crew. *Mafia Wars* spawned a sequel, grew to eight million monthly users, and helped Zynga become the top Facebook app developer in April 2009. The company also moved onto other platforms with its first iPhone release, *Live Poker*. With business booming, Zynga moved to larger quarters a few blocks away from the Chip Factory.

Though fewer than 5 percent of players would spend real dollars to purchase virtual goods, the small purchases added up.

As the venture capital flowed in, Mark took careful steps to avoid diluting his ownership. He created private stock shares with stronger voting power than the common shares, ultimately retaining nearly 40 percent ownership of the company.

The next two years would see mind-boggling revenue growth. Sales shot up more than sixfold in 2009 to over $121 million, and would similarly skyrocket to nearly $600 million in 2010. But it would take until 2010 to achieve Mark's second big goal: profits.

Mafia Wars *was Zynga's first original game hit.*

Zynga values

Zynga had a clear approach in running the business: measure and analyze everything. Interviewed for an online Wharton journal, Andrew recalled: "I believe the differentiator between Zynga and a lot of our competitors [was] the ability to test, analyze, optimize [and] repeat that cycle. Everybody at Zynga—developers, product managers, business people, executives, CEO, everybody—had that focus on metrics and transparency, which really did allow us to innovate quickly, test things really, really aggressively, and ultimately, kind of dominate this space ... "

In shaping Zynga's corporate culture, Mark wanted to avoid creating the stifling environment he'd hated at his jobs. He empowered employees with an "everyone is a CEO" philosophy.

Wanting to pamper his hard-working staff, Mark hired a trainee chef from a nearby culinary school to serve up healthy lunches and dinners. The company offered on-site massage, acupuncture, paid gym memberships and other wellness perks.

Taking their lead from Mark, many employees brought their dogs to work. The company also had no traditional vacation rules. Instead, employees were encouraged to take time off as needed to rejuvenate and avoid burnout.

Doing "every horrible thing"

The next major game would be a game-changer. In summer 2009, *FarmVille* was an instant smash, becoming the first Facebook game to reach 10 million daily users. (The ensuing outpouring of status updates from *FarmVille* players pleading for game items proved so annoying to nonplayers that Facebook would later change its policy to limit the notices.)

But all was not well. Also in 2009, the pay-per-click advertising revenue model that allowed Zynga to log early revenue became notorious for scammy ads. Some automatically signed up visitors for monthly charges, for instance, while others had dubious product offers. At one point, the poker game gave users chips if they downloaded an advertiser's toolbar, which then proved difficult to remove.

The scandal was dubbed "Scamville." Some players filed a class-action lawsuit that would drag on for two years before finally being settled in Zynga's favor.

In a talk given to entrepreneurs at the University of California, Berkeley, that year, Mark said, "I knew that I wanted to control my destiny ... I did

FarmVille was another instant smash for Zynga.

every horrible thing in the book to just get revenues right away."

Coming as it did around the time the Scamville scandal broke, the remark was widely interpreted to mean Zynga knew and didn't care that some advertisers were shady. But Mark later denied this, saying he simply meant entrepreneurs should keep their independence and focus on generating revenue quickly. Whatever he meant, the timing of the comment—filmed and widely circulated on YouTube—couldn't have been worse.

Zynga responded by removing all ads from its platform in November 2009. Ads returned in January 2010, under a more stringent screening process. With the help of a media blitz similar to the one Mark pulled off at FreeLoader, the company rebuilt its reputation. Mark was a willing promoter, posing variously dressed up as a farmer to plug *FarmVille* and playing poker with Zinga.

The company also faced a steady drumbeat of criticism that its games ripped off those of other developers. Disney's Playdom and the independent maker of *Mob Wars* were among many who sued and settled out of court. For its part, Zynga sued Playdom when seven of its employees defected to the company. Zynga alleged the ex-workers supplied Playdom with the "Zynga Playbook," which outlined the company's strategies and plans. This, too, would be quietly settled a year later.

Investors were unconcerned by the legal issues. At the end of 2009, Zynga raised $180 million from a new set of funders including Andreessen Horowitz and Russian mogul Yuri Milner's Digital Sky Technologies. Another investor round from Google and Softbank Capital would pour in $300 million more in June 2010.

As 2010 rolled on, Zynga expanded with new games, new platforms, translations of games into foreign languages, and new geography. The company's first foreign office opened in Bangalore. Zynga launched many new versions of its games, such as *FrontierVille* and *CityVille*. The latter, a permutation of the old *YoVille* game, would become Zynga's most popular game ever.

The company also brought games to Yahoo! and the iPhone. Zynga began allowing corporations to advertise within its games—for instance, 7-Eleven introduced branded items inside *Farm Ville*, *Mafia Wars* and *YoVille*. Branded versions of Zynga games were also unveiled, tied to celebrities such as Lady Gaga and popular movie releases *Rango* and *Megamind*.

As Zynga became more successful, Facebook wanted a bigger cut of the take and wanted Zynga to switch from collecting cash payments to using Facebook Credits. The issue was resolved after a negotiation in May 2010 with the signing of a five-year agreement that saw Zynga switching to Facebook Credits and Facebook gaining a hefty 30 percent cut of the company's Credits revenue.

Fortunately, Zynga's growth rate was so massive that the effect of the cost hit was almost imperceptible. Sales grew nearly sixfold in 2010 to close to $600 million, and Zynga saw its first annual profit of nearly $28 million.

Where are they now?

In February 2011, Zynga topped $1 billion in venture capital raised with a massive, $485 million investment round that included Morgan Stanley, T. Rowe Price, Fidelity Investments, and Kleiner Perkins Caufield & Byers. Five months later, Zynga filed to go public, seeking to raise $1 billion. The company's total value was estimated at between $15 billion and $20 billion. Revenue in 2011 was close to double the 2010 annual figure.

In late 2011, the company's games had 232 million monthly users, and Zynga owned four of the top five games on Facebook. The company went on an acquisition spree in 2010 and 2011, spending nearly $27 million to snap up 14 other game producers including Wonderland Software and Newtoy. To accommodate its growth, the company moved into new quarters, expanding to more than 400,000 square feet of office space in San Francisco's trendy SOMA (South of Market) neighborhood.

The company also faced down criticism that its business model was too dependent on Facebook. Zynga announced Project Z, a planned stand-alone website where Zynga games could be played. New games were slated including Castle Ville, *the company's most lavish game yet, with Hollywood-movie-level graphics and a full orchestral score.*

Despite a late-2011 plunge in the US stock markets, Zynga went public in December 2011, raising a cool $1 billion in the biggest tech IPO since Google's back in 2004.

Chipotle Mexican Grill

Fast food grows a conscience

Founder:	**Steve Ells**
Age of founder:	**28**
Background:	**Culinary Institute of America graduate and chef**
Founded in:	**1993**
Headquarters:	**Denver, Colorado**
Business type:	**Fast-casual restaurant**

Steve Ells never dreamed of creating a fast-food chain with more than 1,000 units. He wanted to open a fine-dining restaurant like Stars, the famed San Francisco restaurant of celebrity chef Jeremiah Tower, where Steve worked as a cook in the early 1990s. Steve had always been interested in food and remembers watching cooking shows on TV with his mom as a kid, rather than cartoons.

Instead, Steve ended up changing the face of fast food and helping to invent a new category in American dining: the fast-casual restaurant. He created Chipotle, one of the fastest-growing chains in America. Today, the company has more than 1,200 outlets in three countries and sales that top $2 billion.

Doing the math

This sort of chain-restaurant success was far from Steve's mind when he started out. The Culinary Institute of America graduate didn't have the cash up his sleeve to open the swank restaurant he envisioned, and he was looking for a venture that might generate the needed funds when he started noticing the long lines outside a cheap burrito eatery that he frequented in San Francisco's Mission District. Steve read the menu and stood outside, counting heads.

He did the math and concluded the business was a cash machine. Steve decided to open a burrito place of his own, but with a couple of twists: the ingredients would be fine-dining quality, and everything would be prepared in the restaurant using classic cooking techniques. He'd use freshly chopped tomatoes, cilantro, black beans and house-made salsa to create a better-tasting burrito.

Steve returned to his hometown of Denver to investigate the idea of opening a burrito restaurant there.

"When I told my friends and family that I was leaving Stars to go open a burrito shop in Colorado, they thought I was crazy, but I had a very strong vision for the way Chipotle was going to look and taste and feel," Steve says in a company video. "I knew it wasn't going to be a typical fast-food restaurant—it was going to incorporate all the things I'd learned at the Culinary Institute and Stars."

Soon, Steve began testing out recipes on friends. College friend Monty Moran, a newly minted lawyer who would eventually become Chipotle's co-CEO, tasted Steve's first burrito.

"Steve prepared it for me at his house," Moran told *ColoradoBiz* magazine. "[He] had created the Chipotle burrito. He even had the mini basket with the basket liner. He prepared it wrapped in foil just like they are today. He was like 'Here's what I'm going to do.' And by the way, you should have tasted that first burrito."

"When I told my friends and family that I was leaving Stars to go open a burrito shop in Colorado, they thought I was crazy, but I had a very strong vision for the way Chipotle was going to look and taste and feel."

For the name of his eatery, Steve looked no farther than one of the menu's signature ingredients: the chipotle, a smoked, dried jalapeño pepper. It symbolized how Steve planned to elevate humble food items by using ingredients in uncommon ways, just as the jalapeño is transformed into a delicacy by being dried and smoked.

Steve's burrito concept impressed his father, a former pharmaceutical executive, who provided an initial investment of $85,000. Steve began scouting sites and noticed several national fast-food chains were checking out a small corner storefront near the University of Denver campus. The big players passed on the long-abandoned former Dolly Madison ice cream parlor because of its small size–just 880 square feet–and its rundown condition.

But for Steve, it seemed the perfect spot to try out his concept with collegiate diners without committing to a big rent. After extensive work to upgrade and remodel the interior, he opened the first Chipotle Mexican Grill on the site in July 1993.

Steve and his father had calculated that the store needed to sell 107 burritos per day to make a profit. In the first weeks, with no funds left for marketing, it was tough to lure customers to try a restaurant type they'd never seen before. Some people would wander in only to turn around again at the unfamiliar food, but Steve did everything in his power to entice them to stay.

Some eventually did, and soon the restaurant was meeting its initial burrito-sales target just off of word of mouth from enthusiastic customers. A few months later, sales exploded after the *Rocky Mountain News* gave Chipotle a rave review. Chipotle soon far exceeded its sales target and began selling 1,000 burritos daily. The company was doing 10 times its projected business plan three months after opening.

The initial menu was simple—just tacos and burritos. Steve knew he was strong on culinary knowledge but weak on business experience, so he wanted a simple business model. However, customers could make 65,000 different combinations of ingredients by calling out their requests as they walked down the restaurant's meal assembly line. This ability to keep the menu simple while still offering customers many choices proved a key factor in Chipotle's success: the concept was easy to operate, yet allowed each diner to have a unique meal.

The company was doing 10 times its projected business plan three months after opening.

Business was booming, and Steve soon added a second Denver unit in 1995. At this point, Steve was still thinking of Chipotle as a funding machine for his highbrow restaurant.

The third unit opened that same year, funded by a bank loan backed by the US Small Business Administration. Five more Denver restaurants followed in 1996, growing the chain to eight units.

Chipotle quickly became a trendsetter in a national shift by many American diners toward better-quality fast food. This restaurant format came to be known as "fast-casual," signifying a fast-food method of serving, but food quality more on the order of a casual, family sit-down restaurant.

The origins of the Chipotle "look"

The choice of a former ice cream shop for the first restaurant ended up influencing the entire chain's design. The interior of the store was bare-bones with an industrial, factory feel, including exposed ductwork in the ceiling. Steve kept this rustic-industrial feel (which he's described as "raw" and "funky"), with many stores sporting corrugated metal walls, halogen lighting, exposed ducts, steel posts, and concrete floors. A legendary perfectionist, Steve worried over every detail that went into the restaurant's ambiance.

Steve aimed for an aesthetic that would feel both durable and timeless, while at the same time exuding a cool factor that signaled the chain was a cut above ordinary fast food. The style also partly evolved out of necessity: cheap hardware-store supplies such as corrugated metal sheets were used in the first store as a way of saving money.

While each Chipotle restaurant is designed to fit its site, all the units have a few common elements, including the use of natural construction materials. Each Chipotle restaurant also has a sculpture by noted Colorado artist Bruce Gueswel, who creates pieces in the style of ancient Mayan culture. Gueswel's wife, Cyndi, was a college roommate of Steve's and introduced the two.

Steve aimed for an aesthetic that would feel both durable and timeless, while at the same time exuding a cool factor that signaled the chain was a cut above ordinary fast food.

Gueswel's art was included in the very first store. The art sets a Mexican mood and communicates to diners that the food is not your typical fast food. Gueswel also designed the eateries' chairs and other furnishings.

Fan-antics and other un-marketing

From the beginning, Chipotle spent little on marketing. Sales grew mostly through word of mouth—rabidly positive word of mouth. Over the years, diners have started fan blogs, sent photos, and made YouTube videos chronicling their passion for the chain's food. Early on, local food bloggers and Chipotle fan bloggers started posting about a new store's progress. By the time a store opened, everyone in town already seemed to know about it, and huge crowds turned out.

The company built close relationships with fans by corresponding with them by email through its website and by using social media platforms. It excels at creating simple, catchy slogans, which appear on plain white backgrounds in rough-printed black letters. Typical slogans are: "Mystery-free meat," "Burrito—or body pillow?" and "Served hot. Not heated."

Under the Golden Arches

Fresh, casual Mexican food became a national craze in the 1990s, and competitors sprang up fast. California-based Baja Fresh had a head start on Chipotle, opening in 1990. In 1995, copycat concept Qdoba started in Chipotle's home town of Denver. The trend caught the attention of major players in fast food, and soon all three chains were being courted by the big brands.

In Chipotle's case, Steve was looking for money to grow the 16-unit chain, which he now saw had national potential. At this point, Steve realized he wanted to focus his attention on growing Chipotle rather than opening a fine-dining restaurant. In the hunt for investors, Steve decided to approach McDonald's in 1997 through a Chipotle board member who had contacts at the world's largest chain. The timing was perfect: sales were flat at the burger giant, and the company was looking for new ways to grow.

A year of negotiations later, McDonald's made its first investment in a brand other than its own, becoming the majority owner of the budding chain by 2001. At one point, McDonald's controlled 92 percent of Chipotle's stock. While some restaurant-watchers thought it an odd pairing, Steve chose McDonald's—after talking to many potential partners—because executives there were excited by the company's prospects and even supportive of Chipotle's natural food values.

Chipotle lost no time capitalizing on the McDonald's Corporation's deep pockets and experienced site-selection team to begin a major expansion push. The first Chipotle stores outside Colorado opened in 2002, in Kansas City and Minneapolis. Other cities followed shortly after.

While some restaurant-watchers thought it an odd pairing, Steve chose McDonald's ... because executives there were excited by the company's prospects and even supportive of Chipotle's natural-food values.

Though now operating under the wing of a brand known for its institutional-grade food, Steve kept striving to improve Chipotle's food quality. In 1999, he read a report about Niman Ranch, a network of 60 or so small US farms and ranches that raise pigs humanely in open fields or deeply bedded barns, without antibiotics.

In 2000, all Chipotle stores began using naturally raised pork, a change that necessitated raising the price of pork burritos by $1. While critics said this would kill business, instead customer reaction was enthusiastic, and sales rose despite the price hike.

Through the years, Steve would continue to raise standards for food quality, adding programs to begin purchasing sustainably raised, antibiotic-free chicken in 2002 and naturally raised beef and dairy products in 2004. In 2008, the chain began buying organic black beans. Steve dubbed this philosophy "Food With Integrity." The emphasis on organic and sustainable ingredients became a major point of differentiation that won Chipotle a loyal audience and helped it trump competing chains.

While Chipotle thrived with McDonald's, other fast-Mexican chains didn't fare as well. Wendy's International, owner of the Wendy's hamburger chain, bought Baja Fresh for $275 million in 2002. Four years later the company sold it off for just $31 million after seeing poor performance. Qdoba was purchased in 2003 by burger chain Jack in the Box, which still owns it today. Qdoba has roughly 500 stores.

While competitors struggled or were forced to tread water under corporate rule, Chipotle made the most of its relationship with McDonald's. The corporate parent provided cash for rapid expansion and helped Chipotle open doors as it entered new markets. With the financial backing of McDonald's, Chipotle continued to grow and had over 500 units as it prepared to go public in late 2005.

The chain also added menu items during the McDonald's years, introducing Burrito Bowls—the burrito without the tortilla—in response to customer demand in 2003. Chipotle sold seven million of them in the first year. In 2005, Steve developed a new recipe for vinaigrette dressing that allowed the company to package ingredients from its service line as salads.

Chipotle did well during this time, with 2004 sales hitting $470 million. Chipotle also reached profitability during this time period, going from a $7.7 million loss in 2003 to a $6.1 million profit in 2004, then jumping to $30.2 million in net profit in 2005.

The company improved its processes and increased "throughput" (the speed at which it could move customers through stores), which allowed stores to serve increasing numbers of customers. The average receipt grew slightly as well, to over $8 per customer, an unusually high figure in fast food. A typical store brought in nearly $1.4 million in annual revenue in 2004, up from just over $1 million the prior year. Today, revenue per restaurant tops $2 million.

Leaving McDonald's behind

By 2006, McDonald's was changing its growth strategy and aimed to divest several chains it had acquired, including Chipotle. Steve was also chafing a bit under what he described as the company's "typical thinking and bureaucracy," so it was a mutually agreeable decision to part ways. In 2006, Chipotle went public in one of the hottest IPOs since 2000: the stock doubled in price on opening day. In sharp contrast to the steep loss Wendy's took on Baja Fresh, McDonald's sold its interest in Chipotle for a cool $1 billion against its initial $330 million Chipotle investment. By 2010, Chipotle's store-count would double and top 1,000 units.

Fears that Chipotle would suffer without the buying power of McDonald's proved unfounded. In fact, the company's profitability stayed strong even after the 2008 economic crash. While other chains—including its former parent—turned to price-slashing and dollar menus to keep customers, Chipotle stuck with its pricing and kept margins up.

Growth without franchising

Chipotle had picked up its first few franchisees during its time with McDonald's. Three McDonald's franchisees took an interest in the concept and opened Chipotle restaurants, too. But ultimately, Steve decided he didn't want to go the franchising route. The franchises were eventually bought back, and today Chipotle is entirely company-owned.

This is a stark departure from the approach of most fast-food chains, which rely heavily on franchising to fund their growth. By retaining ownership of all the Chipotle units, Steve kept more control over how the brand was presented to the public. Instead of selling franchises, he created a "restaurateur" program that rewards managers for excellence, including $10,000 bonuses if they mentor another employee to become a manager.

The program cut employee turnover, saving the chain greatly on recruiting and training costs. The same program also created long-term career opportunities for employees while developing top-performing employees into future leaders for the company.

Testing the waters overseas

Despite its smash American success, Chipotle has only dipped its toe into international markets. Two Toronto outlets opened in 2008 and 2010. In May 2010, Chipotle opened its first restaurant in London, on Charing Cross Road. The biggest change to the concept came in the packaging, with Chipotle managers quickly realizing they needed new packages with Queen's English spellings to appeal to British diners. The food remained virtually unchanged.

Taking a decidedly measured approach to international growth, a second UK unit opened in 2011, on London's famed Baker Street. Paris and Munich have been mentioned by Steve as possible future expansion markets, as the company develops managerial talent in the region.

Confronting controversies

Despite its strong company culture of social responsibility, Chipotle has nevertheless faced criticism at times for its practices. In December 2010, after an audit of the Minneapolis restaurants by US Immigration and Customs Enforcement, 450 employees were fired for presenting fraudulent citizenship documents, a move that led to labor protests.

In May 2011, Steve's commencement address at the graduation ceremony of his alma mater, University of Colorado Boulder, was met with protests over the chain's decision not to join in the Campaign for Fair Foods, which seeks to improve farm-labor conditions. Steve said Chipotle didn't feel a need to support the cause.

The "healthy" positioning of Chipotle's food has also come under fire The Center for Science in the Public Interest has pointed out that with over 1,000 calories, a giant Chipotle burrito is essentially two meals' worth of food. But the negative flak Chipotle has received has made no dent in public enthusiasm for the chain's cuisine.

Where are they now?

By August 2011, Chipotle's stock had grown by more than 500 percent since its IPO in 2006, to nearly $290 a share. The restaurants serve about 800,000 customers per day and take in an average of about $2 million apiece. The company saw more than 10 consecutive years of double-digit growth in comparable-store sales that ended only with the 2008 recession, and by early 2012 it had recovered to see six consecutive quarters of positive same-store sales growth. In 2011, Chipotle ranked #54 on Fortune *magazine's list of the 100 fastest-growing companies. In 2010, Steve's own pay topped $14 million in cash and stock.*

As Chipotle's success grew, Steve became more involved in philanthropy around his pet cause: sustainable, organic food. Over the last couple of years, the company gave over $2 million to organizations including The Nature Conservancy, Jamie Oliver's Food Revolution, Family Farmed.org, and the Niman Ranch Scholarship Fund. The Chipotle Cultivate Foundation was established in 2011 to continue this work.

Rather than putting energy into a big, international rollout of Chipotle, the company has focused on creating a second fast-casual concept that could duplicate Chipotle's American success. ShopHouse Southeast Asian Kitchen offers Thai, Vietnamese and Malaysian cuisine, while employing Chipotle's fresh-and-natural ethos and production-line delivery methods.

The ShopHouse name was registered in early 2011, and the first restaurant opened in September 2011 in Washington, DC. The name came from inspiration Steve found from trips abroad, eating in Asian shophouses, a style of family business in which the owners operate a business on the ground floor of a two-story building and live upstairs. The staple menu items are "bowls" and Vietnamese-style baguette sandwiches known as bahn mi, *seasoned with a choice of mild or spicy curry sauce or a tamarind vinaigrette. As at Chipotle, customers can customize their order as they move down the service line.*

"I always believed that the Chipotle model would work well with a variety of different cuisines," Steve said at the announcement of ShopHouse. "Chipotle's success is not necessarily about burritos and tacos, but rather about serving great, sustainably raised food that is delicious, affordable, and convenient."

Gatorade

Making liquid gold out of dehydration

Founders:	**Robert Cade, Dana Shires, Harry James Free and Alejandro de Quesada**
Age of founders:	**37 (Robert)**
Background:	**Medicine**
Founded in:	**1965**
Headquarters:	**Chicago, Illinois**
Business type:	**Sports drink**

Gatorade is now a PepsiCo "mega brand" generating $7 billion in annual sales for the drinks giant; but it wasn't always the case. Spin back to the 1984–85 NFL season. There were high expectations for the 2012 Super Bowl-winning New York Giants that year too. But a third of the way into their schedule, the Giants stood at a mediocre 3-3 record. Then a curious thing happened. After beating their archrival the Washington Redskins, the Giants' nose guard Jim Burt picked up the team's cooler of Gatorade as the game clock expired and poured it over head coach Bill Parcells.

Fans, teammates and media were shocked. Most saw it as a sign of disrespect. In fact, it was just a bit of playful revenge on Burt's part after Parcells had chided him all week that he would struggle against the Redskins' offensive line. But it was also intended as a celebration of the team's success.

Luckily for Burt, Parcells had a sense of humor and smiled as he was showered with the energy drink. And when the Giants won again the following week, Burt persuaded teammate Harry Carson to join him in another Gatorade bath. Because Parcells was known for being quite superstitious, the dunks continued. And the Giants had thus initiated a celebration that defied the traditional boundaries of coach and player. Little did they know then what an impact it would have on Gatorade and the wider world of sports.

Sports drinks overshadowing sport

The following season, as the Giants stormed to their eventual Super Bowl win, the media followed the unique tradition of soaking coach Parcells in a "Gatorade bath." Suddenly a sports drink was overshadowing their wins. Games were being watched just for that moment when the cooler was tipped over Parcells's head.

The tradition soon spread across professional and amateur sports alike. There it was, at the end of every broadcast game, a Gatorade-branded cooler hefted over the coach's head. And so in perhaps the most remarkable example of viral advertising in corporate history, what began as a little-known sports drink developed on a tiny budget in its creators' spare time grew into a dominant global brand with a name synonymous with success.

The Gatorade story has its roots in the 1960s, when the University of Florida freshman football squad was having a tough time. In August 1965,

25 of the first-year Gators were admitted to the university's hospital with dehydration and heat exhaustion. In fact, this was a nationwide problem, as late-summer heat claimed the lives of a number of young football players. Dewayne Douglas, an assistant coach for the Gators, mentioned his concerns to his friend Dr. Dana Shires, a research fellow at the University of Florida who worked under 37-year-old associate professor of medicine Dr. Robert Cade.

Douglas spoke to Dana about his team's troubles. Even those who weren't becoming ill were suffering. Some tried to rehydrate by drinking lots of water, but were experiencing stomach cramps. Those who consumed too much salt got leg cramps. A desperate Douglas asked if Robert and his team could look into why so many of his players were suffering from heat-related illnesses.

As a specialist in kidney disease, Robert had a lot of experience in mixing rehydration solutions, and though he had other priorities at the time, he agreed to investigate the matter. Joining Robert and Dana were fellow researchers Dr. Harry James Free and Dr. Alejandro de Quesada, the latter having recently arrived from Cuba with just $5 to his name. To the four of them, Douglas's request was intriguing for the riddle that it posed; not one of them dreamed they would get rich from their little side project.

Sweat and tears

Robert and Dana began by focusing their attention on the composition of sweat. Not much was known about it at the time, but after several months of research Robert and his team determined that the players were losing electrolytes and carbohydrates that weren't being properly replenished. Using these findings, they then spent $43 developing a beverage containing sodium and potassium that would move through the body quickly to help re-balance the players' carbohydrate and electrolyte levels. To make it tolerable to drink, the doctors squeezed 20 lemons into the concoction, on Robert's wife's recommendation.

But developing the drink was in some ways the easy part. Next the team had to convince the Gators' head coach and athletic department to let them test it on the players. They faced a prevailing attitude of "tough it out" in those days. Many teams didn't even provide water on the sidelines, instead believing that dehydration would toughen up their players.

Joining Robert and Dana were fellow researchers Dr. Harry James Free and Dr. Alejandro de Quesada, the latter having recently arrived from Cuba with just $5 to his name.

Thankfully Gators' coach Ray Graves didn't subscribe to this school of thought, having endured it himself as a player two decades prior. Graves didn't understand the science Robert and his team pitched to him, but he agreed to try it nevertheless.

With the coach's blessing, Robert and his team recruited two freshmen to be their guinea pigs. After their two-hour practice sessions, they would accompany Robert back to the lab where the researchers took blood and urine samples, recorded body temperatures and analyzed sweat wrung from the players' gloves. In return, Robert took the players out for a steak dinner—the only major development cost Robert incurred, as everything else was done in the university lab.

Soon they began giving the drink to all the freshman players, and as a sort of test, the freshman team played the varsity squad. The freshmen drank the researchers' concoction on the sidelines, while the varsity team drank water. As expected, the more experienced varsity team jumped to a quick lead. But then something quite intriguing happened. The varsity team wore down as the game went on, but the freshmen maintained their stamina and ended up winning.

Impressed, Coach Graves asked the doctors if they could make a batch for the entire varsity team, which was set to play the heavily favored Louisiana State University Tigers the next day. The doctors stayed late in the lab that night making 100 liters of their potion, and the next day the Gators roared to an improbable 52–14 victory.

Drinking to success

They called it Gatorade. All season long the Florida Gators consistently outlasted their opponents and beat teams they weren't supposed to beat. The University of Florida athletic department paid Robert and his team $1,800 to compensate them for the steak dinners and all the late nights.

Founder Robert Cade with an athlete enjoying the promising drink.

Before this point, neither Robert, Dana, Harry nor Alejandro had thought of their concoction as anything more than a little side project that, as sports fans, they enjoyed doing in their spare time. But now Robert began to wonder if Gatorade had commercial value. When the 1966 season started he told Graves he would again produce the drink for the team, but it would cost $5 per gallon. Graves said this was too high. But two days later when 24 of his varsity players were hospitalized with dehydration, he put in a call to Robert.

"Coach Graves called my house and told my wife that he needed Gatorade at whatever cost for both games and practice," Robert recalled. "So I told him he could have it at $10 a gallon."

Surprised to find himself in the position of a businessman, Robert next approached the university and asked if it would like to buy Gatorade from him, or perhaps give him $10,000 to keep the product coming. The university declined; however, administrators gave Robert the green light to continue developing it on his own. And so he did.

Robert borrowed $500 from a local bank in 1966, which he used to make several hundred gallons of the drink. At the same time the Gator football team was performing even better than the previous year. Like any good secret, eventually word of Gatorade made it out of Gainesville, Florida. The media caught wind of the Gators' advantage over opponents. And then Robert realized: it was time to grow the business.

By the time the University of Florida's stunning 1966 season ended with an Orange Bowl victory (which the team publicly credited to Gatorade) a number of copycat products were being produced. Robert sought the services of a lawyer, who helped register a patent for Gatorade's recipe and trademarked its name. The four doctors also filed articles of incorporation in Florida under the name Gatorade Inc., listing each of them as a director.

Orders soon came in from other universities, and for the first time Robert began bottling his drink and brokered a deal with Greyhound to ship it out on the company's buses. He also began giving Gatorade away for free to well-known athletes as a means of getting free publicity.

Becoming business royalty

It was around this time that Gatorade attracted the attention of a Northern company more famous for its cans of Pork & Beans. In 1967, one of Robert's interns left to take a job at Indiana University, where he befriended a vice president of the Indianapolis-based Stokely-Van Camp Co., famous for its canned foods. Alfred Stokely, chairman of the company, was intrigued by Gatorade after watching the successes of the University of Florida's athletic teams. He agreed to a meeting with Dana and the former intern, Kent Bradley.

Dana's request was simple: the doctors wanted $1 million for their sports drink. But Stokely-Van Camp's board balked at this offer, believing they couldn't sell a salty-tasting drink to the mass market. Instead, believing the product had limited potential, they negotiated a marketing deal with a royalty structure that gave Robert, Dana, Harry and Alejandro a $5,000 signing bonus and 5 cents on every gallon of Gatorade sold. The deal would make them very rich.

Surprised to find himself in the position of a businessman, Robert next approached the university and asked if it would like to buy Gatorade from him, or perhaps give him $10,000 to keep the product coming. The university declined.

Soon after the deal, Stokely-Van Camp worked on making Gatorade more palatable for the mass market. While attempting to maintain the integrity of the science behind the product, the new ownership sought to improve its taste. A number of new flavors were trialed, of which only orange was successful, and they added 2 percent more sugar to the original lemon-lime solution.

Many college football and basketball programs began ordering the drink in bulk, and professional sports teams began to take notice, as well. In the year prior, 1967, Stokely executives had quietly signed a $25,000 deal with the NFL for Gatorade to be the league's official sports drink—a deal that in hindsight was quite prescient. The agreement meant that every NFL team, whether they drank it or not, was required to keep Gatorade-branded coolers and cups on the sidelines of every game.

A glowing article about the drink in *Sports Illustrated* pushed its profile even higher. Soon the biggest stars of the NBA were claiming the cloudy drink gave them more stamina in high-pressure games. Tennis star Arthur Ashe even called Stokely's offices personally to see how he could get a shipment of the wonder solution.

Meanwhile, the royalties were pouring in for Robert and the other doctors. By 1969, Gatorade was being sold and marketed nationwide. It was the new official drink of Major League Baseball, and a major marketing campaign with Florida Gators Coach Graves pushed Gatorade ahead of Pork & Beans in Stokely-Van Camp's portfolio of profitable products. Gatorade was even Elvis Presley's drink of choice.

Things were on the upswing until later that year when the Food and Drug Administration issued a ban on cyclamate due to new research showing it was harmful to one's health. Cyclamate, of course, was a key ingredient in Gatorade, and the doctors were forced to regroup. Executives at Stokely-Van Camp were worried about the cost of pulling Gatorade from supermarket shelves, as well as how the product would continue without the sweetener.

Eventually the company replaced the cyclamates with fructose, which, like the banned cyclamates, is sweet and transports quickly through the body. While a number of other companies struggled with their rebranding after the FDA's cyclamate ban, Gatorade thrived. Company research found that very few consumers knew Gatorade contained cyclamates to begin with, and by simply not rebranding the fructose-based Gatorade, as other drink manufacturers did with their own products, very few knew there was a change in recipe.

Making it in the big league

In yet another development in what would be a key year for the company, Florida Gators Coach Ray Graves suggested to his friend Hank Stram, coach of the NFL's Kansas City Chiefs, that his team should drink Gatorade to help cope with the heat and humidity during the team's summer training camp. Stram agreed, and the Chiefs were so impressed with the "Gator coach's aid" that Stram kept it on the Chiefs' sidelines throughout the entire season ... which ultimately led to a stunning victory over the Minnesota Vikings.

Gatorade soared to the number one market position, and to capitalize on its popularity Stokely launched the brand's now-famous lightning bolt logo, which was meant to represent the speed with which the body absorbs Gatorade.

As Gatorade's profile grew, however, so too did the number of people trying to claim credit. Because Robert had stated in company reports that Gatorade had been partly developed using money from National Institutes of Health grants ($80,000 in total over five years), the federal government sent him a letter declaring its potential ownership of the product. Likewise, the University of Florida also sought its share of the profits, despite passing on the product previously.

Robert, Dana, Harry and Alejandro responded by forming the Gatorade Trust and selling their product to Stokely-Van Camp. While the US government backed off its claim, the University of Florida pressed harder, even spurning Robert's offer to give his entire share of the trust–13 percent (valued at $2.6 million)–to the school because University officials believed they could win more in court.

"Gatorade started out as fun," Robert told the *Atlanta Journal-Constitution* at the time. "A lark, just a little probe into man's machinery. It's not a joke anymore."

With the trust's legal fees—and tensions—rising, Robert left the university in 1971. Finally, in 1972, with the help of a US congressman, both sides reached a resolution. Stokely-Van Camp was allowed to keep the Gatorade trademark, while the University of Florida was granted 20 percent of the product's royalties, as well as $237,509 in back pay—and as of 2007, the school had claimed more than $110 million in profit from Gatorade.

With their legal woes behind them, the new ownership got back to the business of selling Gatorade. Throughout the 1970s, Stokely-Van Camp sold hundreds of thousands of gallons annually. The company continued to grow and make a tidy sum from the sports drink until 1983 when, following a bidding war with Pillsbury, the Quaker Oats Company purchased Stokely-Van Camp and Gatorade for $220 million.

Pouring into international markets

This marked a turning point in Gatorade's history. In its first two decades of existence, Gatorade had been marketed solely within the United States, but Quaker Oats saw potential in international markets. Beginning with Canada, Quaker Oats began a program of expanding the drink's distribution to Europe, South America, Australia and parts of Asia. By the mid-1990s these efforts returned more than $283 million in international sales. Gatorade was being sold in 45 countries, and the addition of 10 more in 1997 led to another 18.7 percent boost in sales.

Clever—and free—marketing campaigns helped drive the brand through this period. Having begun with the New York Giants, the tradition of the "Gatorade bath" soon spread to all professional and amateur sports and gave Gatorade an association with premier athletes and success, which it neither had to pay for nor invest much effort in perpetuating.

During this time the company also landed a major coup over Coca-Cola, which had just launched rival sports drink Powerade, by outbidding them to land Michael Jordan as a spokesman. The year 1991 brought Jordan—arguably the most well-known athlete in the world at the time—into the Gatorade fold on a 10-year, $13.5 million deal.

"I think if you had kept Michael with Coca-Cola and the advertising was well done, they would have been able to dramatically penetrate Gatorade's dominance in the marketplace," Jordan's agent, David Falk, said at the time.

The enduring success of Gatorade's "Be Like Mike" campaign had led to top stars from all professional sports associations (Peyton Manning, Tiger Woods, Mia Hamm, Derek Jeter and more) signing on to be product spokespeople.

Gatorade used this period of growth to expand its product line. After 20 years of just two flavors, lemon-lime and orange, Gatorade introduced Fruit Punch in 1983, and followed that up five years later with Citrus Cooler. These sweeter flavors appealed to younger consumers and delivered the product a new market audience. In the 1990s Gatorade expanded its flavors even further with Cherry Rush, Strawberry Kiwi and M'mmmandarina, among others.

Clever—and free—marketing campaigns helped drive the brand. ... The tradition of the "Gatorade bath" soon spread to all professional and amateur sports and gave Gatorade an association with premier athletes and success.

This was followed by Gatorade Frost. Described as an "active thirst" product, it was intended to appeal to consumers outside of the company's traditional team sports market. Flavors like Alpine Snow, Glacier Freeze and Whitewater Splash quickly caught on and far surpassed the company's expectations.

In 2001, another key year for the company, Gatorade marked its first move into the solid food market with the Gatorade Energy Bar. Packed with protein and carbohydrates, the Gatorade Energy Bar was intended to give people the same pick-me-up and endurance that the original drink was famous for. This was followed in the same year by the introduction of the Gatorade Performance Series. This specialist line of sports nutrition products included Gatorade Carbohydrate Energy Drink, Gatorade Nutrition Shake, Gatorade Protein Recovery Shake and Gatorade Nutrition Bar, aimed at elite athletes.

Gatorade was at its peak. It was seemingly going from strength to strength, and in a somewhat surprising move, also in 2001, the Quaker Oats Company was acquired by the mammoth multinational food and drink company PepsiCo. The deal, for $13 billion, solidified Gatorade's top spot in the market, with even greater marketing and R&D budgets, as well as further expansion into overseas markets. Gatorade was introduced to India, Ireland and the UK. By 2010, Gatorade was being sold in more than 80 countries worldwide, often marketed with localized flavors.

Where are they now?

While Robert Cade sadly passed away in 2007, Gatorade continues its climb and lays claim to being the number one sports drink by annual retail sales in the US, Canada, Brazil, Argentina, Mexico, Italy, Indonesia, the Philippines and a host of other nations.

New products continue to be released, aimed at new audiences. A low-calorie Gatorade drink called G2 was released and continues to be successful, earning expanded production in seven flavors. Dubbed "the top new food product of 2008" by an industry body after its launch, G2 generated more than $150 million at the cash register in its first year alone.

Then in 2010 PepsiCo embarked on a rebranding of Gatorade, introducing the G Series. The G Series consists of Gatorade Prime 01, billed as a pre-game drink; Perform 02: Gatorade Thirst Quencher, the original Gatorade drink; Perform 02: G2, the low-calorie version of the original; and Gatorade Recover 03, marketed as a post workout drink with additional protein added to help you "recover."

Later that year the G Series was expanded to include G Series Pro, aimed at professional athletes, and G Natural, which is made with natural flavors and ingredients. Meanwhile, 2011 has seen the launch of G Series FIT, a product line consisting of pre-workout fruit-and-nut bars, electrolyte replacement drinks and a post-workout protein smoothie.

Gatorade remains one of PepsiCo's "mega brands" within the company's portfolio, generating around $7 billion in annual sales for the company, and is still writing its stunning legacy in both professional sports and popular culture.

Jamba Juice

Whipping up a winner

Founders:	**Kirk Perron, Kevin Peters, Joe Vergara and Linda Ozawa-Olds**
Age of founders:	**All mid-20s**
Background:	**Real estate investor, college student, smoothie-store employee and newly minted MBA**
Founded in:	**1990**
Headquarters:	**San Francisco (originally San Luis Obispo), California**
Business type:	**Smoothies, fresh juices, healthy snacks**

As 1990 dawned, Kirk Perron was a health-conscious 26-year-old with an idea: he thought fruit-filled smoothie drinks could have popular appeal. The scrappy California native, who'd only made it through a two-year junior college, had no idea just how popular his new company—first known as Juice Club and later as Jamba Juice—would become. Today it's the largest smoothie chain in the US, with more than 700 stores and over $260 million in annual sales.

How did a young entrepreneur and three of his friends in the small Northern California town of San Luis Obispo come out on top in the smoothie wars, despite scant retail or restaurant experience? It took hard work, networking, a well-timed flat tire, and a fortuitous visit to put Jamba Juice on its way to success.

Portrait of a young entrepreneur

Growing up in Los Angeles, and later in San Luis Obispo, Kirk showed his entrepreneurial bent early. At 17, he put together a buyer syndicate of adults he knew at school and bought an acre of land in nearby Paso Robles, California, which he soon sold, Jamba Juice co-founder Kevin Peters recalls. With his share of the profits, Kirk purchased a triplex apartment, and later built and sold a duplex next door.

After graduating from Cuesta College, a local two-year junior college, Kirk was drifting. He was working at a Safeway grocery store, and hating it; he was looking to get out and start his own business.

In his 20s, Kirk had become a health and fitness buff, into gym workouts and long bike rides. After exercising, Kirk sometimes cooled off with a smoothie at one of the local stands. At the time, the few smoothie shops in the area were mostly shacks on the beach or hole-in-the-wall places.

Kevin recalls the shops of that era as "strictly geared for the granola people." In other words, they appealed to only a small segment of the population.

Ever on the hunt for his next business idea, Kirk began to think about the potential for introducing smoothies to mainstream consumers. It was 1990, and the low-fat health craze was just taking hold. Smoothies were a low-fat product. Kirk reasoned that if smoothies were sold in a clean, well-designed, friendly, well-located store, they could attract a broader audience.

There was a growing smoothie chain in the south—Smoothie King had started in 1973—but no established chain on the West Coast. No one had created a systematized *business* around smoothies, with appealing stores and consistently tasty products.

Drinking a smoothie one day, "something inside me clicked," Kirk recalls in his co-authored book *Jamba Juice Power*. "I realized then and there that freshly made smoothies and juices were the ticket. You can enjoy smoothies on the run, they taste fantastic, they don't cost a lot, and their health benefits are undeniable."

Opening the first store

After driving the California coast to check out existing smoothie stores for ideas, Kirk was ready to open his own store under the name Juice Club. He bought a few industrial-grade blenders and started experimenting with smoothie recipes. For his founding employee in the smoothie business, Kirk looked no farther than his longtime romantic partner, Kevin, then 24, who was studying business at California Polytechnic State University at San Luis Obispo.

For the first location, the duo focused on the neighborhood around the Cal-Poly campus, figuring it would give the store good traffic from college students and faculty. There was only one snag: the pair had to find a landlord willing to rent them a retail storefront. Few shopping-center owners were enthusiastic about taking a chance on a couple of young kids with no retail experience.

"Kirk was having a hard time getting landlords to pay attention," Kevin recalls. "He's 6'4" and kind of imposing, but they'd still look at the business model and think, 'Maybe not.'"

After months of pitching their plan to landlords without success, Kirk caught a break. An old family friend knew the landlord of one small shopping center near campus, Ferrini Square.

The owner put them through their paces. How many customers did they anticipate? How much sales did they expect to do in the first year? Kirk said his goal was to do $2,000 a day at the store.

The landlord was convinced, and the pair signed a lease for a small store. After fitting in the refrigerators and freezers needed to store the smoothie ingredients, Kevin recalls there was less than 800 square feet of retail space left.

Next, Kirk cobbled together the money needed to build the first store, using his own cash flow from the triplex, as well as loans from friends and family. Construction was originally estimated at $170,000, but ran over and neared $200,000.

Now that the store was taking shape, Juice Club needed someone who knew the smoothie business. For an operations manager and second founding employee, Kirk picked another aspiring young entrepreneur he'd met in the checkout line at Safeway: Joe Vergara, who was managing a local smoothie shop for a small chain.

In creating the first store, Kirk and Kevin had a chance to indulge a personal passion for design and architecture. Every detail was belabored—the curve of the counter, the shade of white for the walls, the way wheatgrass was displayed in the case, the stain color on the wood floors. The effort paid off immediately, Kevin says.

"People were invigorated as much by stepping into the space as by drinking the smoothies," he says. "People started asking from the very beginning, 'Wow—is this a chain?'"

Cruel summer

Juice Club opened on April 7, 1990. From the start, the store had a dozen employees, Kevin recalled, as the shop's hours were long (7 a.m. to 11 p.m.). Kirk would often open the doors in the morning, while Joe would take the day shift and Kevin would arrive after classes at Cal-Poly to work and then close up. Business grew gradually but steadily, and within 60 days the employee count was closer to 30.

> *"Team members in the early days, their job description was very simple—do whatever it takes to make the customer's experience the best."*

With essentially no initial marketing budget, Juice Club relied on word of mouth. Kevin noticed a trend: women would come in, have a smoothie, and then return with their boyfriends. From the beginning, Juice Club smoothies had sexy names such as Hawaiian Lust, Boysenberry Bliss and Pacific Passion, so there was a romantic angle to coming into Juice Club that worked to draw more customers.

From Juice Club's early days, customer service was a huge focus. In a company video, Kirk recalls, "Team members in the early days, their job description was very simple—do whatever it takes to make the customer's experience the best." Staff worked to build personal rapport with each visitor.

This approach was paying off in a growing audience of enthusiastic, repeat customers. It seemed an auspicious time to open an eatery that sold cold drinks, as a hot California summer lay just ahead. Kirk was certain business would boom. But when June rolled around, the green Juice Club team got a nasty surprise.

With the conclusion of the spring semester, the Cal-Poly campus emptied out as most students decamped back home for the summer. Most of the first customers were from the college; year-round residents in town had yet to catch on to Juice Club.

Traffic at the store plummeted. The next two and a half months were nerve-wracking as the team strategized how to keep the shop going until the fall, when the students would return.

While there were still some sales coming in, expenses had to be covered in part by Kirk's rental income and family aid. To save money, staff was cut back to a skeleton crew, with one of the founders often holding down the early-morning and late-night hours alone, Kevin recalls.

But aside from staff cuts, the founding team looked for positive ways to use the slow time.

It was during this tough first summer that Juice Club launched a marketing program, selling reusable Juice Club-branded plastic mugs for patrons who didn't want to create waste by getting Styrofoam cups. Soon, Kevin recalls, San Luis Obispo's streets teemed with cyclists and joggers with Juice Club mugs clipped onto the outsides of their backpacks, essentially creating walking ads for the store.

"We were both biting our nails a bit, Kirk especially," says Kevin. "But I'll never forget how keeping our game face on encouraged customers to keep coming back."

Inquiries were also made at the college, and Juice Club was added to a city tour Cal-Poly provided to new students during Welcome Week. This canny move would deliver prospective customers straight to the shop's door at the start of school in the fall. Product quality was also under scrutiny, and Kirk worked to find relationships with the best fresh- and frozen-fruit providers to make sure the smoothies were the best tasting.

Despite the financial stress, the team tried hard to maintain the upbeat, friendly atmosphere Kirk sensed was essential to setting Juice Club apart from other smoothie stores. The few customers that did come in were met by smiling, attentive staff and never guessed the company was experiencing a cliffhanger of a summer.

"We were both biting our nails a bit, Kirk especially," says Kevin. "But I'll never forget how keeping our game face on encouraged customers to keep coming back."

The home office

In September, school resumed, the weather was still warm, and word spread quickly about Juice Club. "Sales just exploded," Kevin recalls.

From their initial goal of doing $2,000 a day of business, Juice Club now often brought in five times that figure. At the end of the first year, sales were roughly $600,000, Kevin recalls, and the store turned a profit. Within two years, the annual figure would hit $1 million at the original store.

As Juice Club's sales volume grew, the small store quickly proved inadequate to house all the smoothie ingredients. Kirk and Kevin ended up renting a small house next door to Ferrini Square, which they used as living quarters and office. The garage served as overflow storage space for the store.

It was decided the best way to grow Juice Club was through franchising. Kirk pinned up a large US map at home and put the first pin in San Luis Obispo. It took until 1992 to get all of the franchise paperwork squared away, and then the founders started visiting franchise trade shows to pitch their concept to prospective franchise buyers.

To help drive their franchising effort, the trio brought on a fourth founding employee—another local resident and Cal-Poly acquaintance of Kevin's, Linda Ozawa-Olds, who had just completed an MBA at the school. The house's kitchen became her office while Kevin, who'd enjoyed his business-writing classes at Cal-Poly, wrote the four-inch-thick franchise operations manual in a spare bedroom.

In a surprising twist, the young team with two gay men in leadership roles ended up selling their first franchise to a retired Marine colonel in his forties, Robert McCormick. The connection: he was a health and fitness buff, too. He opened the first franchise store in Irvine, California, in 1993, and another pin went into the map at Kirk and Kevin's house.

By 1994, meetings with prospective franchisees were increasing and Kirk wanted a more professional-looking office. Juice Club took over an empty storefront next door to the store, outfitting it with wood floors and crown moldings. As word spread that Juice Club was franchising, top-caliber prospects began to visit the new office—a carload of Pepsi executives at one point, and even a member of the royal family of Bahrain, Kevin recalls.

That same year, Scott and Celia Denig got a flat tire in San Luis Obispo, and wandered into Juice Club while they waited for a tire change at a nearby repair shop. The young couple ended up staying in town overnight to investigate the concept further, and opened the third store in Palo Alto, California, in 1994.

Venture capitalists come knocking

The accidental visitor to the Palo Alto Juice Club store would prove to have an even greater impact on Juice Club's future. The wife of Technology Venture Investors general partner Bob Kagle came in for a smoothie and then, like so many women before her, came back with her husband. Kagle saw lines out the door and enthusiastic customers, and thought he had found the next Starbucks—an analogy that came readily to mind, as Kagle was also a Starbucks investor.

"It seemed like everyone had a tremendous sense of affirmation about buying this smoothie," he told the *Los Angeles Times*.

Franchisees continued to sign up, and Juice Club had commitments for a total of 20 stores when Kagle led a $3 million investment round in Juice Club in late 1994. Also participating: Starbucks founder Howard Schultz.

As they got to know the business, the new investors saw two troubling problems. One lay in the business model—because Juice Club was cash poor, it couldn't provide franchisees with location build-outs or purchase the land under their stores, as many franchise chains do. The franchise fee Juice Club could ask under these circumstances was too low to generate the cash needed to build a robust franchise support team.

Instead, Schultz wanted Juice Club to follow the same model as his company and own its stores. The funding round was delivered on the promise that Juice Club would stop franchising and use the money to build its own stores.

A new name

The other problem was the name. Schultz and other board members impressed upon the team that "Juice Club" was too generic and didn't successfully convey all the qualities of the brand—health, fitness, fun, great service. Most importantly, it included no words that could be trademarked to help protect the brand's identity from imitators. This was a problem the founders were well aware of, as they'd seen copycat smoothie bars popping up near their stores named Juice Bistro, Juice Bar, and more.

The search for a new name would be a tortuous one. Two different ad agencies were employed to come up with a brand name and logo, one after the other, but their ideas were rejected. Finally, Kirk, Kevin, Linda and Joe decided to do it themselves. The pressure was on: new stores were being built and signage was on hold until the new name was chosen.

"We were doing pretty sophisticated focus groups and marketing to button up what the brand meant, so we could change the name and launch the rocket," Kevin says. "But it had to feel right."

The other problem was the name ... "Juice Club" was too generic and didn't successfully convey all the qualities of the brand—health, fitness, fun, great service.

They brainstormed. They went to the Cal-Poly library and looked through books, including dictionaries in other languages. Finally, they went out for fish and chips together and came to the Swahili word "jama", which means "to celebrate." This evolved into "jamba." To go with the new name, they chose the now-familiar swirl, which represents a smoothie being mixed in the blender.

Prepare for take-off

After rebranding as Jamba Juice in 1995, the company quickly jumped to 30 stores. The following year, Jamba Juice made a valuable alliance with upscale-organic juggernaut Whole Foods Market. This allowed Jamba Juice to operate smoothie bars inside the grocery stores, creating a new channel for expansion.

In the late 1990s, the company began adding more food to the menu, adding Jambola pastries in 1998, and a Souprimos soup line in 1999. As profits increased, the chain also returned to selling some franchises, while still keeping the majority of its stores company-owned. In 1998, the chain cracked 100 stores; in 2000, sales neared $100 million, but per-unit sales weren't what they once were. Saturation had brought average sales down to about $324,000 a year, a report from Coriolis Research found. During this time period, the chain opened at least one store a week for several years running.

By the turn of the 21st century, the founding team at Jamba Juice was departing. In 2000, former Burger King executive Paul Clayton was brought in as CEO. Kevin left in 2001 to go into architecture and design full-time, and Linda partnered with fellow founder Joe to run eight franchise Jamba Juice stores on the Central Coast, including the original store. Linda also taught marketing at Cal-Poly. By 2004, the overall Jamba Juice chain had grown to more than 350 units.

To fuel this growth, over the years Jamba Juice raised an additional $44 million from venture investors, including Microsoft co-founder Paul Allen's Global Retail Partners. It turned out that the investor group would need patience—Jamba Juice did not go public until 2006, a 16-year wait for the early investors.

As it prepared for the IPO in 2005, Jamba Juice had 532 stores, of which just over 200 were franchises. Also in 2005, the first international Jamba Juice store opened, in the Bahamas. By this time, Kirk had also left the company.

Jamba Juice went public in 2006 using a somewhat unconventional method: the company was acquired for $265 million by a publicly traded "blank check" acquisition company, Services Acquisition Corp. International, which was created expressly to buy up companies. SAC then changed its name to Jamba Inc. The maneuver allowed Jamba to skip the grueling investor "road show" that usually precedes an IPO and avoid making detailed financial disclosures.

Where are they now?

Flush with new cash from the IPO deal, Jamba grew quickly to over 730 units by 2008 and nearly $334 million in sales. But there was trouble brewing: Jamba racked up losses each year, hitting a high of nearly $150 million in 2008, just in time to confront a major economic recession.

Jamba was in a poor position to withstand the downturn on the heels of its rapid growth and losses. CEO Clayton resigned and Safeway executive James White was named as Clayton's replacement in late 2008.

The company's policy of owning most of its stores had come back to bite it, causing revenue to plummet, along with the company's stock price. A re-franchising initiative found franchise buyers for more than 140 company stores, which generated franchise fees and cut the number of company-owned units. Revenue fell to $255 million in 2010, but losses also fell, shrinking to under $21 million.

Turnaround efforts have focused on repositioning Jamba as a health and fitness brand with food for all three meals of the day. Hot beverages were introduced in stores for the cold months to shore up winter revenue. White also cut deals to license the Jamba name to grocery goods makers to bring Jamba products, including smoothie mixes and fruit chips, to grocery shelves.

By year-end 2010, comparable-store sales had stabilized. The company returned to profitability in mid-2011.

One bright spot in Jamba's recent struggles is that one founding employee returned to the fold. In 2009, Linda returned and, with her husband, bought and still operates nine Jamba franchise stores in California, including the original store.

Pinkberry

Creating a swirl in the market

Founders:	**Hyekyung "Shelly" Hwang and Young Lee**
Age of founders:	**31 and 39**
Background:	**Restaurant manager and architect**
Founded in:	**2004**
Headquarters:	**Los Angeles, California**
Business type:	**Frozen yogurt shops**

After the turn of the 21st century, frozen yogurt was a fading American fad. By 2005, the volume of frozen treats produced in the US had fallen by half compared with 1990, the International Dairy Foods Association reported.

Then along came two entrepreneurs from South Korea, former restaurant manager Shelly Hwang and architect Young Lee. They had a new twist on frozen yogurt that would win them wildly enthusiastic fans and help reinvent the category to suit modern tastes. But that triumph came only after the pair faced down problems including irate neighbors, unhelpful relatives and nasty lawsuits.

School ... and school of hard knocks

Shelly came to the US in 1992 to study business at the University of Southern California. After she graduated, Shelly's father put her in charge of an LA franchise restaurant he owned with some business partners. Then just 26, Shelly soon realized she was in over her head.

The full-service restaurant had many different menus—steaks, pastas, desserts, a buffet. Shelly tinkered with the offerings, but customers were still confused. Was it a steak house? A pasta bar? Sales were only about $500 a day, she recalls. She lasted two years before the restaurant closed down.

"I kept increasing the menu, instead of specializing it," Shelly recalls. "I lost a lot of money—not my money, but our money. And after that, my father stopped supporting me."

Shelly next started a textile business, an enterprise that ultimately failed as well. She made many trips abroad while learning the business, especially to Italy. It was there, on a visit to the affluent northern Italian town of Reggio Emilia, that she says she encountered tiny, mom-and-pop frozen yogurt shops.

The yogurt they sold wasn't like sweet, heavy American yogurt—it was non fat, tart and often topped simply with fresh fruit. She learned that some of these small, utilitarian shops had been operating for 25 years or more. They were successful businesses on a small scale, Shelly saw, but the owners didn't have the vision to build a chain.

Intrigued, Shelly tracked down the local shops' Italian yogurt manufacturer and brought samples back to the USA to test. She missed the restaurant business and still dreamed of opening her own restaurant.

"I didn't have a research-and-development person," she recalls. "I had a tiny office, one machine, and I'd just drop in the yogurt and milk and taste it and throw it out, again and again and again."

Dealing with rejection

Meanwhile, Shelly thought she would try a time-tested dining concept first, to give her a more assured success. She laid plans to open an English-style teahouse.

Scouting locations, she located a funky, 650-square-foot West Hollywood storefront on Huntley Drive, just south of main thoroughfare Santa Monica Boulevard. The storefront was a converted two-car garage that had formerly served as a tattoo parlor. The store was set back from the street, which Shelly thought would help create a relaxing, secluded feel for the teahouse.

Shelly signed a lease for the space, a move she would soon regret. Her application for the teahouse's liquor license was opposed by local residents. The store's neighbors turned out in force at numerous public hearings to voice their objections. They didn't want their quiet street disrupted by loud drunks. The process dragged on for nearly a year before her application was denied.

The original store in West Hollywood.

By now, Shelly had experimented with her yogurt recipe until she hit on a formula she liked. Already under lease for the West Hollywood store, she decided to go to Plan B: she would open a frozen yogurt shop. This would not require a liquor license, so she would be free to open the doors as soon as the shop interior was built.

"I didn't have a research-and-development person. I had a tiny office, one machine, and I'd just drop in the yogurt and milk and taste it and throw it out, again and again and again."

Shelly was excited by the prospect of moving forward to open her own eatery. But her father, who had since returned to South Korea, didn't think much of her idea.

"My father didn't call me for a year," she says. "'You are embarrassing to my family members,' he said. 'You are going to be sitting behind the counter, reading a magazine and selling a couple yogurts. Do not call me anymore!'"

Cold start

Mindful of her previous restaurant failure, Shelly envisioned a simple menu for her yogurt store. Initially, there would be just two flavors, "original" or plain, and green tea. There was also shaved ice with flavored syrup, as an alternative for the lactose intolerant. The store wouldn't even sell bottles of water to go with the yogurt—just a variety of toppings, mostly fresh fruit. The yogurt came in four sizes, from extra-small to large.

With the menu in place, Shelly sought a designer. She wanted an eye-catching, memorable look that imparted a refreshing, restful feeling. She interviewed several architects before choosing Young, whom she knew by reputation.

Young told her the Huntley Drive site was the worst retail location he'd ever seen. Parking was scarce, the store was hardly visible due to its setback, and the tiny store was off the main drag for pedestrians. But Shelly told Young he had to figure out a design for the existing store.

Shelly sought a designer. She wanted an eye-catching, memorable look that imparted a refreshing, restful feeling.

Together, they brainstormed a name for the concept. Shelly says they came up with Pinkberry "because pink is a very positive color, and the word had a nice rhyme to it. We wanted people to picture fresh, happy berries."

While the big yogurt chains of the 1980s had a cheap, fast-food feel, Young created a sleek, "fun," high-style look for Pinkberry. The décor featured lots of white, with sherbet-colored dots of pink, orange and green for accents.

Young selected top-drawer, name-designer furnishings: sleek, translucent Philippe Starck Victoria Ghost chairs; Le Klint light fixtures that evoked a ball of swirled yogurt; white, oval Isamu Noguchi tables; and minimalist wood-strip Case Study benches. A pebbly floor evoked the beach and summertime. The company logo was a simple pink swirl topped with a fruit leaf. The feeling he was going for, Young said later, was not unlike the makeup counter at Bloomingdale's—warm, flattering lighting and an environment that makes customers feel special.

Pinkberry opened on January 10, 2005, staffed by Shelly and one part-time employee hired through a classified ad. Midwinter wasn't the best time to open a frozen-treat shop, but Shelly didn't want to wait.

When she put out the "Open" sign, a couple from the neighborhood came in—not to buy, but to offer their condolences. They told her bluntly that a yogurt shop was not going to make it in this odd locale. Then they bought a cup of yogurt, just because they felt bad for her.

For the month of January, total sales were $70. "I was really depressed," Shelly recalls. "I thought, I've got this home equity loan from the bank and if I lose this business, I'll lose my house, and I'll have to go back to Korea and beg my parents to live with them."

Confident that she could get customers by handing out free samples, Shelly loaded a cooler with yogurt and began walking up and down the street. But few pedestrians were willing to accept her free samples. She literally couldn't give the yogurt away.

They told her bluntly that a yogurt shop was not going to make it in this odd locale. Then they bought a cup of yogurt ... they felt bad for her.

The only hopeful sign: the neighbors who were her first customers returned to buy more yogurt. When she asked why, Shelly recalls they said, "You know, I keep thinking about it. After dinner, I want to have it."

The low-calorie, non-fat, yogurt was a perfect fit for the capital of compulsive dieting. Diners felt good about treating themselves to Pinkberry regularly—in some cases three or more times a week. Where many dessert shops saw more occasional business, Pinkberry quickly developed a stable of regulars. There was no advertising campaign whatsoever, but word of mouth began to bring a slow trickle of customers in the door, despite the fact that it was a particularly nasty California winter with lots of rain.

One rainy night, Shelly and Young—who had become romantic partners as well as business partners—were dining out when they got a call that the store's roof was leaking. They drove to Pinkberry to find the windows

Hordes of people would queue up for their "fix" of Pinkberry yogurt.

fogged from moisture. It was hard to see what was going on inside. When they opened the door, they found the small eatery packed with patrons. Shelly and Young started to feel more hopeful. They forgot all about the roof leak.

One gray morning shortly afterward, it was raining heavily. The Pinkberry store wouldn't open until 11 a.m., but by 10:30 a.m., Shelly found 20 people were already lined up outside, waiting in the downpour.

"That's when I thought, 'This is something. This is going to happen,'' Shelly recalls.

The yogurt that launched 1,000 parking tickets

As winter gave way to spring, the buzz grew about the little yogurt store with the light, tangy yogurt. Food bloggers began to take notice. A mention in the influential blog *Daily Candy* in August 2005 touted the low-calorie, nonfat aspect of the yogurt. Traffic grew and began to include celebrities. Soon, Salma Hayek, Paris Hilton, Leo DiCaprio and others appeared in gossip magazines with a Pinkberry cup in their hands.

Suddenly, Pinkberry went from interesting to red-hot. Fans dubbed it "Crackberry." Popular food blogger Rosie O'Neill wrote, "I would get Pinkberry IV'd into my veins if I could." Customers wrote fan letters and signed them "Groupie for life."

The budding business broke even by about mid-year when it hit $400,000 in total sales. By the end of that first year, sales topped $1 million.

Salma Hayek, Paris Hilton, Leo DiCaprio and others appeared in gossip magazines with a Pinkberry cup in their hands.

A stampede of other media outlets called after the *Daily Candy* mention. One piece about Pinkberry appeared on Korean television and caught the eye of Shelly's father, who flew out for a visit. He took one look at the shop's long lines and revised his opinion of her business idea. "He said, 'I'm proud of you,'" Shelly says. "It reunited our family."

Customers began to arrive from farther away, driving in from Baldwin Hills, from Koreatown, from Santa Monica. With nowhere to park, they'd double-park or block driveways, then dash inside only to find a 20-minute wait. The city of West Hollywood's parking enforcement cops began handing out $50 and $60 parking tickets.

By the following summer, the city was handing out $175,000 a month in parking tickets to Pinkberry devotees. It became known as the $60 yogurt–it was $5 for the yogurt and $50 for the ticket.

The parking-ticket situation caught the eye of a *Los Angeles Times* reporter. The resulting article, "The taste that launched 1,000 parking tickets," alerted the entire city to Pinkberry's runaway success. Shelly was immediately inundated with offers to invest in the company and offers to open Pinkberry locations: a typical day would bring 100 phone inquiries and 150 faxed-in applications. It was a situation most entrepreneurs would have killed for, but Shelly put off signing any deals.

To market, to market

Before expanding, Shelly wanted to develop a marketing plan and improve the branding for Pinkberry. After a search, she hired Singapore native Yolanda Santosa of design firm Ferroconcrete. A visual artist who would go on to design the title credits for TV shows *Ugly Betty* and *Desperate Housewives*, Santosa asked for a $250,000, one-year contract. Shelly agreed immediately.

"I felt this is money I have to invest in our brand image," Shelly says. "She's a genius. She made every little thing have meaning."

Santosa created branding for every item at Pinkberry, down to the bathroom-door signage. Inspired in part by the film *2001: A Space Odyssey*, early ads featured the original white yogurt against a white background in a white Pinkberry cup with the logo showing, with a couple of raspberries on top.

The company's reward program was dubbed "Pinkberry Groupies", rather than a fan club. "Pinkberry is a rock star," Santosa explained in a 2008 presentation on the chain's branding.

At this time, "swirly goodness" became the company's trademarked slogan. Team members are "swirlers" and attend Swirly College. Signs with store hours announce: "Swirling daily 11 a.m.–11 p.m."

The final branding masterstroke: Pinkberry has a theme song. The bouncy, rap-style tune was created by Lady Tigra of the '80s hip-hop duo L'Trimm. Among the lyrics:

Sorry ice cream, I'm dreaming of a different dessert
Pinkberry shaved ice and frozen yogurt
It doesn't feel like I'm cheating when I'm eating it
Cuz it's healthy; I'm feeling better already ...
Sorry ice cream—I'm on my way to Pinkberry ...

Branching out

In September 2006, Shelly and Young opened a second store financed by the company's cash flow, in LA's Koreatown. It quickly became as mobbed as the original store.

At this point, Shelly felt stretched to her limits. She was working full-time in the first store, getting up early to purchase and cut up fruit for toppings, and now also managing a second store. So for a third location on trendy Melrose Avenue, she sold a franchise to a trio of brothers who owned a small chain of 10 video-rental stores. Soon after, several more franchises expanded the LA market and brought Pinkberry to New York City.

Visitors to those stores told their friends about Pinkberry, too. Some of these fans turned out to be friends of Starbucks CEO Howard Schultz and his investing partner Dan Levitan, who together had co-founded Seattle-based venture capital firm Maveron. In late 2006, Levitan had his first meeting with Shelly and Young.

"We were just totally struck by the consumer reaction to it," says Levitan. "We met with them a few times, and thought the business was very much on trend and satiating a modern consumer sensibility. We kept a dialogue going and got to know them over time, and a personal friendship developed."

In October 2007, Maveron finally inked a deal to invest $27.5 million and build a professional management team to develop the strategy for Pinkberry's global expansion. How did Shelly and Young choose an investment partner from the crowd of possible suitors?

"Dan was a true believer in our brand," Shelly says of Levitan. "And Howard could help us expand into other countries, which really helped us, too."

"We were just totally struck by the consumer reaction to it," says Levitan. "We met with them a few times, and thought the business was very much on trend and satiating a modern consumer sensibility."

With the investment came the appointment of a new CEO: Ron Graves, a Maveron partner and former Air Force fighter pilot. He had worked alongside Schultz and Levitan for eight years before joining Pinkberry. Graves focused on creating a clear strategy to transform Pinkberry from a hit chain in two US markets into a successful global brand.

Graves immediately sought to partner with the founders and add discipline to franchising practices. An important change was a switch from seeking individual franchise owners to relying on area developers who build multiple units. Choosing fewer, more experienced franchisees helped the chain expand rapidly.

With a new board of directors and the addition of experienced managers to execute the anticipated growth curve, a bold strategy was crafted to expand

Shelly with new CEO Ron opening Pinkberry in Kuwait.

internationally immediately, by opening in Kuwait City before Chicago. Pinkberry was a smash hit in the scorching-hot climes of the Middle East, and would add more stores in the region through a 2009 agreement with experienced regional franchise operator M.H. Alshaya Co.

But is it yogurt?

While Pinkberry was basking in its favorable press, growing its audience of loyal patrons, and adding more stores, success bred many competitors. Another California chain, Yogurtland, started in 2006 and would grow to be a major competitive force.

The backlash hit in 2007, when a class action lawsuit was filed, alleging the chain engaged in deceptive marketing. It turned out that Pinkberry's frozen treat technically wasn't frozen yogurt under California law. Unlike in the vast majority of US states and the rest of the world, to be called "frozen yogurt" in California, the product had to be made in a certified off-site facility. Pinkberry wasn't the only company caught in the confusion, with the state notifying several frozen yogurt manufacturers in a clarification of the rules. Once the founders of Pinkberry knew about the certification requirements, they quickly complied.

The timing wasn't great, as Pinkberry had already expanded to its second major market, New York City. At the same time, another competitor was entering the fray.

Red Mango had a head start on Pinkberry, opening first in South Korea in 2003. It grew to 100 locations there before opening its first American store in LA's Westwood neighborhood in July 2007, a full 18 months after Pinkberry opened. Red Mango USA founder Dan Kim shared his suspicions with the media that Shelly and Young had really gotten the idea for Pinkberry not from Italy, but from seeing Red Mango stores back in Korea. Kim told the *New York Post*: "Pinkberry borrowed a lot of our design elements."

Pinkberry viewed such comments as competitive sour grapes and noted that the signature design elements Pinkberry became famous for weren't present in any Red Mango stores.

The lawsuit was a major media event—"The All-Natural Taste That Wasn't," blared the *New York Times*—but customers didn't seem to care. Sales continued to soar. In 2008, the lawsuit was settled with Pinkberry donating $750,000 to various charities. Pinkberry won official recognition from the National Yogurt Association and the scandal was put to rest.

Pinkberry's rapid success spawned copycats—referred to by Pinkberry staff as Fakeberries—resulting in Pinkberry, too, instigating lawsuits to protect the company's trademarks. In 2008, Pinkberry sued yogurt startups Kiwiberri and Yogiberry for trademark infringement. In Yogiberry's case, the chain made changes to its logo and store décor, while Kiwiberri's case was quietly settled.

The company's focus soon returned to its products, and seasonal yogurt flavors began to be introduced, starting with pomegranate. In the years to come, additional unusual flavors would be added, including peanut butter & jelly, salted caramel, and blood orange.

Reflecting back on the company's success, Shelly says her best move was choosing the right investor who could provide not just money but expertise to help her grow her idea into a global brand. Her biggest mistake, she says, was letting the chain grow too quickly in the early days before having the infrastructure to scale the business.

Where are they now?

In April 2009 the company announced $9 million in new private financing. Shelly departed as an active manager of Pinkberry that year, but remains on the board of directors.

It turned out that parking and visibility really do matter in retail: in April 2010 the original Pinkberry store in West Hollywood was converted to a research-and-development lab, leaving neighbors in peace at last. Young left the company around the same time, ending his ties to Pinkberry in May 2010. Graves continues as CEO, implementing Maveron's global expansion strategy.

Having opened its first store in 2005, Pinkberry ended 2011 with more than 170 stores in 17 countries, with more growth ahead. More than 40 of the stores are overseas.

In the past few years, Pinkberry has faced increasing competition from another frozen yogurt trend: self-serve. While other competitors including Yogurtland allow customers to create a custom-sized serving and pay by the ounce, Pinkberry has stuck to its original model, focusing on quality yogurt products, inspirational design and customer service.

Whole Foods Market

A food awakening

Founder: **John Mackey**
Age of founder: **26**
Background: **College dropout living in a vegetarian commune**
Founded in: **1980**
Headquarters: **Austin, Texas**
Business type: **Natural and organic foods supermarkets**

Texas in the late 1970s and early 1980s wouldn't seem like the best place to start a business dedicated to natural and organic foods. A state dominated by the beef industry and famous for its barbecued ribs, it was hardly the place where an innovative, organic grocery store like Whole Foods Market would spring to life. Its founder, John Mackey, tough and combative, championed a brand and a direction that few would contemplate anywhere, let alone in a state where meat counts so much toward the local economy. Yet today the company has more than 300 outlets and has spread as far as Europe, boasting $10.1 billion in revenues for the full year to September 2011.

John and his then-girlfriend Renee Lawson Hardy went through a rollercoaster ride before attaining their success. Not only did they survive a tough recession and a skeptical consumer base, but also a flood, an eviction, and battles of conscience—not to mention many of the other challenges that can hit any business—before making a success of their natural food vision.

An organic awakening

John had no training in business; indeed, there was very little on his résumé prior to Whole Foods that would have foretold his huge future success. By the time he set up in business in 1978, he had dropped out of no fewer than three colleges across Texas. John was a hippie: just before establishing his first company, he was living in a vegetarian co-op that was essentially a hippie commune.

He wasn't really interested in business and spent a lot of his time reading philosophy, cooking natural foods, and being outdoors. "I got interested in food when I was in my early 20s and moved into this vegetarian co-op. I wasn't a vegetarian, but I figured the co-op would have a lot of interesting women living there," he laughs in retrospect.

One of the interesting women he met there was Renee Lawson Hardy, who soon became his girlfriend, and sometime later helped co found Whole Foods Market. John remembers that his time at the co-op was very important to him: "I learned how to cook and I became the food buyer. I got very interested in food; I sort of had an awakening about what's happened to our food over the years," he says.

John became increasingly dissatisfied by what modern culture had to offer in terms of food and the way it was produced. He found himself at odds with the high-yield, low-cost approach that most US food producers adopted. He became concerned about health and the impact that food has on a person's well-being. Also, he was troubled by the way animals were treated and became a vegetarian as a result. Later in life he would go even further and restrict himself to a vegan diet.

Garage business

In 1978, John and Renee were just 25 and 21, respectively. John's "food awakening" had a profound effect on him. He went to work for a small natural foods store, which was his first taste of working in a retail environment, and he loved it so much he eventually decided to open a similar store himself.

John remembers, "I pitched the idea to my girlfriend: 'Hey, why don't we go do our own small store?' She loved it, and we went out and hustled everybody we knew and raised $45,000 and opened the first store."

To raise the money, John and Renee approached family, friends and acquaintances at the co-op—many of whom were hippies and were lured by John's energy and passion for natural foods but still expected a modest return for their cash.

John's biggest benefactor was his father, from whom he borrowed a crucial $10,000 that gave him a foundation. Later that same year, he was able to raise an additional $35,000 of equity investment with which he and Renee were able to officially co-found their first store, SaferWay Natural Foods (a pun on ubiquitous supermarket chain Safeway). The first SaferWay store opened its doors in Austin, Texas, in 1978 and was little more than a small shop in a garage.

Two years later, in 1980, he and Renee would team up with two other young entrepreneurs to create Whole Foods Market, launching their first store, a 10,000-square-foot outlet on Lamar Boulevard in Austin. As one of the very first supermarket-style natural foods stores in the country, the store thrived from its opening day.

"I pitched the idea to my girlfriend: 'Hey, why don't we go do our own small store.' She loved it and we went out and hustled everybody we knew and raised #45,000 and opened the first store."

Nevertheless, it was a big gamble. At the time there were just a handful of supermarkets in the US only selling organic foodstuffs. At the time, the term "organic" hadn't even been properly defined or regulated by the US Department of Agriculture (and wasn't until 2002, with the help of Whole Foods). John and Renee were pioneering a new concept of food, focused on production methods that emphasized the use of renewable resources, treated animals humanely, and didn't use genetically engineered pesticides or genetically modified ingredients or synthetic preservatives.

It was fun: local farmers would drop off produce in old pickup trucks, and John would buy nut loaves and muffins from hippie bakers. The shop was strictly vegetarian like its founders and achieved some $300,000 in sales in its first year. This didn't equate to making a profit, however.

"We didn't know what we were doing; we managed to lose $23,000," John says. "We lost half of the money which was invested in the first year. But I'm a quick learner, so we made a small profit in the second year. The first thing I realized was that the store was too small and we needed to get to a larger location if we were really going to be successful."

The small store didn't always have enough storage space, so Renee and John kept some of their vegetables at their rented home. However, their landlord objected to this and the couple were subsequently evicted. With cash tight and with few other options available to them, they opted to live at the store. Life was far from glamorous. The store didn't have standard bathroom facilities so they had to be inventive when it came to personal hygiene. In order to bathe, they used a Hobart commercial dishwasher to which they attached a water hose.

Organic growth

After two years, John had learned a lot from running a business and decided that he needed to think bigger if he was to be successful. However, some of his initial investors were not so sure: they were more interested in growing the SaferWay shop slowly and making some of their investment back. But John was determined to change locations. As he explains: "I didn't think we'd be competitive there over the long term."

"The first thing I realized was that the store was too small and we needed to get to a larger location if we were really going to be successful."

The investors were adamant, though, and refused to put any more money in unless John could find other investors. "Their basic strategy was that they didn't think anybody would be stupid enough to invest in this business ... but I was very persuasive," he recalls.

John was friends with the owners of another natural foods store and suggested that they merge to form a larger business. In some ways it was an offer that the other business couldn't afford to refuse.

"They were a competitor but they were friends of mine. So I didn't go up there and threaten them and say, 'Join with us or we're going to drive you out of business,'" he explains. "I went up there and said, 'We're going to open a 10,000-square-foot store about a mile from here. Wouldn't it be a lot more fun to join forces together rather than compete when our store's going to be four times bigger than yours?' And they saw the logic of that argument."

Ethical roots

John's first store, SaferWay, had been a wholly vegetarian-focused business, but he realized that he couldn't sell just vegetables if he was going to run a supermarket. He opted to stock other products, too, such as meat, seafood and dairy products. For a vegetarian this wasn't an easy decision, and some criticized him for this.

John explains, "When we made the decision to open a bigger store, we made a decision to sell products that I didn't think were healthy for people, such as meat, seafood, beer, wine and coffee. We didn't think they were particularly healthy products, but we were a whole food store, not a 'holy food' store. We're in business not to fulfill some type of ideology, but to service our customers."

However, John did steer clear of the many brands and suppliers that other supermarkets buy from and always focused on buying from more ethically defensible sources. Typically this meant smaller farms where animal welfare was paramount.

Floods of interest

The new store opened in 1980 in Austin as Whole Foods Market. It was the first supermarket-style natural foods store in the country with 10,500 square feet of space and a staff of 19. The store was a hit with customers–sales started pouring in and the store was profitable almost straightaway.

Word of mouth quickly spread about this new, sizeable health store, and people took notice–there were fewer than half a dozen natural foods supermarkets throughout the whole of the US at the time. Consumers who had grown tired of processed foods flocked to buy Whole Foods Market's healthful, high-quality, natural vegetables and groceries. In some cases the goods were more expensive, but customers still bought them and became very emotionally attached to the company. Pleased by his customers' loyalty, John didn't yet know how important it would become.

"We were a whole food store, not a 'holy food' store. We're in business not to fulfill some type of ideology, but to service our customers."

Within a year of opening, a spring flood almost wiped out the whole business. The shop was filled with water and mud and $400,000 of stock was lost. The company, which didn't have insurance to cover the damage was brought to the brink of extinction. But that same day, loyal customers began to arrive with brushes and buckets and began work clearing the floor of the store that they loved. Even the bank lent a hand, rapidly arranging financing to keep the business afloat. Within 30 days, Whole Foods Market was back up and running.

A growing business

John and his colleagues knew they were on to a winner and looked to expand the business as quickly as possible. The second store opened in 1982, and the business soon crossed state lines and has since moved into 38 states. It did this through a mixture of organic growth and acquisitions. Since its formation the business has made 16 major acquisitions, buying companies such as Whole Food Company, Wellspring Grocery, Bread & Circus, Mrs. Gooch's, Fresh Fields, Bread of Life, Amrion, Merchant of Vino, Allegro Coffee, WholePeople.com, Nature's Heartland, Food for Thought, Harry's Farmers Market, Select Fish, Fresh & Wild and Wild Oats Markets. For the latter, Whole Foods Market fought a seven-month battle with the Federal Trade Commission, which scrutinized the merger with an eye to potential anti-trust concerns before green-lighting the deal in August 2007.

Primarily, these have been businesses that already closely matched the outlook and ethics of Whole Foods. However, some have criticized Whole Foods, suggesting that as it grows it is likely to lose its ethical spirit. John denies that this has been the case and believes that big businesses can be a force for good.

"America has a romance with small businesses. And it has mistrust of the large businesses," he says. "Whole Foods is out to prove that wrong. I don't see any inherent reason why corporations cannot be just as caring and responsible as small businesses."

But as its business has expanded, so has its range. It now offers a wide range of alcoholic drinks, meats, seafood, and even novel items such as yoga mats, as well as its traditional fare of organic fruit and vegetables. The business has grown and expanded while its founders have learned and adapted to the world around it.

Although expanding his range has had dramatic effects on the growth of his business, it has also ignited controversy among his early, strictly vegetarian backers, leading John to become something of an anti-hero in that community. In the beginning, local farmers and hippies dropped off produce at his small garage shop. When he started offering beer and wine, steak and lamb, and air-freighted fruit in the winter in order to grow interest in his business, he invited some criticism.

Whole Foods Market now offers it all, from beer to rack of lamb, but John has helped fend off criticism by doing so in the most ethical manner possible, even setting the benchmark that competitors have been forced to follow. Working with organizations like People for the Ethical Treatment of Animals (PETA) and the Animal Welfare Institute, John has set more rigorous standards of humane treatment for the animals it sources from local farmers.

> "I don't see any inherent reason why corporations cannot be just as caring and responsible as small businesses."

For instance, animals must have access to clean water and the outdoors, be allowed to hunt for their food and be free from mutilation. In some cases this has required suppliers to adapt their production facilities, but John says that the Whole Foods team has met little resistance.

"I think one of the most misunderstood things about business in America is that people are either doing things for altruistic reasons or they are greedy and selfish, just after profit," John has said. "That type of dichotomy portrays a false image of business. It certainly is a false image of Whole Foods. The whole idea is to do both: the animals have to flourish, but in such a way that it'll be cheap enough for the customers to buy it."

The dividends are undeniable, as the company continues to grow, with revenues of $12 billion in its sights for the end of its fiscal year 2012 (a staggering sum in an organic food retail industry that is worth around $30 billion in the US).

But John says that he never had any clearly defined plan for growing the business. "Twenty-five years ago? No. I mean, we didn't have this in mind until a year or two before we opened the store up. There's a misconception somehow or another that there was some master plan and I've been fulfilling the master plan that we made up 25 years ago, but ... it's a discovery process. We've been making it up as we go along.

"We didn't have a plan," he adds. "My girlfriend and I started it because we thought it would be fun. It was an adventure. Imagine a couple of young people that are taking backpacks and going to Europe and they know they've got three months over there but they don't necessarily have a complete itinerary worked out, exactly where they're going to go, because they don't know who they're going to meet and they don't know what kind of adventures they're going to have. The plan will unfold as they go along."

Where are they now?

In 1992, with 12 stores and $92 million in sales, Whole Foods floated on the NASDAQ stock exchange to raise money for growth and acquisitions. Today, Whole Foods Market is the world's largest retailer of natural and organic foods with more than 300 stores in North America and the UK. It also employs about 60,000 staff, or "team members." Importantly, Whole Foods Market has maintained its ethical stance with regard to farming and sustainable practices. It also engages and supports projects and charities that promote sustainable and equitable food production. Impressively, while doing *all this it has remained a great place to work and was named one of the best companies to work for by* Fortune *magazine.*

The company continued its expansion through the early 2000s, breaking into the UK market in 2004 with the acquisition of seven Fresh & Wild stores. As of 2011, the company had signed 52 leases for new stores to add to its already existing fleet of 300 outlets. It lays claim to being the ninth-largest food and drug store in the US.

Despite his company's rapid growth, John kept an open mind toward new business ideas. In recent years, for instance, he has offered $10 million in low-interest loans to local farmers and food producers to help them expand their enterprises, while other ventures such as his Whole Planet Foundation have taken on a more global agenda to help end poverty in developing nations.

Unlike many other successful entrepreneurs, John still sits at the helm of the company, retaining an active role in the company's affairs as its CEO. However, he now draws little money from the company and in 2006 announced that he was reducing his salary to just $1 a year. John also sold his stock portfolio to charity and established a $100,000 annual emergency fund for staff facing personal problems.

He wrote: "I am now 53 years old and I have reached a place in my life where I no longer want to work for money, but simply for the joy of the work itself and to better answer the call to service that I feel so clearly in my own heart."

Dubbed "the Bill Gates of organic foods", John's lack of experience led him to try things that others might be afraid to do. Inexperience can actually be an advantage, not a drawback: "I didn't have any biases. I didn't know how it was 'supposed' to be done. I didn't have any preconceptions about how business had to be. This meant I made mistakes. We reinvented the wheel a few times, but I didn't know what I couldn't do. And so I was free. We were free to be creative and inventive and to try new ways of doing things."

BlackBerry (RIM)

Wireless success

Founders: **Mike Lazaridis (shown) and Doug Fregin**	
Age of founders: **Both 23**	
Background: **Engineering students**	
Founded in: **1984**	
Headquarters: **Waterloo, Ontario, Canada**	
Business type: **Mobile communications**	

Mike Lazaridis is every inch the inventor. Since co-founding Research In Motion (RIM), one of the most profitable device makers in history, he has earned a reputation for being a true visionary of mobile communications—with good reason. This is the man who was studying wireless technology in the late 1980s, before most people even had a home PC. The primary fruit of this research, the BlackBerry device, now enables millions of users around the world to check, send and receive emails while on the move. RIM generated revenues of more than $19.9 billion in the fiscal year ended February 2011.

Now 51, Mike is still heavily involved in one of the most successful and pioneering technology businesses in the world. It wasn't until the first weeks of 2012 that Mike handed over day-to-day operations to RIM Chief Operating Officer Thorsten Heins, and he has stayed on as vice chair of the board, and chair of the board's new Innovation Committee. He is as determined as ever to maintain RIM's position as a technology pioneer.

The early days

There were signs of Mike's inventive talents long before the world started to hear about them. The man who helped develop the world's first reliable portable email device made a record player out of Lego blocks at the tender age of four. When he was 12, his fascination with engineering and with the way things work became clear when he was awarded a prize at his local public library in Windsor, Ontario, for reading every science book on its shelves.

Perhaps unsurprisingly, Mike's peers remember that even as a teenager he had a seemingly endless bank of new ideas and inventions. In 1984, while studying electrical engineering at the University of Waterloo in Ontario, he set up a company with childhood friend Doug Fregin to develop some of his ideas. This company was backed by Mike's parents and a New Ventures Loan from the government of Ontario. RIM was born.

Founded as an electronics and computer science business, RIM caught a lot of people's attention, and Mike, certain of its potential and desperate to devote all his time and energy to it, dropped out of college just a month before graduating to work on the business full-time. It was around this time that RIM won a major $600,000 contract with General Motors, one of the largest car companies in the world, to create an electronic display system. The creation of user-friendly electronic displays has since proved to be a particular strength for Mike, as evidenced in the BlackBerry.

After his first big project with General Motors, a series of successive contracts generated revenue for RIM, and by the late 1980s sales hit $1 million, with the company having grown to employ 12 people. In 1987, a contract with Rogers Cantel Mobile Communications Inc., a mobile phone and pager operator, marked the beginning of the company's journey into wireless communications. RIM was the first wireless data technology developer in North America. Tasked with researching digital wireless devices, RIM developed a wireless radio modem. It was later used in products such as computers and vending machines, and for business communications such as credit card transactions.

Funding growth

Throughout the 1990s, RIM focused its energy on the challenge of making mobile wireless emailing a reality. The company began working with Ericsson to enable its wireless data network to support two-way paging and wireless email, as part of a three-way partnership with Anterior Technology. In 1992, Mike hired James Balsillie to develop and run the business, freeing him up to focus on what he does best: engineering. Harvard MBA graduate Balsillie soon became RIM's chairman and co-chief executive.

Balsillie invested CA$250,000 into the business himself and later helped secure CA$2 million from COM DEV, a technology firm in Waterloo, Ontario. The company also received CA$100,000 from the University of Waterloo's Industrial Research Assistance Program in 1994. Further research and development was funded by venture capitalists who invested in the company in 1995. In the first round of venture capital funding, Working Ventures Canadian Fund made a CA$5 million investment, which was used to complete the development of RIM's wireless hardware and software. During this time, RIM also received substantial investment in the form of loans and grants from the Canadian Government

RIM was the first wireless data technology developer in North America.

In 1996, RIM developed a plug-in card for computer-enabled wireless email. By the following year, the company had created a relatively small handheld

people learned how to use it in literally a few seconds. Within minutes of having their BlackBerrys set up, people were comfortable using them, unlike most other competitive devices trying to do the same thing.

Expanding overseas

By 2001 the BlackBerry, which now had its signature thumb-controlled keyboard, was beginning to make an impression on the European market. Agreements with telecommunications companies such as BT Cellnet, Digifone and Telfort Mobiel meant BlackBerry devices became available in the UK, Ireland and the Netherlands, respectively. Meanwhile, expansion in the home market continued at a fast pace, helped along by more distribution agreements with the likes of IBM. By the end of 2001, more than 12,000 organizations in North America were using BlackBerrys.

Within minutes of having their BlackBerrys set up, people were comfortable using them, unlike most other competitive devices trying to do the same thing.

RIM's head office in Waterloo, Ontario, Canada.

By this point, RIM had sold over 200,000 devices and had forged a partnership with AOL to provide its email service through RIM's handheld devices. While Palm's range of PDAs were the biggest sellers in the overall market, the BlackBerry was fast becoming the device of choice for business people who needed fast and reliable access to their corporate emails.

The early years of the new century brought stiff competition, not least the introduction of Nokia's SMS service. To remain competitive, RIM in 2002 began enabling third-party developers and manufacturers to enhance their products and services with wireless communications. It also began licensing its keyboard technology (which was uniquely controlled by a user's thumb) to its rivals Palm and Handspring.

A decision to partner with Hutchison—one of Australia's biggest media technology companies, which operates the mobile phone brand 3G—signaled the arrival of the BlackBerry "down under." Hutchison Telecoms offers an industry-leading international roaming service that operates in over 149 countries. In 2001, Hutchison was beginning to expand outside its native Australia and promoted the BlackBerry device heavily throughout Asia and the Antipodes.

BlackBerry's launch in the European markets was helped by its development in 2002 of the 5810 model that incorporated mobile phone functions. In the UK, this led to a huge deal with the cellphone network provider Vodafone, and a similar agreement followed with Deutsche Telekom in Germany. Over the following months, BlackBerry was launched in France, Italy, Spain and Switzerland. However, by 2002, RIM had net losses amounting to $28.3 million as a result of the mounting costs of product development and international expansion. The company therefore made the decision to cut 10 percent of its staff.

By 2004, the company was back on course, and there were now 1.7 million BlackBerry subscribers worldwide. With 82 percent of these still based in North America, the company took steps to ramp up its international expansion plans. Europe was a particular focus, and in 2004 RIM had secured deals with most of the major European networks, including Orange and BT, which doubled sales in this region. Key to this success was the fact that BlackBerry sales staff were giving free trials to companies that wanted to give the devices to their workers. Around 90 percent of these companies ended up as paying customers.

Also in 2004, RIM released a new version of its email server to support Chinese and Arabic alphabets. In 2005, Hutchison's Hong Kong branch partnered with language support company Onset to introduce Japanese and Korean language support functions for BlackBerry users in Hong Kong and Macao. This partnership ensured BlackBerry could make significant headway in Japan and Korea.

Cracking the mass market

Throughout its history, RIM has continually raised its game when it comes to product development and has remained a true pioneer in the design, manufacture and marketing of mobile communications tools, winning numerous awards for product innovation.

While the BlackBerry was an instant hit with executives and fast-paced business people, the company has now adapted the model, with video cameras and music players, to draw in more retail customers. The BlackBerry Pearl 8100 was introduced in 2006, and helped BlackBerry shed its heavily corporate image. It's now quite common to see people on trains and planes playing games on BlackBerrys.

RIM has worked hard to make its email portals as secure as possible. Since becoming the first product to offer dependable mobile email in 1997, the brand has become synonymous with data security and is used by many customers who are sending sensitive, "for your eyes only" material, be they celebrity A-listers or government officials. The company has also faced several legal battles to protect its multiple-award-winning patented technology from being used by competitors (serial inventor Mike holds more than 30 patents).

BlackBerrys are now used all over the world, and the company has offices in North America, Europe and Asia Pacific. The devices, which run on nearly every network, have become so successful that many users (typically senior executives of large companies and business owners) now wonder how they ever lived without them. Unofficially dubbed the "Crackberry," the BlackBerry is known for being addictive. With the option to receive an alert whenever a new email arrives, many business people are unable to resist the temptation to check out the latest addition to their inbox, no matter where they are or what the time is.

The brand has become synonymous with data security and is used by many customers who are sending sensitive, for your eyes only material.

In 2007, RIM was named one of Canada's Top 100 Employers, as published in *Maclean's*, Canada's leading business magazine. What's more, it was the only wireless technology company on the list. Meanwhile, the BlackBerry continued to be synonymous with the concept of email on the go, and the device's ability to synchronize with its owner's desktop proved a valuable feature.

RIM also created a dedicated corporate philanthropy program to donate money to help students in the fields of science, engineering and business to commercialize their ideas or inventions.

Where are they now?

BlackBerry is now available in more than 140 countries worldwide, and its subscriber base has nearly 75 million customers globally, made up primarily of senior executives and business owners who use BlackBerry for email on the move. By partnering with some of the world's leading mobile phone producers, including Sony Ericsson, to help it develop its ranges of smartphones, BlackBerry has maintained a strong position—although a key partnership with Nokia fell through when Nokia decided it wanted to move forward alone.

The Blackberry Bold 9900 is one of RIM's latest models in their range of smartphones.

BlackBerry does have a fight on its hands, primarily as a result of the incredible rise of Apple's iPhone, as well as Google's Android operating system. Recent data from Nielsen show that Android's market share in North America has now reached 29 percent, while BlackBerry's has slipped to 27 percent.

At the beginning of 2012, RIM dramatically announced that Thorsten Heins will take over as president and chief executive officer. Mike has become vice chair of RIM's board and chair of the board's new Innovation Committee. James Balsillie remains on the board but does not have any operational role.

On Thorsten's transition to CEO, Mike said: "There comes a time in the growth of every successful company when the founders recognize the need to pass the baton to new leadership. Jim and I went to the board and told them that we thought that time was now."

As BlackBerry experienced a number of setbacks in 2011, and with its share price continually falling, a shake-up was deemed necessary.

Despite a tumultuous 2011, which culminated with launches of versions of RIM's BlackBerry Bold touchscreen smartphones. RIM is releasing the BlackBerry PlayBook 2.0 tablet and the BlackBerry 10 mobile operating system in 2012. With a change at the top it is continually striving to compete with its rising competitors. In fact, Mike is so confident of RIM's future that he announced plans to purchase an additional $50 million of the company's shares.

Dropbox

Out-of-the-box success

Founders: **Drew Houston and Arash Ferdowsi (shown, left to right)**	
Age of founders: **24 and 21**	
Background: **Self-admitted "computer geeks"**	
Founded in: **2007**	
Headquarters: **San Francisco, California**	
Business type: **Online file-hosting service**	

Sometimes the best business ideas come from simple solutions to life's small problems. Conceived in 2007 and officially launched by co-founders Drew Houston and Arash Ferdowsi a year later, Dropbox is a Web-based file-hosting service that uses cloud storage to let its users share and back up files using file synchronization capability.

Drawing comparisons with pioneers Apple, Google and Facebook, Dropbox's growth has been nothing short of stunning. And it grosses far more per employee from its 70-strong team than those luminaries do. Despite the fact that 96 percent of the company's approximately 50 million users pay nothing for their service, Dropbox is said by analysts to be on course to take in revenue of $240 million in 2011. What's more, it's been said that the company can double its sales in 2012 without recruiting a single new customer, as users exceed their "freemium" allowance.

But as the company prepares to move into a new 87,000-square-foot headquarters early in 2012, and while rumors abound that the company is in the process of raising between $200 million and $300 million in funding at a whopping $5 billion valuation, it's clear that Drew and Arash have no need to be modest.

The precociousness of youth

The story of Dropbox begins with a precocious child who grows into an overachieving teenager. As a mere 5 year old in suburban Boston, Drew began messing about on an IBM PCjr, and not long after, he started writing his first code.

Drew recounts that his mother, a high-school librarian, sensed his burgeoning computer "geekiness" and did her best to help him fit in with other kids by refusing to let him skip grades. Things changed, however, when Drew was a teenager. At just 14, he signed up to beta test an online video game. In the process, he made a detailed list of all of its security flaws. Impressed, the company hired Drew as their networking programmer in exchange for equity in the company. Drew continued to work with small startups throughout high school, and when he wasn't working he was still coding.

Drew says he knew then, in high school, that he wanted to run a computer company. But inspired by Daniel Goleman's book *Emotional Intelligence*, he knew that just being smart wasn't enough to make a company succeed, and so he spent the summer before his freshman year at MIT reading business books.

"No one is born a CEO, but no one tells you that," Drew has said of that time. "The magazine stories make it sound like [Facebook founder Mark] Zuckerberg woke up one day and wanted to redefine how the world communicates with a billion-dollar company. He didn't."

Drew's first hands-on education in managing people came when he rushed the Phi Delta Theta fraternity, and took on a leadership position as treasurer for the sole purpose of gaining that experience. But when fellow fraternity brothers left to go pursue their own entrepreneurial visions, Drew was left frustrated. He had the desire and was building his skill set, but he was waiting for that moment of divine inspiration. He needed an idea. And then he got one.

"No one is born a CEO, but no one tells you that."

In January 2007, Drew boarded a bus going from Boston to New York City. He'd brought his laptop and planned to do some work during the four-hour trip. But as the bus pulled away he realized he had forgotten his USB memory stick, and without those files he wouldn't be able to get anything done. It was actually a frequent problem of his, but this time, on the bus, he had a moment of clarity. There must be a way to sync your important files to devices over the Web. Immediately Drew began doing what he did best: writing code.

Driven by frustration

Driven by the frustration of working from multiple computers, Drew sought to create a service that would let people bring all their files anywhere, with no need to email attachments. Drew coded a demo of his idea. Four months later, in June 2007, Drew left Boston for good and flew to San Francisco, where he pitched the idea to Paul Graham of the highly regarded startup incubator Y Combinator. Graham had seen a demo of Dropbox that Drew posted online and was keen to learn more.

The model Drew pitched was simple: Dropbox makes all of your important files available to you wherever you may be in the world. Using cloud technology, files are synced and accessed from any computer or phone. Working late at the office? Just add the file you've been working on to your Dropbox folder and pick it up later at home. What Dropbox was selling was never again having to remember a USB stick or think about where your files are.

Drew wrote software that users could download and install for free, creating a special folder on the user's computer. Anything added to this Dropbox folder would automatically save to all of that user's computers, as well as to the Dropbox website. The true innovation, however, was its social nature, with users able to invite people to share any folder in their Dropbox, making it essential for a wide range of users, such as teenagers who want to share music, or businesses sharing information and designs with colleagues and clients.

What Dropbox was selling was never again having to remember a USB stick or think about where your files are.

Ultimately, everything hinged around a business model called freemium. Users would pay nothing to sign up for Dropbox, and just by signing up they would get 2GB worth of space. Drew knew this would lure people in. But Drew also knew the nature of the Internet and that users would blow through 2GB. At that point, the Dropbox model would offer users upgrades to 50GB and 100GB with monthly fees of $10 and $20, respectively.

The potential was huge. And Paul Graham was impressed. On behalf of Y Combinator, a seed-stage start-up funding firm, Graham agreed to give $15,000 in seed funding to develop the business further and take it to the next stage. The amount was modest, but Y Combinator as a rule provides very little seed money, reflecting Graham's theory that with the Web and free software available, the cost of starting an IT firm has greatly decreased. In addition to the seed money, Graham's firm offered advice and the opportunity to build connections. But there was a catch—Graham insisted that for the idea to work, Drew needed a co-founder.

Drew didn't have long to search for the right person. Things were moving quickly. He polished his demo of Dropbox and ultimately decided to show it to his friend and fellow MIT student Arash Ferdowsi. So impressed was Arash that he dropped out of MIT—with only one semester left before graduating—so that he could help Drew make Dropbox a reality.

With Arash on board and Graham's funding in the bank, Drew had the tools he needed to move forward. With the $15,000, he rented an apartment and bought a Mac, which he spent 20 hours a day reverse engineering in his attempt to make his Dropbox application work on every computer and on the growing number of "smart" devices such as phones and tablets. Then, three months later, Drew and Arash were invited to a meeting that would accelerate the business even further and change their lives forever.

So impressed was Arash that he dropped out of MIT—with only one semester left before graduating—so that he could help Drew make Dropbox a reality.

After a Y Combinator event, Arash, the son of Iranian refugees, was approached by a man who started speaking to him in Farsi. The man was Pejman Nozad, a famous dot-com-era investor, notable for funding startups such as PayPal.

Nozad got to know the young entrepreneurs and believed in their plan. He persuaded them that they needed to think bigger and started representing the pair, telling investors that they were already fielding a number of offers from venture capital firms. "Basically, he was our pimp," Drew has joked.

It worked. In September 2007, the pair got a meeting with Sequoia Capital, the firm that famously funded Internet giants Google and Yahoo. Drew and Arash were seeking only a few hundred thousand dollars, and they admit they were quietly nervous when it became apparent at the meeting that they would be talking about much larger sums.

"On a Friday afternoon, we walked into the Sequoia offices, and on the walls were the original stock certificates of Apple and Cisco. It was daunting," Drew writes. "I was thinking, 'Holy shit, I'm just some kid. What the hell am I doing here?'"

Pitch of a lifetime

Keeping their nerves at bay, the pair made their pitch, and the next day they were visited at home by legendary investor Michael Moritz, who heard the same presentation. Another meeting followed–this time, dinner with fellow investor Sameer Gandhi–and for the first time they began to talk specific numbers. Moritz had told his partners to go forward with the deal, and Gandhi revealed that they would be investing $1.2 million in Dropbox.

"We got an email a few days later from Sequoia requesting instructions for a wire transfer," Drew continues. "Arash and I just looked at each other. We thought, 'It'd be really embarrassing if we started–or quickly ended–this relationship by not even knowing how to get the million dollars into our bank account.'"

Drew recounts the humorous episode of the two of them venturing into their bank and asking if there was a limit to how much one can deposit into a bank account.

"It's hard to describe the feeling of looking at your checking account online and continuously hitting Refresh, watching the balance increase from $60 to $1.2 million," Drew writes. "You really have $1.2 million. And now it's up to you to figure out how to use it."

"We got an email a few days later from Sequoia requesting instructions for a wire transfer. ... We thought, 'It'd be really embarrassing if we started–or quickly ended–this relationship by not even knowing how to get the million dollars into our bank account.'"

Soon they had more. In total, Drew and Arash raised $7.2 million from a combination of Sequoia Capital, Paul Graham at Y Combinator, Accel Partners and a host of other prominent investors, such as Amidzad (Nozad's firm), and brothers Ali and Hadi Partovi who sold their startup iLike to MySpace in 2009.

Every other file storage service at the time suffered problems with Internet latency, large files or bugs, Drew had told them, and Dropbox was the first to conquer them all. Perhaps crucially, the service supports revision history, so a user's files deleted from the Dropbox folder may be recovered from any of a user's synced computers. Past versions are saved for 30 days; however, users can purchase a "Pack Rat" option of unlimited version history. Finally, the version history uses an encoding technology that helps conserve bandwidth and time. If a user makes changes to a file, Dropbox, when syncing, uploads only the elements of the file that have been changed, not the whole file.

"I've seen a variety of companies attacking parts of his problem," Moritz later told *Forbes* magazine. "Big companies would go after this, I knew. I was betting they had the intellect and stamina to beat everyone else."

Fine-tuning the model

The next step for the pair was fine-tuning their model, which they eventually presented in a private beta launch video on the popular social news website

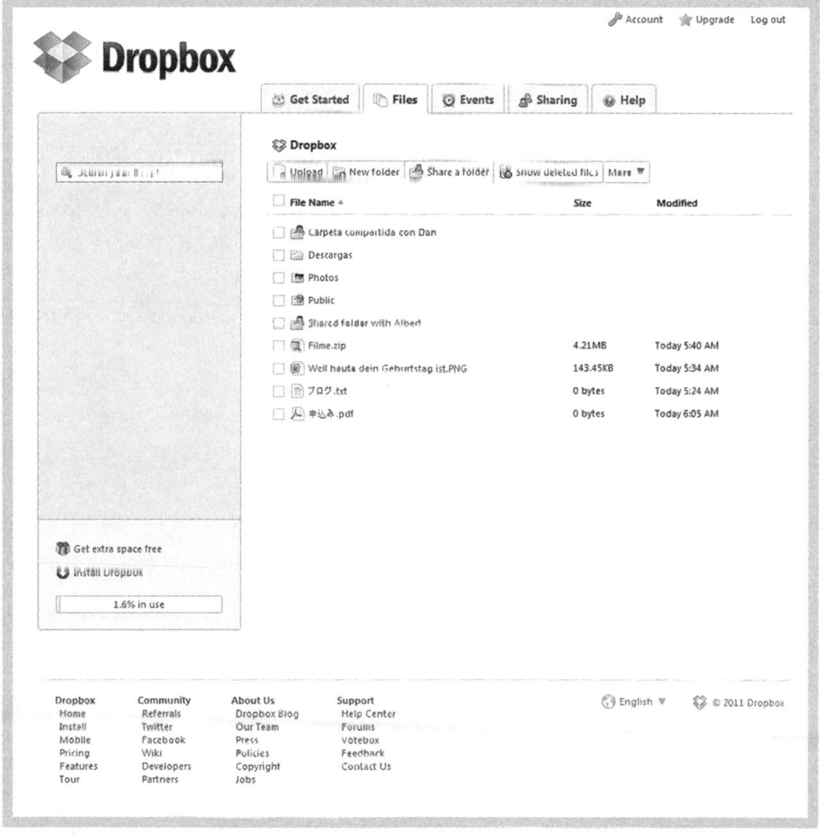

A screenshot of Dropbox online.

Digg in March 2008. Hoping to get around 15,000 user requests from the video, Drew and Arash were stunned to find 75,000 people wanting to test their service.

Not wanting to risk the bad press that could ensue from 75,000 people trying still-uncertain software, Drew hand-picked a number of people to test Dropbox through a series of private invites. The invite-only strategy was successful in bringing in tens of thousands of new users, and the company added to that figure by drawing some 300,000 new users alone from its newly launched iPhone app.

Using social media sites such as Twitter and Facebook, the Dropbox team netted another 50,000 users almost immediately. Drew and Arash also used Google AdWord placements to help spread the word in a more targeted manner and build viral momentum among an audience it knew was paying attention.

In short, Drew has said, the early growth strategy was simple: go where your first followers hang out and make yourself visible. Dropbox did this with their private beta launch and saw their users jump from 5,000 to the previously stated 75,000 in just one day, and they continued with a strategy of winning over their niche users first and riding that momentum.

The pair were also quite media savvy. Knowing journalists are busy people, they've said that part of cultivating Dropbox's momentum was helping reporters find the angle when reporting on their growth. To this end they met journalists in person, and Dropbox has always included a thorough media resources page on its site.

Significantly, Drew and Arash resolved that Dropbox should focus on doing a couple of things really well rather than many things poorly. They poured their time into making their service as easy as possible for its users, not asking them to think too much when using it, but openly inviting feedback. This ease of use, and a referral program that increased sign-ups by some 60 percent in the first year eventually helped Dropbox surge past the all-important benchmark of a million users.

The early growth strategy was simple: go where your first followers hang out and make yourself visible.

Using a video on a social news site like Digg to introduce themselves was a bit unconventional and is something Drew concedes they couldn't do now. But at the time, the people they were trying to sign up for their service were Web 2.0 geeks who resided on sites like Digg and Reddit—Reddit itself being a fellow Y Combinator startup.

The buzz to go global

On advice from its investors, Dropbox finally officially launched later in 2008 at the TechCrunch50 technology conference, a global competition for start-up companies. Fifty entrepreneurs are invited to present at the event, and the winner receives $50,000. The event is supported by Sequoia Capital, one of Dropbox's key investors, who thought the young company could make a name for itself.

Dropbox didn't win the competition, but the event provided enough exposure to create buzz. The company counted just nine employees when it formally debuted—eight engineers to monitor the servers and deal with customer queries, and one designer—despite boasting a number of registered users soaring well past the million mark.

For the remainder of 2008, Drew, Arash and their small team pulled all-nighters, working out bugs and perfecting the small details, even down to the shades of color on its icons. Registered user numbers continued to grow tenfold that year, as the company weathered the sharp economic downturn that fall thanks to their small number of staff, limited overhead, and a service that was essentially free. By April 2009 they could claim 10 million members, while in their modest offices investors Hadi and Ali Partovi were showing Drew and Arash how to recruit talented staff and more effectively market themselves.

Looking back, Drew says their main challenge that first year was marketing. "We sucked at it," Drew recalls. He's said that they knew they had a great product, but the company's biggest obstacle was selling a product that solved a problem most people didn't know they had.

But Drew and Arash didn't want to rely on a marketing firm. Nothing can kill momentum like an overly slick marketing message. Instead, they turned to their customers. Research showed Dropbox users were very loyal to the firm, and so Drew and Arash offered 250 megabytes of extra storage free to each customer who gave them a referral.

"Most of our growth is word of mouth/viral, so free users are still valuable: we grow faster, and they refer people who might pay," Drew has said of their strategy. The move, in fact, was so successful that 25 percent of all new registered users still come to Dropbox this way.

Privacy issues and public problems

The company experienced a few more contentious challenges, however. Dropbox drew criticism for harboring those who infringe on others' copyright, and as a result it had to adjust its terms to comply with the Digital Millennium Copyright Act, which establishes a notification-and-takedown system for addressing claims of copyright infringement. To comply, Dropbox has reserved the right to delete or remove any file from users' accounts in response to claims from copyright owners.

The company was also forced to fend off claims its staff could access its users' files at any time. Questions over its privacy and security policy reached a fever pitch when a complaint was filed with the Federal Trade Commission concerning Dropbox's system of checking whether a file has been uploaded before by another user and alleging that linking to the existing copy exposed users' files to intruders. In response, Dropbox tightened its security measures and clarified its terms of service.

These were only minor blips, however. Dropbox's rapid growth saw the firm expand its team to 20 people to cope with all of the queries and requests coming from its paying customers in 175 countries. By 2010, its team grew to 60, and Dropbox began launching new services targeted toward businesses, such as Dropbox for Teams, and a new one terabyte storage option.

As Dropbox expanded, Drew's time began to shift away from coding to more traditional CEO fare: people management. Uninspired by stereotypical cubicle life, Drew wanted to create a new corporate structure and has broken Dropbox's staff engineers into small teams, while just three managers handle the company's thousands of servers.

With the company reportedly looking to expand from 70 to upwards of 400 staff, Drew has said that the biggest challenge Dropbox faced is internal communication, since messages from the top have typically been shouted across the room. Times have certainly changed for Drew and Arash, who just a few years ago were coding in their small shared apartment in

Dropbox pokes fun at its foolproof system.

North Beach, San Francisco. Perhaps the defining moment for Drew, when it became apparent just how far he'd really come, arrived in December 2009 when he received an invitation to meet his hero, Steve Jobs.

The meeting was at Apple's Cupertino offices, and Jobs was interested in buying the plucky startup. After pleasantries, Jobs made his pitch. But Drew told him to stop. He was well and truly flattered, but he wasn't selling. He wanted to grow the company. And as Dropbox surged past the 25-million-user mark in the months following and has today breached 50 million, Drew is well on course to achieving his dream.

Where are they now?

After reaching the 25-million-user threshold, Dropbox signed deals with mobile carrier Softbank and handset maker Sony Ericsson in a bid to attract more customers in Asia and Europe. As the company cruised past 50 million users in 2011, Drew and Arash announced even bolder plans.

In August 2011, the pair invited seven top venture capital firms with a history in Silicon Valley to visit their offices and make an offer for further investment by the following Tuesday. According to interviews with insiders, just before midnight on Monday, Dropbox's head of business development expressed his concern that only one offer had arrived and suggested that Drew and Arash pull the funding round.

But Drew declined. He would see it through. And as he expected, every firm came back with an offer in the morning. They eventually closed a mammoth deal in September with Index Ventures, Sequoia, Greylock, Goldman Sachs, Benchmark Capital, RIT Capital Partners and Accel Partners that netted the company $250 million on a $4 billion valuation. According to Forbes, *Drew's own estimated 15 percent stake is worth some $600 million dollars.*

Dropbox's rapid growth has seen it ranked as the world's fifth most valuable Web start-up company, falling in line after luminaries like Facebook, Twitter, Zynga and Groupon. And industry observers have noted that people save more files on Dropbox than there are Tweets on Twitter.

Drew, who remains CEO, has said he envisions a day not too far off when Dropbox does more than just store, for instance, people's photos. He sees his system taking it a step further and reading the metadata and embedded location information on these photos, which can then be indexed to allow users to arrange all the pictures taken within a 20-mile radius. Named the best young tech entrepreneur by Business Week, *there seems to be little doubt he will achieve this and much more.*

Google™

Google

Organizing the world's information

Founders:	**Sergey Brin and Larry Page (shown, left to right)**
Age of founders:	**24 and 25**
Background:	**Stanford PhD computer science students**
Founded in:	**1998**
Headquarters:	**Mountain View, California**
Business type:	**Search engine**

Google. We all know its name and use its website probably more than any other. We also know that it is extremely successful and that its founders have become billionaires. Yet amazingly, in 1999, almost none of us had heard of it, let alone used it. Its growth has been more substantial than most of the world's greatest business success stories, and it happened faster, too.

The birth of PageRank

But Google hasn't always been such a gold mine. In fact, when they started, Google's co-founders Larry Page and Sergey Brin weren't even sure how their site would make money.

The pair met at Stanford University in the spring of 1995, where they were both enrolled in its prestigious Computer Science PhD program. Located in Silicon Valley, Stanford had already spawned some of the world's most successful technology companies, such as Hewlett-Packard and Sun Microsystems, and the academic environment encouraged risk-taking and entrepreneurship. Its office of technology licensing offered technologists resources, advice and assistance with the patent process to help its students commercialize their research projects in return for a stake in the businesses. It was also a stone's throw from Sand Hill Road, home to some of America's most successful venture capital firms.

Sergey and Larry had both grown up surrounded by science and technology. Larry's father was one of the first-ever recipients of a computer science degree from the University of Michigan. His mother was a database consultant with a master's degree in computer science. Sergey was born in Moscow and came to the US when his parents moved here; his mother was a scientist at NASA and his father a mathematics professor at the University of Maryland. Sergey had completed his BS in Mathematics and Computer Science at the University of Maryland by the age of 19, while Larry had built a working inkjet printer out of Lego blocks in high school. So by the time they met, both were highly accustomed to computers and how they worked. They struck up a strong friendship at Stanford, fueled greatly by their shared love of academic debate and discourse.

At the time, several rudimentary search tools existed, but a search on one of them would generally yield thousands of results, which were not ranked in any order of relevance. Fellow Stanford PhD students Jerry Yang and David Filo had developed Yahoo! to tackle the problem, but they employed a team of editors to assemble a Web directory and were already struggling to keep up with the mushrooming World Wide Web. Convinced there was a better way, Sergey, an expert in extracting information from vast amounts of data, joined forces with Larry, who was studying the leading search engine Alta Vista. Never short of ambition, Larry set out to download the entire Web onto his PC to study the relevance of Web links, which Alta Vista didn't appear to be taking into account. The project took far longer than expected and cost the computer science department around $20,000 every time they sent out a crawler program to capture online data—but the effort was definitely worth it.

Never short of ambition, Larry set out to download the entire Web onto his PC to study the relevance of Web links.

They concluded that the number of links pointing to a site was a measure of its popularity. Furthermore, they decided that links could be weighted. For instance, if CNN (which itself receives high volumes of traffic and has many links pointing to it) links to your Website, this is worth more than a link from a less popular site. Naming it after himself, Larry called the algorithm he developed to establish this pecking order PageRank. By adding this to traditional search methods (which matched keywords on pages with those in the search terms) the pair devised a search engine that produced results that were highly accurate and relevant to the user's request. Google was conceived.

Looking for a buyer

The founders did not set out to build a business. Coming from backgrounds where academia was revered, they were more excited to have stumbled across the basis of a killer thesis. They developed a prototype of their search engine, called BackRub, which was renamed Google in 1997. The term was a play on the word "googol," a mathematical term for the number 1 followed by 100 zeros, and it represented the vast amounts of data on the Web. Working day-in, day-out from a room on campus, the founders unleashed their creation on Stanford's student body via the university's intranet. Its popularity among this information-hungry population soared through word-of-mouth recommendations, as users quickly discovered how much faster and more relevant its search results were.

Not wanting to get too distracted from their academic pursuits, but certain they had created something far superior to anything else available at the time, they attempted to sell their technology to Excite, Yahoo! and then market leader Alta Vista for up to $1 million before patenting it. Amazingly, each company passed on the opportunity. Search did not present any obvious revenue-generating opportunities, and Google's goal to produce results in a split second did not make it an ideal space for advertisers. Feeling passionately that they had developed something that people truly needed, Sergey and Larry were left with no choice but to take Yahoo! co-founder David Filo's advice and take Google to market themselves.

By amassing email feedback from their academic peers, they refined their offering before seeking funding to make it scalable. In August 1998, they met private investor Andy Bechtolsheim, a co-founder of Sun Microsystems who had sold another business to Cisco for hundreds of millions of dollars. Despite the lack of a clear business model, Bechtolsheim was so taken with the idea that he wrote out a check to Google Inc. for $100,000 on the spot, compelling Sergey and Larry to incorporate the company. Google was born.

Scaling it up

Bechtolsheim was particularly impressed with Sergey and Larry's plans to rely solely on the strength of their product and word-of-mouth recommendations to market the brand, instead of blowing huge sums on advertising. Instead, they planned to invest in IT as no other company had done before. From the outset, Sergey and Larry had been extremely efficient in their use of computers. They were downloading, indexing and searching the Internet using a network of off-the-shelf PCs they had custom built and linked together themselves. On them ran the software and algorithms they had also designed to crawl through and rank Web pages. The intention was to continue with this strategy, scaling it up cost-effectively by adding more and more PCs to the network to ensure their lightning-fast search results kept up with the growing number of websites and users.

The well-known Google home screen.

Google's stated mission is "to organize the world's information and make it universally accessible and useful."

Following Bechtolsheim's endorsement, several friends and family members also backed the pair, who were able to raise a total of $1 million. After running their operations from a garage for a while, where they hired their first staff member, the duo moved into offices in Palo Alto, California, in 1999. A mention in *PC Magazine*'s top 100 websites created a huge surge in user numbers, and before long, Google was dealing with upwards of 500,000 searches each day.

Struggling to maintain the level of IT investment they needed to keep up, the team was forced to seek further backing before long. Luckily for them, the economic climate worked in their favor. Google's story is set against the backdrop of the dot-com rise (and subsequent fall). Following the buzz created by the stock market flotation of Internet browser producer Netscape in 1995, which valued the company at $3 billion after the first day of trading, Wall Street stockbrokers were on the prowl for more Internet success stories.

In 1999, Google closed a deal with two of the world's most prestigious venture capital firms, both based on Sand Hill Road in Silicon Valley: Sequoia Capital, which had backed Yahoo!, and Kleiner Perkins Caufield & Byers, which had backed Amazon and many others. In an unprecedented move, the renowned venture capitalists agreed to invest equally in Google, with neither having a controlling interest. So eager were they to back the search pioneer while they had the chance (despite it still not having a successful business model) that each firm put up $12.5 million, while Sergey and Larry remained in sole charge of the company they had created—a non-negotiable condition for them.

Going global

Following the buzz this created, Google experienced a major growth spurt. Larry and Sergey continued in their method of custom-building server racks using parts from low-cost PCs and stacking them one on top of the other, getting maximum value per square foot in their data centers. At this stage, their business model was to earn income by licensing their search technology to other partners. This wasn't bringing in sufficient revenue, so they began to consider other ways to turn their growing search engine into a sustainable business.

They were initially hesitant to allow advertisers onto the site because they worried that users would doubt the search results' impartiality, and Sergey and Larry remained resolute that they would never allow companies to pay to rank more highly, as other search engines had done. They came up with a compromise which was to revolutionize not only their own business, but also their competitors'—and the world's advertising industry. Their idea was that whenever someone searched for a topic, they would display small text ads relevant to the subject of the search alongside the more prominent "natural search engine results."

Sergey and Larry remained resolute that they would never allow companies to pay to rank more highly. ... They came up with a compromise which was to revolutionize the world's advertising industry.

This soon evolved into the current pay-per-click model, whereby Google would earn money whenever a user clicked on one of these "sponsored links." The rate paid per click was set by the advertiser in a fair, automated online auction process.

This worked spectacularly well for several reasons: it was extremely simple and quick for an advertiser to set up; it could be tested for a tiny investment (far smaller than any other advertising method); it enabled advertisers to present their message to a very highly targeted audience; it was free unless someone clicked on the advertiser's link; it was easy to measure how successful it was; and, above all, it worked. Advertisers got excellent results from people clicking on their ads.

In 2000, the founders hired Dr. Eric Schmidt as chief executive to take over the day-to-day running of the business. Although Sergey and Larry were hesitant at first for fear of losing control of the company they had created (after all, this was a condition of the investment to which they had reluctantly agreed) Schmidt's appointment proved to be extremely successful. In particular, his business expertise played a key role in Google's overseas expansion. One of the first things he noticed was that, while 60 percent of its searches came from outside the US, just 5 percent of ad revenues came from overseas advertisers. While the searches had been available in foreign languages for some time, and the business was truly serving a global audience, it had yet to make money from this. Under Schmidt's supervision, sales offices were duly established in London, Hamburg, Tokyo and Toronto. Revenue soared.

Google's stated mission is "to organize the world's information and make it universally accessible and useful." Hardly a modest ambition! As its revenue grew, it started adding new services to deliver more of this mission. By 2004, in addition to the core search engine, it offered Google

Images, a huge library of searchable images, and Google News, a service that aggregated stories on any particular subject from around the world. It also introduced Gmail, a Web-based email service.

Going public

In August 2004, the founders reluctantly listed the search engine on the NASDAQ stock exchange, raising $1.2 billion. Going public was actually the last thing Sergey and Larry wanted to do. Apart from the fact that their independence had helped them weather the dot-com bust, they were extremely hesitant to make their financial information available to competitors.

Up until 2004, analysts had grossly underestimated just how big the search giant had become, and the last thing Google wanted was for the world to know how much money they were making, or more information on how they were making it. However, they now had so many investors that US law required them to disclose their financial information. Given that they would have to spill the beans anyway, they felt it prudent to take the company public and give their early employees and investors a tangible return.

No other company has created such phenomenal influence, profit and wealth in such a short time.

But shortly before its IPO, a number of factors coincided to bring down Google's share price. First, the company had to deal with backlash from rival Overture, a subsidiary of its largest competitor, Yahoo! Overture pioneered the idea of selling ads to accompany search results using a pay-per-click model, and accused Google of infringing its patents. Conscious of the negative effect of the ongoing legal battle in the run up to its stock market debut, Google's founders gave Yahoo! 2.7 million shares in an out-of-court settlement.

Secondly, Google's recent entry into the email market with Gmail was steeped in controversy. The founders sought to offer a service that was far better than anything else out there. Using their search technology, you could easily search for and find a stored message within Gmail, and Google offered what was then a colossal one gigabyte of space with an account. However, their plans to make money through contextual ads, which were generated by scanning messages and matching ads to keywords, were slammed by privacy advocates.

The combination of factors meant that Google's IPO valued shares at just $85 each. But this didn't last for long. Despite these setbacks, Google's share price rose to $100 by the end of the first day of trading, valuing the company at $23.1 billion. As with many new companies in Silicon Valley, many of Google's early employees had been given share options (instead of high salaries, which helped keep costs down for the young business while it was trying to become profitable. This made early hires millionaires when the company went public.

Part of Google's phenomenal growth has come from a scheme it created called AdSense. This allows other websites to install a Google search box on their site; when users click on the contextual ads that Google supplies, the partner website earns some of the fee advertisers pay to Google. AdSense has been enormously popular with other websites, including giants such as AOL and the *New York Times*. AdSense is typical of Google's progressive approach and its belief that working alongside competitors can grow the market for all.

Continued growth

Google has used its success to make a number of significant acquisitions. Examples include its $1.65 billion purchase of user video clip phenomenon YouTube in October 2006 and its purchase of online advertising network Doubleclick in April 2007. The latter was bought for $3 billion, lengthening its reach into the display advertising market on the Web.

The company's founding principles have also played a key part in the company's success, not least the founders' determination to make Google a great place to work. Its motto, "Don't be evil," is world famous, as is the award-winning culture that Sergey and Larry have fostered. On site at its Mountain View headquarters, staff can make use of a wide range of facilities, including pool tables, swimming pools and volleyball courts, as well as being well fed with free gourmet food.

Engineers are given 20 percent of their time whereby they are actively encouraged to work on their own projects. Both Google News and Froogle, an online shopping service, are the result of this initiative. Google now has sales offices all over the world, and this culture of creativity pervades them all. As a result, the company receives more than 1,300 job applications every week.

Its motto, "Don't be evil", is world famous, as is the award-winning culture that Sergey and Larry have fostered.

No other company in history has achieved such brand awareness without spending heavily on advertising and marketing. No other company has created such phenomenal influence, profit and wealth in such a short time.

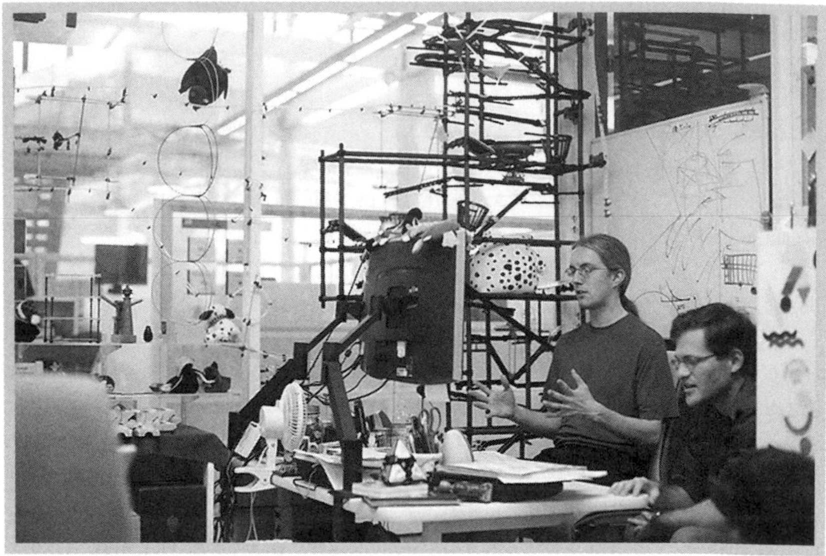

Technicians hard at work in the Google office, in Mountain View, California.

Where are they now?

At the height of its success in 2007, shares in Google were being sold for $741.80, but its price began to tumble amid fears that its ad revenue was falling (newspapers reported fewer people were clicking on its ads). But, true to form, Google laid waste to those claims when it brought home $1.3 billion in profit between January and March 2008, on revenue of $5.1 billion.

In April 2011, a Google share would set you back $577. Its market capitalization (the current value of all its shares) at that time reached a staggering $185.6 billion. Annual revenues hit just shy of $30 billion for 2010, with net income of $8.5 billion for the period.

Google's website now processes hundreds of millions of searches every day. Google's homepage has retained its design simplicity, despite the fact that it could potentially be a source of considerable extra income. As a result, it loads quickly, improving the customer experience. Likewise, Google has steered clear of Flash features and other elements that would slow it down. It is estimated that Google's network now consists of considerably more than 500,000 servers, a computing power unmatched by any other company. Its employees still assemble and customize the PCs the company uses to carry out its searches. No enterprise has more computing power than Google.

Sergey Brin and Larry Page moved to their Mountain View, California, headquarters in 2004, and that is where the company remains to this day.

From April 2011, Larry resumed his position as chief executive, with Eric Schmidt becoming executive chairman. Sergey, meanwhile, devotes his time to strategic projects and developing new products to solve great problems.

The Coca-Cola Company

The Coca-Cola Company

The Coke side of business

Founders:	**John Pemberton (creator) (shown) and Asa Griggs Candler (business founder)**
Age of founders:	**55 and 35**
Background:	**Pharmaceuticals and sales**
Founded in:	**1886**
Headquarters:	**Atlanta, Georgia**
Business type:	**Beverage manufacturer**

Everyone has sampled the "Coke side of life." Its trademark scripted, bright red logo can be seen all over the world—from English pub umbrellas to football stadiums, from Chinese shop signs to a 20-foot-tall neon sign in Times Square. It's no exaggeration to say that The Coca-Cola Company has a presence in every country in the world, and arguably it was the world's first truly global brand. It has been declared both the world's most recognizable trademark and the world's most popular branded drink.

Making medicine

Yet this amazing success story had very humble beginnings. A pharmacist from Atlanta named John Pemberton invented a new "medicine" called Coca-Cola. One afternoon in 1886, when workers were building the Statue of Liberty in New York Harbor, John was experimenting in his backyard with combinations of ingredients in a three-legged brass pot to try to develop a new medicine. He came up with a fragrant, caramel-colored liquid. Out of sheer curiosity, he took it to neighboring Jacobs' Pharmacy, where he

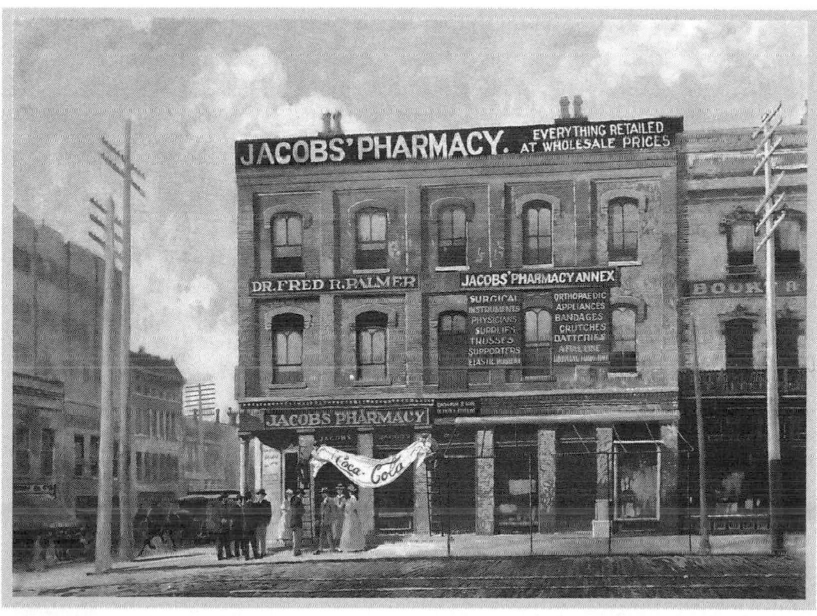

Coca-Cola was first sold as "medicine" for 5 cents a glass in pharmacies.

added carbonated water. After testing it on customers, who all thought it was something special, Jacobs' Pharmacy started selling it as a medicine for 5 cents a glass (the equivalent of about a dollar today). John claimed his new drink cured diseases, including morphine addiction, dyspepsia, neurasthenia, headache, and even impotence.

In the first year, John sold just nine glasses of Coca-Cola a day, making around \$50 in total (\$1,170 today). It had cost John \$70 to create and advertise the drink, so he incurred a loss. But he persevered. Encouraged by the drink's popularity with customers, John remained convinced he would eventually make something of it.

First named Pemberton's French Wine of Cola, the alcohol in the drink was quickly replaced by sugar to make it more appealing to drink. The drink was renamed Coca-Cola by John's bookkeeper, Frank Robinson, who also wrote the name for the logo in the distinctive script that is still in use today. The name is derived from two key ingredients: leaves from the coca plant and the caffeine-rich kola nut. Until 1905, the drink even contained traces of cocaine, added for its medicinal effects.

John's young company started to grow sales of its drink by getting other pharmacies to sell Coca-Cola too. It sold 25 gallons of syrup to drugstores and made sure that all the stores that sold the drink had hand-painted Coca-Cola signs to help promote it. John persuaded six local businessmen to invest in the company to help him finance this expansion.

Coca-Cola's famous advertising campaigns have roots in its early history: soon after the drink was created, John placed the first newspaper ad in the *Atlanta Journal*, inviting people to try "the new and popular soda fountain drink."

Sadly, John died in 1888 and never saw his drink concoction taken to the masses. The person to do this was Atlanta businessman Asa Griggs Candler, who bought the rights to the drink for \$2,300 (\$54,400 today). It took Asa three years to secure rights to the business, as a very ill John had also sold rights to another businessman and given exclusive rights to his son, which took some time to unravel.

Asa had a vision for the product: to turn the now-popular drink from a beverage into a business. He disbanded the pharmaceutical arm of the company and partnered with his brother, John Candler, and John Pemberton's bookkeeper, Frank Robinson. Together they raised \$100,000 (\$2,370,000 today)—then a very substantial sum—to kick-start the business.

In 1891, Asa had full control of the business, and within a year he had increased sales of Coca-Cola syrup tenfold. In 1893, the company was incorporated and The Coca-Cola Company was officially born.

The company soon began a huge marketing campaign, using new advertising techniques. To spread the word, Asa gave away coupons for free Coca-Cola samples in newspapers, and offered pharmacists two gallons of the syrup if they agreed to give away one gallon's worth when people produced his coupon. He supplied the pharmacists with urns, clocks, calendars, and scales all bearing the brand name. The combination of strong branding and a drink that appealed to so many people worked wonders, and sales grew fast.

Just four years later, in 1895, Asa had grown demand for his product so much that he needed to build syrup plants in Chicago, Dallas and Los Angeles. He declared to his shareholders that "Coca-Cola is now drunk in every state and territory in the United States." Given the far reach of today's mass media, it might be easy to miss just what a major achievement in advertising this really was. This, after all, was an era in which it took days to travel across the country. Likewise, there was no radio or television, and so to achieve product placement in every state so quickly was quite phenomenal.

The combination of strong branding and a drink that appealed to so many people worked wonders, and sales grew fast.

Until 1894, Coca-Cola was sold only by the glassful. But then a Mississippi businessman named Joseph Biedenharn had the idea to bottle Coca-Cola at his factory. He sent a dozen bottles to Asa; Asa hated the product and quickly dismissed it. He overlooked this crucial development again in 1899 when two lawyers from Chattanooga, Tennessee, Benjamin F. Thomas and Joseph B. Whitehead, secured exclusive rights from Asa to bottle and sell the beverage in nearly all of the states, for only $1. In fact, Asa was so sure that this idea would amount to nothing that he didn't even bother collecting the dollar!

This was the start of Coca-Cola's unusual corporate structure, which continues to this day. The Coca-Cola Company supplies syrup, called concentrate, to customers all over the world. Some of these customers are restaurants and bars, which sell the drink by the glass, much like the original pharmacy customers. The other group of customers are bottling companies, which add carbonated water to the syrup in a factory and bottle it for sale in shops.

Thomas and Whitehead began by opening bottling plants in Chattanooga and Atlanta, but soon realized there was a far better way for them to distribute bottled Coca-Cola across the country. The two Chattanooga lawyers were joined by John Thomas Lupton and the trio split the US into three territories, selling bottling rights to local entrepreneurs. Not only did this reduce the amount of capital the lawyers needed, as local entrepreneurs used their own money, but it also provided local knowledge and the commitment of business owners, which would have been very hard to set up any other way. The first sub-licensed bottler began in 1900, and by 1909 there were 400 Coca-Cola bottling plants across America.

By the turn of the century, Asa had increased Coca-Cola's sales to 40 times its 1890 level, and his continuing advertising campaign and his free samples had spread the name "Coca-Cola" across the country.

Coca-Cola's bottle progression over nearly a century.

Bubbling overseas

The drink was first taken overseas by Asa's son, Charles, on a trip to London. Charles took a jug of syrup with him and gathered modest orders for five gallons. Coca-Cola was first sold in England on August 31, 1900, and gradually it built enough momentum to be sold in London's prestigious Selfridges department store and the London Coliseum.

After seeing the success of the bottled drinks, The Coca-Cola Company decided to license out bottling rights to overseas territories itself. The first international bottling plants began in Canada, Cuba and Panama in 1906; plants in the Philippines and Guam followed shortly afterward in 1912. As he had done so effectively in America, Asa supported the new supplies of drinks with a thorough marketing campaign, to ensure that Coca-Cola's bright-red logo was seen in stores and cafés everywhere.

Of the companies granted rights to bottle Coca-Cola around the world, most were brewers. This worked well, as the brewers already had bottling plants and expertise, so it was relatively easy and quick for them to add the new drink to their range. The brewers also already had distribution networks through their existing customer base, which meant that Coca-Cola had access to stores, bars and restaurants far faster than it would have done had it set up a brand-new business from scratch in a new country.

As he had done so effectively in America, Asa supported the new supplies of drinks with a thorough marketing campaign, to ensure that Coca-Cola's bright red logo was seen in stores and cafés everywhere.

The drink had become very well known, and it was clearly successful, so inevitably a number of competitors appeared—though, of course, none knew the precise recipe for the drink, which was kept secret. The Coca-Cola Company grew concerned that it was too easy for customers to be given a different drink and mistakenly think it was "The Real Thing"—which meant not only that Coca-Cola would lose out on the sale but, if customers didn't enjoy the rival drink, that it would lose out on future sales, too. Something had to be done. So the company decided to come up with a distinctive bottle to ensure its product stood out. In 1915, following a design contest, the now-famous bottle was introduced. Created by the Root Glass Company of Terre Haute, Indiana, the winning design was chosen for its attractive and original appearance and because, even in the dark, people could easily identify it.

New leadership, new vision

After nearly three decades of turning the drink into a substantial and successful business, Asa eventually sold the business in 1919 to Ernest Woodruff for $25 million (worth roughly $315 million in today's money); his son Robert Woodruff became president in 1923. The company was reincorporated as a Delaware corporation and listed on the New York Stock Exchange, selling 500,000 shares to the general public at $40 per share. Coca-Cola was now firmly established as an American icon, but Woodruff's mission was to go global. His vision was to create a brand that was "in arm's reach of desire."

During the 1920s and 1930s, Woodruff set his sights on international expansion. When he took over in 1923, Coca-Cola was strongly established in North America, had some bottling arrangements in South America, and had just opened its first European bottling plant in France. From this base, Woodruff's Coca-Cola went on to open additional plants in Guatemala, Honduras, Mexico, Belgium and Italy in the 1920s. In 1926, Coca-Cola set up a Foreign Department, which became the Coca-Cola Export Corporation in 1930. In all the countries Coca-Cola expanded into, a creative, vibrant and culturally relevant advertising campaign followed.

A significant international move occurred in 1928, when Woodruff began a partnership with the Olympic Games in Amsterdam. A thousand bottles of Coca-Cola accompanied the US team, and the drink was on sale in the Olympic stadium. Vendors wore caps and coats emblazoned with the Coca-Cola logo, and the drink was also sold at surrounding cafés, restaurants and stores.

Elsewhere, Woodruff affixed the company logo on everything from Canadian racing dog sleds to bullfighting arenas in Spain. By the start of World War II, Coca-Cola was in 44 countries. A marketing genius, Woodruff continued to develop the company's successful, but limited, line. He introduced the six-pack (making the drinks more transportable and encouraging people to buy in bulk) and the open-top cooler. Coca-Cola was available in vending machines from 1929 and was advertised on the radio from 1930. In 1935, bottlers hired women to act as door-to-door salespeople for the drink, with a target of 125 calls per day.

In all the countries Coca-Cola expanded into, a creative, vibrant and culturally relevant advertising campaign followed.

In a marketing scheme that was to have repercussions for little children everywhere, Coca-Cola's famous red-suited Santa Claus made his debut at Christmas 1931, banishing the long-established and previously unchallenged green Santa into the mists of time.

Santa Claus dressed in red is now a globally recognized figure.

Coca-Cola's wartime effort

Throughout World War II, Coca-Cola continued to manufacture, offering the drink for 5 cents to any serviceman, whatever country he was in, regardless of the cost to the company. Bottling plants were opened to supply troops with the drink, following a request from General Eisenhower himself on June 29, 1943. Eisenhower asked for the shipment of materials for 10 bottling plants to be sent to North Africa along with three million bottles of Coca-Cola and enough supplies to make the same amount twice a month. Coca-Cola responded within six months, setting up a bottling plant in Algiers.

In all, 64 bottling plants opened during the war, and more than five billion bottles of Coca-Cola were consumed by service people. Mobile service stations were also taken to the battlefields, and people throughout Europe and the Pacific had their first taste of the drink. These wartime bottling plants were later converted and run by local civilians, who continued to produce and sell the drink even after the Americans had left.

Promoting global happiness

Postwar America was the perfect place for Coca-Cola to expand: people were embracing a carefree lifestyle, and Coca-Cola's advertising mirrored this desire, with images of loving couples at the drive-in and happy families driving around in shiny cars. Coca-Cola continued to be served at soda fountains and was now added to the menu in ice cream parlors.

The company still had just one product, albeit an extraordinarily successful one, and it began experimenting with new flavors. In the 1950s the company introduced Fanta (which was originally concocted in wartime Germany), followed by Sprite in 1961, Tab in 1963 and Fresca in 1966. Coca-Cola acquired the Minute Maid Company in 1960, branching out into juices. New lines of Coca-Cola were also introduced in 1960, along with bigger bottles and metal cans.

The 1950s and 1960s saw bottling plants built in more countries, expanding into new markets in Cambodia, Montserrat, Paraguay, Macao and Turkey. During the 1970s and 1980s, many of Coca-Cola's small and medium-sized bottlers joined forces to better serve their growing international customer base. By 1969, for the first time, Coca-Cola sales in international markets exceeded those in the US.

In 1971, Coca-Cola created a particularly special television advertisement, which featured young people from all over the world gathered on a hilltop in Italy to sing, "I'd Like to Buy the World a Coke." Coca-Cola had made its mark on the international market, and for a time it was seen as an icon of unity in an era that had not yet grasped the consequences of globalization. Significantly, in 1978, the People's Republic of China declared The Coca-Cola Company as the only company allowed to sell packaged cold drinks in China.

Intelligent risk-taking

In 1981, Roberto C. Goizueta became chairman of the board of directors and CEO of The Coca-Cola Company. Goizueta's mantra was to take the company forward with a strategy he called "intelligent risk-taking." This began with the introduction of Diet Coke on Independence Day 1982, the very first extension of the Coca-Cola trademark. Coca-Cola's archrival, Pepsi, had released its diet version of the drink in 1963 with great success. Despite its comparatively late entry, within two years Diet Coke had become the top low-calorie drink in the world. Coca-Cola might have been slow on the uptake, but it quickly followed Diet Coke's inception with a range of alternatives, including Caffeine-Free and Cherry Coke.

Goizueta's riskiest initiative began in 1985, when he released what was deemed "New Coke," which marked the first change in recipe in 99 years. Why fix something that isn't broken? The data suggested there were cracks at the seams. Coca-Cola's share of the soft drinks market decreased from 60 percent at the end of World War II to less than 24 percent in 1983, in large part due to its new rival, Pepsi. Coca-Cola's share price had also decreased by 2.5 percent in the preceding four years (that might sound like a small percentage, but it represented a drop in market capitalization of $500 million). Pepsi had directly challenged Coca-Cola's success in the marketplace by conducting blind taste testing on the streets of America, with many people opting for the sweeter Pepsi. This marketing campaign helped Pepsi overtake Coca-Cola in supermarket sales.

New Coke passed taste testers' approval in extensive testing before launch, as most preferred it to Pepsi; however, it didn't succeed in the marketplace. In an unprecedented expression of brand loyalty, people demanded their old Coke back. Coca-Cola received over 40,000 letters from customers pleading for the old recipe, and the company's phone lines were continually overloaded. After the reintroduction of Coca-Cola Classic, the market share of New Coke in the Cola beverage segment (which continued to be sold alongside Coca-Cola Classic), ultimately fell from 15 percent to 1.4 percent. Pepsi declared itself the victor of the so-called "cola wars." The company listened, and after 87 days of New Coke, the company started supplying the original Coca-Cola again under the banner of "Coca-Cola Classic."

Its return was momentous: ABC News anchor Peter Jennings interrupted regular programming to share the news with viewers, and speaking in the US Senate, Senator David Pryor called the reintroduction "a meaningful moment in US history." More importantly, Coke's sales leapt up, reclaiming the top spot, which it has never lost since. New Coke was eventually discontinued, and the original recipe is still used today.

The company listened, and after 87 days of New Coke, the company started supplying the original Coca-Cola again under the banner of "Coca Cola Classic."

In an effort to help manage the now-substantial network of bottlers, the company set up Coca-Cola Enterprises Inc. in 1986. This new public company was intended to organize the bottling partners and ensure that they could meet the international demand for Coca-Cola. The company follows the same approach today: Coca-Cola works with local bottlers, some of which are public companies while others are independent and family-owned. Significantly, the majority of them are not owned by Coca-Cola. The bottling plants (of which there are now nearly 300) package, distribute and market the product.

Coca-Cola Classic was brought back due to public demand.

In 1985, Coca-Cola became the first independent operator in the Soviet Union, and throughout the early 1990s it invested heavily in building bottling plants in eastern Europe.

Flying high

During the 1990s, Coca-Cola made its presence known in the sporting world, sponsoring the Olympic Games, the NBA, FIFA World Cup and Rugby World Cup. In 1993, the company launched its catchy "Always Coca-Cola" advertising campaign, and by 1997 it was selling a billion servings of its products every day.

The 1990s also marked the return of Coca-Cola to India, following a liberalization of trade laws. The company pulled out of the market in 1977, when Indian law forbade companies to trade if they withheld trade-secret information, something Coca-Cola insisted upon to protect its formula. In 1991, India changed its laws regarding trademarks, and Coca-Cola went on sale again in 1993. A populous and hot country, India seemed fertile ground for the international giant, but surprisingly it struggled to capture the market. Its slow growth was aided by the acquisition of Indian brands Limca, Maaza and Thums Up. The company followed this pattern of growth by acquisition in other countries, too, including Barq's Root Beer in the US, and Inca Kola in Peru.

In 1999, The Coca-Cola Company purchased the soft drinks brands of Cadbury Schweppes PLC in various countries, including the UK. This expanded the existing product range of Coca-Cola, Diet Coke, Cherry Coke, Fanta, Sprite, Lilt and Five Alive to include the Schweppes range, Dr Pepper, Oasis, Kia-Ora and Malvern water.

Where are they now?

The Coca-Cola Company celebrated its 125th anniversary in 2011, now owns more than 500 brands and sells 1.7 billion beverage servings each day. Since it began, it has produced more than 10 billion gallons of syrup.

Of all the countries that Coca-Cola dominates, the highest per capita consumption is in Mexico and Iceland. The company employs over 90,000 people and is headed up by Muhtar Kent, chairman and CEO. To celebrate its heritage, The New World of Coca-Cola, an attraction dedicated to the brand, opened in 2007, and remains one of Atlanta's main tourist attractions.

Now a major global corporation, Coca-Cola faces new challenges: changing patterns of demand for soft drinks in many developed countries, and enormous and fast-growing potential in increasingly affluent countries such as China.

In the past decade, Coca-Cola has continued to add to its extensive brand list, including the launch of Coke Zero in 2005, and acquisitions, including water and tea companies. In 2008, Coca-Cola launched its first-ever clothing range of sustainable apparel. Sold in Wal-Mart, the T-shirts are made of recycled Coca-Cola bottles.

Coca-Cola Company and subsidiaries' full-year results to December 31, 2011 showed revenues of $46.5 billion, a year-on-year increase of 33 percent. Today, 72 percent of Coca-Cola is sold outside of the USA, and Coca-Cola's share price continues to rise, based on expectations of continued profitable growth to come.

IBM

Computing success

Founders:	**Thomas Watson, Charles Flint and Herman Hollerith**
Age of founders:	**40, 61 and 51**
Background:	**Salesman and executive for National Cash Register (NCR) Company, serial businessman who negotiated first overseas sales of Wright Brothers' planes, and statistician and owner of Tabulating Machine Company**
Founded in:	**1911**
Headquarters:	**Endicott, New York**
Business type:	**Computer hardware**

Unlike most business stories, the founding of IBM is not simply a tale of one man with an idea. Rather, it is a story of several men, three in particular, whom history brought together and who laid the building blocks of a vast technological business. It is the story of Herman Hollerith, a brilliant inventor and flawed genius, who would envisage and develop the tabulating machines that IBM would later sell across the world. And it is the story of Charles Flint, a maverick investor and adventurous businessman, who would buy several companies, including Herman's, which would be forged together to form the International Business Machines Corporation. Thirdly, and most crucially, it is the story of Thomas Watson Sr., a brilliant leader and salesman, who would bring order to Charles's messy acquisitions and create a strong and vibrant culture that resonates at IBM to this day.

For many, Thomas was IBM. He was its leader from 1914 to 1956, setting its course, and he was the man who gave the company its name. But Thomas was no engineer or inventor—he barely understood how his company's machines worked, beyond the information he needed to tell his customers. His path to the helm of IBM is an intriguing one, but to appreciate his journey it's necessary to return to the beginning and look at how the company came into being, formed from the sparks of genius decades before.

Crunching the data

In 1879, Herman, a 19-year-old college graduate, took a job at the US Census Bureau, compiling statistics. The census was taken every 10 years, and it was a tiresome and cumbersome affair for all involved. The data, recorded by hand, took years to process, and Herman became determined to find a more efficient method. He conceived of a machine that would process data automatically, and he spent the next few years of his life inventing it.

Inspired by the way ticket conductors punched holes in train tickets to record information such as destination and age, Herman predicted that the same process could be used to collect the census data. He saw that the position of a hole on a line of paper could represent answers to census questions, such as male or female, or whether a person lived in the US or was from abroad. He imagined a machine that automatically fed the paper through its processors, and a board with buttons that would electrically punch the holes in the paper. As the paper was fed through the machine, it would pass over a drum, completing an electrical circuit for each hole.

The data would then come rolling out automatically, without the need for human intervention. The "tabulating machine" would, in time, revolutionize data processing, and on September 23, 1884, Herman submitted his first patent application.

But an invention alone does not a business make, no matter how great it is. Herman still needed to prove his machine worked in an office environment; he needed to manufacture it and to sell it to the world, and this required investment. Herman worked out that he would need around $2,500 ($60,000 in today's money) to develop his invention, and a family friend agreed to put up the cash. Herman then visited the census offices and asked if they would consider using his machine to work on some past census data–in effect asking the government to fund the invention by providing the manpower (in the form of government clerks) to test it–to which census officials agreed.

Herman's first version of the tabulator in 1890.

Things were going well, but the machine itself was not perfect, not by any means. For one thing, the paper Herman was using would tear easily, and it was difficult to read the information recorded. To solve this, Herman switched to using punch cards the size of $1 bills. The advantages over paper were clear: the size of the cards meant they were easier to sort and collate, and they did not tear so easily. The process of trial and error to iron out problems took years of dedicated work, and during this time, investors were not easy to find or keep. Government departments were intrigued by the potential of Herman's machine, however, and they continued to test his machines. Meanwhile, Herman kept himself going financially by consulting on patents and working on other inventions.

In 1888, the War Department decided to rent one of Herman's tabulating machines for $1,000 for the year. Herman was told that if it was successful, there was the chance the Navy would also be interested, as the Office of Records and Pensions wanted to compile data on the health of its servicemen. The machine performed well, Herman signed a contract with the Navy that same year, and he began to rent out his machines to other clients. Then, in 1889, Herman's patent application was finally approved and he took his machine global, exhibiting it at the Paris Universal Exhibition of that year.

Herman developed his invention to include a motorized card feeder.

By this time, the 1890 census was fast approaching, and as the US population had grown considerably in the 1880s, it was estimated that it would take 13 years to complete. The Census Bureau trialed Herman's machine against two competitors'—and Herman's won. The Bureau placed an order for six machines at a yearly rate of $1,000 each. A year later, in 1890, an order for 50 more machines was placed by the Bureau.

The data collection for the 1890 census was completed in a staggeringly short six weeks, and the whole census itself was finished in just two and a half years. Herman's invention saved taxpayers $5 million and earned him a PhD from Columbia University.

By 1891, demand for the machines soared and Herman won contracts from other countries such as Austria, Canada, France and Russia, following his appearance at the Paris show. Every country was keen to use his invention to gather and process census data, and the machines now had a great track record. There was also demand from private companies, as Herman expanded the commercial uses of the machine to encompass freight and agricultural data.

The data collection for the 1890 census was completed in a staggeringly short six weeks, and the whole census itself was finished in just two and a half years. Herman's invention had saved taxpayers #5 million.

At the end of 1896, Herman founded the Tabulating Machine Company to continue making and licensing out his machines. However, he was a far better inventor than he was a businessman, and he struggled to cope with the demands of managing a business. Herman also possessed a difficult temperament, often antagonizing both his staff and his customers. By 1911, he was finding it increasingly difficult to manage a growing business, was suffering from poor health, and had competitors biting at his heels. Herman decided to sell the business to an investor named Charles Flint, who was putting together a collection of businesses that would become IBM.

Fair means or foul

The man whom many regard as the face of IBM, Thomas, couldn't have been more different from Herman. While Herman was awkward in social situations, Thomas proved to be a savvy manager and motivator. Also, unlike the well-read and educated Herman, Thomas was a man of humble beginnings who never went to college and who started full-time work as soon as he could. After a few jobs, his working career began in earnest in 1896, when he joined the National Cash Register Company (NCR), based in Dayton, Ohio, as a sales apprentice. Thomas was taken under the wing of John Range, who taught him all about sales, and his career began to flourish.

By 1903, Thomas had made a real impression with senior management and they called on him to work on a special project. With NCR backing, Thomas set up the American Second Cash Register Company, which was little more than an NCR front designed to crush the competition by fair means or foul. NCR's business was selling new cash registers, and the company was therefore threatened by companies that bought and sold secondhand ones. Thomas's goal was to drive out the competition by overpaying for used registers and even acquiring rival businesses on condition that they would not re-enter the market. The operation was highly successful, although later NCR would gain the unwanted attention of the federal government on charges relating to monopolistic activities. Indeed, thanks to Thomas's work, NCR had gained 90 percent of the market by 1910.

Thomas's work gained him a promotion at NCR to sales manager, where he worked directly beneath the company's founder, John H. Patterson. From him, Thomas learned much about leadership and running a business, and NCR's founder was to have a profound influence on Thomas's own leadership of IBM. Patterson was an uncompromising and tough leader, who instilled both fear and respect in his staff. Although he was often ruthless and controlling, he extolled the importance of believing in his staff and developing teams. Patterson also taught Thomas how to win at all costs. The two became close—so close, in fact, that Thomas became one of the few people who could contradict Patterson and get away with it.

It was through NCR that Thomas heard about Herman's tabulating machines. He was impressed with how they could be used to transform company data, and he hired some machines for his offices. It is clear that at this stage Thomas understood the importance of being able to measure performance, as well as the benefits of having a scientific approach to business.

In 1912, NCR's management was indicted by the federal government for its corrupt and monopolistic practices, and John H. Patterson and Thomas Watson were among those indicted. The charges were made criminal and Thomas faced up to a year in prison. The indictment began a dark period in Thomas's life and would go on to haunt him throughout his career. At the first trial, the company was found guilty. The defendants appealed, and eventually a deal was made. Thomas never admitted he had done anything wrong.

By the end of 1913, Thomas was finished with NCR. However, with federal charges still hanging over him while he awaited the appeal, he found it difficult to find work. He would have liked to set up his own business, but no one was likely to back someone who could soon end up in prison. However, after many trips between Dayton and New York looking for a job, Thomas would eventually enter the offices of Charles Flint.

Leader in the making

Charles Flint is a colorful character in the history of IBM. He had been an adventurer, an explorer, an investor, an arms trader and a friend to high society, to US presidents and to dictators. Prior to meeting Thomas, Charles had acquired several businesses: the Tabulating Machine Company, International Time Recording, Bundy Manufacturing, and Computing Scale of America. The new company became known as the Computing Tabulating Recording Company (CTR). However, the acquisitions were not working out, and Charles needed a strong manager to turn his sinking ship around. It was a brave decision to make, bearing in mind the charges still standing against Thomas, but Charles saw in him a true leader in the making. The two struck a deal whereby Thomas would be manager until charges against him were dropped, and then he would become president.

Thomas understood the importance of being able to measure performance, as well as the benefits of having a scientific approach to business.

Thomas began work at CTR but found the experience a miserable one. Unlike the well-oiled machine of NCR, his new company was structurally flawed. Its founder's messy acquisitions did not sit well together, and the company had no discernible culture. It had 1,200 employees based at several locations, which made managing the business virtually impossible. Financially, the business was hemorrhaging money: it was valued at $3 million but had over $6 million in debt. Technically, it was bankrupt. Instinctively, Thomas wanted to impose on it the rational management techniques he had learned at NCR, but two big obstacles stood in his way: Herman, who had remained at the company, and CTR's chairman, George Fairchild.

Herman had sold his business but retained a role at the company that gave him the right to approve or veto any new technological advance or product. The effect was to stifle the company's innovation and prevent gifted engineers from bringing forward the next phase of products. Innovation was needed, as Herman's patents were running out and competitors were cutting into the company's markets. However, Thomas needed Herman, as his name was synonymous with the tabulating machines and the business traded off it. George Fairchild irritated Thomas with his interference, demanding to be consulted and informed while also being unavailable. However, as a member of the House of Representatives, he brought some respectability to the company, which offset Thomas's questionable past at NCR. Thomas had little choice but to play the long game and placate them both.

Nevertheless, Thomas got to work on his sales team and soon proved himself a powerful motivator. He wanted to transform the approach his managers had toward their staff, encouraging a more nurturing approach. "Every supervisor must look upon himself as an assistant to the men below him, instead of looking at himself as the boss," he told his managers.

The Man Proposition

Thomas also introduced what became known as "The Man Proposition." On a blackboard, he wrote out the words "manufacturing," "general manager," "sales manager," "sales man," "factory manager," "factory man," and so on, covering all the positions within the business. He then crossed out all the words apart from "man," suggesting that all were equal in the company. "We are just men," he said. "Men standing together, shoulder to shoulder, all working for one common good."

The Man Proposition would be repeated regularly at IBM for the next 40 years or more, and is one of Thomas's biggest contributions to the company's culture.

By 1915, the federal case against the management of NCR had concluded, and while most of those involved accepted a minor penalty for what they had done, Thomas never admitted to any wrongdoing. The federal government declined to pursue him any further. He therefore became president of CTR on March 15, 1915, and was determined to turn the company around and to run it in as moral a way as possible. It was a grueling challenge, as the US economy was then in decline as World War I raged in Europe.

Imbued by the Man Proposition, Thomas looked to find talent within his existing staff rather than recruit from outside. "The directors told me, 'You'll have to hire outside brains before you can build up this company,'" said Thomas. "I told them, 'That's not my policy. I like to develop men from the ranks and promote them.'"

Thomas's own personal style and morality affected those around him. He never drank alcohol, and soon it became the norm for the executives to refrain from drinking as well. Thomas also had a love of fine clothes, and pretty soon those under him adopted his style of suits. However, while he espoused democracy and equality, he could also behave like a tyrant, subjecting staff to brutal tongue-lashings and tirades. At the same time, he engendered a love in his staff, which meant that most forgave or tolerated him, and he developed many loyal employees.

"The directors told me, 'You'll have to hire outside brains before you can build up this company,'" said Thomas. "I told them, 'That's not my policy. I like to develop men from the ranks and promote them.'"

In many ways, Thomas was becoming more and more like John H. Patterson, his old boss at NCR, aping some of his ideas as well as his management style. NCR had a Hundred Point Club whereby salesmen who hit targets would be treated to a weekend at a country club. Similarly, Thomas created the Hundred Percent Club, which served the same purpose. He strove for unity and cohesion, which wasn't easy while managing what were effectively separate companies. "We want all of our subsidiary companies to feel that they are all one thing, one big family," he said.

The thinking company

Against the odds, by the end of the decade, CTR was growing and beginning to really show its potential. Herman's influence was declining, and later Thomas would establish a robust engineering department that would work on and improve the tabulating machine. Although he was not an engineer himself, he managed to get the best out of his men. Sometimes, he would secretly set them the same task and then choose the best product, believing that rivalry brought better work. He tried many different techniques to bring out the best from his team, and repeated whatever seemed to work the most effectively. He also liked to have the slogan THINK displayed at various places across the company, another vestige of his NCR days.

On a blackboard, he wrote out the words "manufacturing," "general manager," "sales manager," "sales man," "factory manager," "factory man," and so on ... He then crossed out all the words apart from "man," suggesting that all were equal in the company.

In 1917, the company moved into Canada, and Thomas decided to call that company International Business Machines (IBM). He later used that name as the company moved into South America. In 1924 the CTR name was dropped completely and IBM floated on the New York Stock Exchange. Also that year George Fairchild died, and the last remaining barrier to Thomas's dominance was removed. IBM was now truly Thomas Watson and would remain that way for the better part of 30 years.

Where are they now?

During the Great Depression of the 1930s, IBM managed to grow and even launch new products such as the Electric Writing Machine (a typewriter), while other businesses struggled. In the 1940s, the business made its first foray into computing, and a decade later introduced its first computer. By the 1960s, IBM recognized the potential that computers would bring to business, and, accordingly, the business was transformed from a medium-sized manufacturer of tabulating equipment to the technology industry leader more familiar to us today.

Today, over 100 years since the founding of the business, IBM has grown to become the world's largest computer manufacturer, operating in over 200 countries with more than 425,000 employees. In 2011, it was ranked by Forbes *as the 18th-largest firm in the US and the 7th most profitable, with annual revenues breaking the $100 billion barrier at the end of 2011. The company has also branched out into diverse markets in recent years, and can now boast of being the largest IT services provider in the world, as well as the largest IT financier.*

The Walt Disney Company

Creative to the core

Founders:	**Walt Disney and Roy Disney**
Age of founders:	**21 and 29**
Background:	**Cartoonist and naval officer**
Founded in:	**1923**
Headquarters:	**Burbank, California**
Business type:	**Entertainment**

Disney is the largest entertainment company in the world. While we might naturally associate the company's origins with Mickey Mouse, the real story involves a rabbit, and several years of hard work, creditor disagreements and mutiny. With a failed business behind him at just 21, Walt Disney and his brother Roy started their company from their uncle's garage in California in 1923. Armed with a truckload of talent and little else, the Disney brothers' story is littered with highs and lows reminiscent of a rollercoaster found at Disneyland. The business, which today brings in more than $40 billion a year and employs 150,000 people, is a remarkable story of survival and creativity.

Hard knocks

As you might expect, Walt Disney had always been fascinated with illustration. He took an active interest in drawing from a young age; he was even commissioned to draw his neighbor's horse. Aged 10, he continued his love of drawing, attending Saturday school at the Kansas City Art Institute. But Walt soon realized he was not good enough to pursue traditional illustration and turned his attention instead to caricatures and cartoons.

When the family moved to Chicago, the teenage Walt became cartoonist for his school's newspaper and took night classes at the Art Institute of Chicago. After leaving school, Walt intended to become a cartoonist. But with the advent of World War I, he joined the Red Cross as soon as he was old enough and served in France for a year in 1918. Throughout this time, he continued to hone his drawing skills, submitting numerous pieces to national magazines. Upon his return home in 1919, he started a concerted effort to find a job in illustration.

Walt received numerous rejections, but eventually got a job at a commercial art studio that produced marketing materials and corporate stationery. Here he met Ub Iwerks, the man who would later become his first business partner and eventually a loyal member of the Disney empire. Both men were quickly let go from the studio once a busy period ended and, at a loose end, they decided to set up their own company in January 1920.

Iwerks-Disney Commercial Artists was a short-lived venture but gave Walt valuable business experience. The pair won a few small contracts producing content similar to that of the studio they had been fired from. However, it was all over within six weeks, when Walt accepted a position at the Kansas City Film Ad Company for $40 a week and persuaded his bosses to take on Iwerks, too.

The company made silent cartoon advertisements, mostly in black and white, and working at the ad company gave Walt a real taste for bringing his artwork to life. He decided to become an animator. He found he was able to improve the company's basic and somewhat lackluster animation significantly, and started to work on his own cartoons in his spare time. His boss at the ad agency let him borrow a camera with which to experiment at home.

Walt began working on a series of cartoons with the aim of selling them to the nearby Newman Theater. He called them the Newman Laugh-O-Gram Films, and presented them to the theater manager, who was impressed enough to ask how much they cost. For all the time he'd spent on the cartoons, Walt hadn't actually worked out how much he'd need to charge to make a profit. Without thinking, he offered up a price of 30 cents per foot—the price it had cost Walt to produce them—and the theater manager promptly accepted.

The deal was done, and it was too late to renegotiate the price to try to make a profit, but Walt had his first commission and didn't intend to waste the opportunity. Walt needed to get help to produce the cartoon strips, but with no money to pay staff, he had to come up with another way of attracting talent.

A scratchy start

As a way around his staffing problems, Walt placed an ad looking for boys who wanted to learn to animate. He offered applicants training and a share of any future profits. He put together a small team, including colleagues from his work, and they spent evenings after work creating a series of cartoons that could be made into films and sold to theaters. The Laugh-O-Grams were a great success and became popular in theaters throughout Kansas.

Walt's team began working on other projects and created an animation of *Little Red Riding Hood* that proved a hit at local theaters. This success gave Walt the courage to leave his job at the Kansas City Film Ad Company and concentrate on his fledgling business full-time. He persuaded some of his former colleagues to invest in the business and set up Laugh-O-Gram Films in 1922, having raised $15,000. At 20 years old, he owned his first company, although he later joked that it "was probably illegal" to be president of a company at that age. Now in charge of a "proper" company, Walt rented some studio space, brought in his former colleague Ub, and took on another handful of budding young animators who earned very modest wages.

The team began to work on more animations and worked nearly every hour of the day, producing some excellent results. But Walt desperately needed to find someone to distribute his products. With no advertising budget, Walt struggled to get his company noticed and eventually had to hire salesman Leslie Mace. Leslie took the films to New York and secured a deal with Pictorial Clubs of Tennessee, a company that hired out films to schools and churches. The deal was for a series of fairytale cartoons. Walt accepted a down payment of $100 on the understanding that a further $11,000 would come through once the series had been delivered.

But six months later, just as Laugh-O-Gram Films was about to deliver the finished series, Pictorial Clubs of Tennessee went out of business. With no income and salaries to pay, Walt saw his employees begin to quit. He was kicked out of his apartment for failing to pay rent and soon became the only member of the company.

At 20 years old he owned his first company, although he later joked that it "was probably illegal" to be president of a company at that age.

Walt spent the next year accepting meager commissions, including one from a local dentist who wanted a film encouraging children to brush their teeth. The dentist offered him $500 and asked Walt to come by and finalize the deal, but Walt couldn't even afford the trip. Times were tough and his only pair of shoes was being held ransom by the cobbler until he could pay his bill. He finally admitted this to the dentist, who promptly paid the cobbler's bill, and the cartoon deal was completed. The money allowed Walt some breathing space and he soon began working on a new idea—one that would eventually lead to the creation of the Disney Brothers Cartoon Studio.

Alice's Wonderland

Walt began to develop ideas for a new cartoon series based on Lewis Carroll's *Alice's Adventures in Wonderland*. New York distributor Margaret Winkler had expressed interest in the cartoon after Walt wrote to her describing it. However, Laugh-O-Gram's debts were holding him back, and he didn't have anywhere near enough cash to finish *Alice*. He had little choice but to declare the company bankrupt and move on. It was a tough period for Walt, but he later said he thought it was "important to have a good hard failure when you're young."

In 1923, Walt set off for Los Angeles, believing it to be the only place he could really bring his visions to life with any success. At the age of 21 and with just $40 in his pocket, he arrived in Hollywood, renting a room from his uncle, Robert Disney. His brother Roy was also in LA, having been transferred to a hospital there to receive treatment for tuberculosis.

Walt first approached the big movie studios to offer his services, but was turned down categorically. Encouraged by Winkler's interest in the *Alice* cartoons, Walt decided once again to set up his own studio, this time in his uncle's garage. He wrote back to Winkler informing her that he was "no longer connected with the Laugh-O-Gram Films Inc." and that he was setting up a studio to produce the cartoons she was interested in. On October 16, 1923, a deal was made for the *Alice* series: six cartoons for $1,500 each, but with no advance.

Walt realized from his experience with Laugh-O-Gram Films that his skills did not lie in cash flow management. The solution was to bring in Roy, who discharged himself from the hospital, put up $200 of his own savings, and borrowed an additional $500 from their uncle. With both their sons at work on the same project, the boys' parents also chipped in, re-mortgaging their home to put up another $2,500.

Walt and Roy then hired a small staff of animators, bought a second hand camera, and hired a one-room apartment before setting to work on the cartoons. Disney Brothers Cartoon Studio was up and running. At this point, Walt declared to his father that the name Disney would eventually be famous all over the world.

Although the studio had a steady income from Winkler, the distributor proved to be a tough client. Continually demanding tweaks and improvements to the cartoons, Winkler soon reduced the company's profits to virtually nothing. To stem losses, Walt decided he needed a more professional animator to join his team alongside the junior staff. His old friend Ub Iwerks had returned to the Kansas City Film Ad Company after the collapse of Laugh-O-Gram. Walt offered him a salary that was $10 a week less than what he was earning in Kansas, but Ub accepted it and moved out to Hollywood to join him.

Walt declared to his father that the name Disney would eventually be famous all over the world.

By 1924, payments from Winkler were becoming increasingly late, and the fee for each cartoon soon went from $1,500 to $900. Winkler had recently married, and her new husband, Charles Mintz, had taken over her business operations, much to the dismay of the Disney brothers. As their profit margins evaporated, the brothers had to face their client. Walt pleaded with Mintz, insisting that the quality of the *Alice* series could not be maintained if the right amount of cash was not proffered. His frankness appealed to Mintz's better nature: another 18 *Alice* cartoons were commissioned for $1,800 each as well as a share of any subsequent profits.

The arrangement continued for another three years and more than 50 *Alice* cartoons, although this period was fraught with fee negotiations and more late payments on Mintz's behalf. By 1927, the New York distributor grew tired of the *Alice* series and requested something new, possibly involving a rabbit ...

Oswald the Lucky Rabbit

Tired of the *Alice* series himself, Walt found a new lease on life with his creation Oswald the Rabbit. Over the previous three years, Walt had realized that his talents were best placed as the creative force of the company, not in the animation itself. He declared, "Around here, we don't look backwards for very long. We keep moving forward, opening new doors, and doing new things, because we're curious."

The Oswald series soon became immensely popular, and before long Mintz was paying $2,250 per cartoon. The production schedule was tight, and Walt later recalled, "In the early days of making these pictures, it was a fight to survive. I used to throw gags in because I was desperate. I didn't even like them but I had to get one out every two weeks." Despite the pressure on the studio, things were running smoothly.

"Around here, we don't look backwards for very long. We keep moving forward, opening new doors, and doing new things, because we're curious."

By February 1928, it really looked as though the company, recently renamed Walt Disney Productions, was starting to make an impact. Walt convinced Roy that his name alone on the cartoon credits would make for a more trusted brand. Roy agreed that a single name would convey more confidence: audiences would associate the enjoyment they gleaned from the cartoons with one entertainer, as opposed to a factory-style corporation churning out commercial entertainment.

But the company was heavily reliant on its Oswald contract with Mintz, a contract that was up for renewal. Walt set off for New York to negotiate a new deal. He left with high hopes, but what was to follow was one of the darkest periods in the history of the Disney organization.

Mutiny in the ranks

Walt had been working his staff hard over the preceding few years, and the fortnightly collections of the Oswald reels meant he had to make tough leadership choices. He joked, "Every once in a while I just fire everybody, then I hire them back in a couple of weeks. That way they don't get complacent. It keeps them on their toes."

However, some of the staff did not appreciate his methods. The animators began talking in secret with Winkler, who was working on behalf of her husband, and she offered them better pay to come and work for Mintz directly.

When Walt arrived in New York to meet Mintz, he asked for an increased fee of $2,500 per cartoon—what Disney thought was a fair increase as the cartoons were so popular—but Mintz had other plans. He offered a mere $1,800, which Walt immediately rejected. However, it was too late. Mintz had hired almost all of Walt's animators out from under him. Ub Iwerks was the only animator to remain loyal. But the company had not only lost its staff, it lost Oswald, too. The terms of the original contract clearly stated that Walt Disney Productions did not own the rights to the cartoon, Mintz did.

Goodbye Oswald, hello Mickey

With no cartoon character, no distributor and virtually no animators to come home to, Walt returned to Hollywood. He sent a telegram to Roy from New York, insisting that it would all be OK and that he would tell him all the details when he returned. But the reality was stark, and even he could not have predicted the eventual turnaround in the company's fortunes.

There are several versions of what came next for the company. One version is that Walt began doodling a new character on the train back home from New York. However, the more accepted version of the story is that the studio's next creation was the result of crisis meetings back home in LA with Ub and Roy.

Stung by the disloyalty of his staff, Walt kept the ideas quiet for some time, holding secret meetings and idea sessions with his brother and loyal friend. Even the drawings for the new cartoon were hidden under Oswald sketches if others entered the room. This new character provided the inspiration Walt needed to get back on his feet and put the Oswald fiasco behind him.

The character was a little mouse, dressed in white gloves and buttoned pants. He was named Mortimer Mouse, but Walt's wife, Lilly, eventually persuaded her husband to rename him Mickey.

In 1928, Ub began creating two new Mickey Mouse cartoons. But 1928 was a groundbreaking year for motion pictures, and the first film with synchronized sound, *The Jazz Singer*, was released. Walt was impressed and poured all the studio's resources into a third cartoon that would have fully synchronized sound. They decided to scrap the first two creations and concentrate their efforts on this film, entitled *Steamboat Willie*.

While Ub produced the drawings, Walt provided the voice of Mickey. A Disney employee at the time described how "Ub designed Mickey's physical appearance, but Walt gave him his soul." Walt continued to be the voice of Mickey until 1946.

Walt partnered with businessman Pat Powers, and with his help *Steamboat Willie* premiered at the Colony Theater in New York on November 18, 1928, and was a roaring success. Mickey Mouse proved to be a worldwide hit, and Walt released the first two Mickey cartoons after adding a soundtrack.

Booming cartoons

The success of Mickey Mouse did not mean easy sailing for the business, however. In 1929, Walt Disney Studios released the Silly Symphonies, a series of comedy animations, each one containing different characters. During this time, Walt was becoming increasingly annoyed by Powers, who he thought was taking too large a cut of the distribution profits. In 1930, he struck a new deal with Columbia Pictures. Disgruntled, Powers persuaded Ub to leave Disney and open his own studio, thus poaching Disney's chief animator.

"Ub designed Mickey's physical appearance, but Walt gave him his soul."

Mickey's popularity rocketed throughout the 1930s, overtaking silent film-era cartoon character Felix the Cat in popularity, but the Silly Symphonies were not as popular as Walt hoped. In 1932, Walt was approached by engineer Herbert Kalmus, who persuaded him to redo one of the Symphonies using new technology that would allow the black-and-white animations to be in full color. *Flowers and Trees* proved a phenomenal success and won the Academy Award for Best Cartoon in that year. Disney Studios went on to win this category for the rest of the decade.

From then on, all Silly Symphonies would be produced in color, and the series grew in popularity. The most famous Symphony of all, *Three Little Pigs*, was released in 1933 and contained the classic song "Who's Afraid of the Big Bad Wolf?," which became the anthem of the Great Depression; it ran in theaters for many months.

Faced with the popularity of a new character, Popeye the Sailor, from a rival studio, Walt turned Mickey colorful in 1935 and soon launched the familiar spin-off characters, Donald Duck, Pluto and Goofy. Never one to rest on his laurels, Walt announced plans to create a feature-length full-color animation of *Snow White and the Seven Dwarfs*. This would take years of production, and Roy and Walt's wife Lilly both tried to persuade Walt against it.

Meanwhile, competitors dubbed the project "Disney's Folly," and were sure this would be the end of the Disney success. They were nearly right, as by 1937 the studio had run out of money and had to show a rough version to Bank of America to get a loan to finish the animation.

Snow White and the Seven Dwarfs premiered at the Carthay Circle Theatre on December 21, 1937, and received a standing ovation from the audience. It went on to become the most successful motion picture of 1938 and earned over $8 million from its original release.

Where are they now?

The success of Snow White *marked the start of the golden age of Walt Disney Studios. With the profits, Walt was able to build new studios in Burbank, and family favorites such as* Pinocchio, Fantasia *and* Bambi *followed in quick succession starting in the early 1940s.*

The onset of World War II saw Disney create training and instructional films for the military. After the war, Disney produced a few mediocre films until the release of Cinderella *in 1950 and* Peter Pan *in 1953. Around this time, Walt came up with the idea of a theme park full of Disney characters, after wishing he had somewhere fun to take his daughters on his day off. Funded by a loan from Bank of America, Disneyland was officially opened on July 17, 1955.*

Walt Disney died in 1966, but Disney continued its global expansion in his absence, with his brother Roy replacing him initially. Shortly before Roy's death in 1971, the company's second theme park, Walt Disney World, opened in Orlando, Florida, continuing Disney's commitment to the new arm of the business.

The early 1980s proved to be a trying time for the company, however, with declining revenue from films forcing the firm into cost-cutting measures and narrowly resisting a hostile takeover bid from financier Saul Steinberg in 1984. After this, Disney saw an upturn in its fortunes, with the animation studio enjoying a string of critical and commercial successes under the new leadership of Ron W. Miller as CEO and Michael Eisner as chairman.

The 1990s saw a further expansion of the Disney theme park franchise with the opening of Euro Disney (now Disneyland Paris), MGM Studios in Florida and a new park in California. Miller died in a helicopter crash in 1994, and Eisner was replaced in 2005 by his long-standing assistant Robert Iger.

Today, The Walt Disney Company is one of the world's leading entertainment corporations, with an annual revenue of around $40 billion. In recent years, it has completed a number of high-profile acquisitions, including 3-D animation partner Pixar for $7.6 billion in 2006 and comics giant Marvel for $4.24 billion in 2009. The Disney juggernaut shows no signs of slowing, with plans to open a new theme park in Shanghai by 2014. As Walt once promised his father, the name of Walt Disney is forever cemented in history.

KFC

Recipe for success

Founder:	**Harland Sanders**
Age of founder:	**56**
Background:	**Farmhand, railroad operator, justice of the peace, insurance salesman**
Founded in:	**1952**
Headquarters:	**Louisville, Kentucky**
Business type:	**Fast-food chicken restaurant and take-out**

When Harland Sanders opened a small roadside restaurant in the 1930s specializing in fried chicken, he could not have predicted the legacy he would create. That one site, in Louisville, Kentucky, has today grown into Kentucky Fried Chicken (more recently renamed KFC), a business with 16,300 company-owned and franchised restaurants in more than 100 countries. The business has expanded from its humble origins into a global superbrand and is as famous now for its chicken as it is for its tagline—"finger-lickin' good"—and the snow-white bearded image of its founder, more commonly known as Colonel Sanders.

Home is where the business is

Harland was born in Indiana in 1890, with a taste for fried chicken honed from an early age. He enjoyed cooking the food his mother had taught him to make, including pan-fried chicken, country ham, fresh vegetables and homemade biscuits.

But it was some time before he could put these homegrown skills to use. Harland left school at the tender age of 12 and displayed his entrepreneurial bent by trying all kinds of jobs—including stints as a farmhand, railroad worker, insurance salesman and even justice of the peace. He also gained experience by starting two companies: one, a steamboat ferry company that operated on the Ohio River between Jeffersonville, Indiana, and Louisville, Kentucky, and the other, a manufacturing business.

His real love, however, was for what he knew best: cooking. In 1930, despite the fact that America was in the grip of the Depression, he opened his first restaurant in the front room of a gas station he had acquired in Corbin, Kentucky. It was a modest set-up, consisting of one table and six chairs. The idea came from conversations with his customers: Harland had spotted an opportunity after customers who stopped for gas asked if they could get food nearby. He named the site Sanders Court & Café, and his entrepreneurial skills were put to good use as he juggled several roles, including station operator, chief cook and cashier.

Word soon spread about his cooking, so much so that in 1935, Kentucky governor Ruby Laffoon made Harland an honorary Kentucky colonel in recognition of his contributions to the state's cuisine. Customers were soon turning up in droves for the food alone, which prompted Harland to expand to bigger premises across the street, a building that housed a 142-seat restaurant as well as a motel and gas station. He enrolled in an eight-week course in restaurant and hotel management at Cornell University to learn more about the business, and forged ambitious plans to start a restaurant chain by expanding to two additional locations. However, both of the new sites failed soon after opening, so he concentrated on improving the existing business.

Spice of life

Some might say that Harland was a late bloomer: it wasn't until 1940, when he was 50 years old, that he created the recipe for which the business is so famous today. But as he said in his autobiography, *Life as I Have Known It Has Been Finger Lickin' Good* (Creation House, 1974), "no hours, nor amount of labor, nor amount of money would deter me from giving the best that was in me."

Fried chicken, too, might not have been a new concept, but Harland proved that not all successful ideas need to be new by coming up with his own original recipe of herbs and seasoning. It gave a new twist to fried chicken, one of the nation's favorite foods. He claimed that the 11 herbs and spices he used "stand on everybody's shelf," ensuring the chicken had that home-cooked feel about it. "I hand-mixed the spices in those days like mixing cement," he once said, "on a specially cleaned concrete floor on my back porch in Corbin."

Some might say that Harland was a late bloomer: it wasn't until 1940, when he was 50 years old, that he created the recipe for which the business is so famous today.

Not satisfied with perfecting the herbs and spices for fried chicken, Harland decided to experiment with the way it was cooked. He braved the pressure cooker, a new invention at the time, in his quest for the perfect fried chicken. He developed a method of pressure-frying the chicken so that it cooked much faster than when using traditional frying methods in an iron skillet—cutting the cooking time by more than a third. Again, this was in response to his customers' needs: they weren't prepared to wait a long time for their food. Testament to his success: in 1939, the motel and restaurant were endorsed by food critic Duncan Hines in *Adventures in Good Eating*, a guide to America's finest roadside restaurants. The listing sent the restaurant's popularity soaring.

Testing times

In the years that followed, though, a series of events that were out of his hands forced Harland to radically alter his original business plan. In 1939, a fire destroyed the original building, but Harland rebuilt and reopened the restaurant. The advent of World War II, however, posed an even bigger challenge: gas rationing forced Harland to close the motel. Undaunted, he reopened after the war, and business boomed for many years, as his restaurant and motel were a popular stop for travelers driving along what was then the major north-south route.

Harland even became an early pioneer of the franchising model. He traveled from town to town cooking batches of his fried chicken for other restaurant owners and employees. Sales were slow, but his dogged perseverance paid off and resulted in his first franchise operation in 1952, when Harland gave Pete Harman of Salt Lake City, Utah, the first KFC franchise. The deal was done the old-fashioned way—a handshake agreement stipulated a payment of 4 cents (about 41 cents today) to Harland for each chicken sold.

Not all progress had a happy ending, however. Transportation development in the late 1950s proved too big a hurdle for even Harland to overcome and hurt his business in more ways than one. The completion of an interstate highway provided travelers with an alternative north-south route, one that completely bypassed the restaurant. The value of Harland's site plummeted as customer numbers dwindled, and he was forced to sell the business and try his luck elsewhere. The sale—for $75,000 ($581,000 today), half the asking price of the previous year—was completed on the day he officially "retired" and picked up his first social security check for $105.

Harland gave Pete Harman of Salt Lake City, Utah, the first KFC franchise. ... A handshake agreement stipulated a payment of 4 cents to Harland for each chicken sold.

After paying off debts, he was virtually penniless, but ever the entrepreneur—even in his 60s—and armed with a strong belief in his fried chicken, Harland adapted his business plan. If customers weren't able to come to his restaurant and try his recipes, he would have to take the idea to them. It was at this point that the KFC franchise began to gather momentum.

The road to success

With the first franchise in Salt Lake City going well, Harland went on the road to sell his recipe to restaurants, but he had to go right back to basics. "Lots of nights I would sleep in the back of my car so I would have enough money to buy cookers the next day if someone took a franchise," he recalled in his autobiography.

It was also a case of all hands on deck: Harland's wife, as he put it, acted as "my packing girl, my warehouse supervisor, my delivery person—you name it. Our garage was the warehouse. She'd fill the day's orders in little paper sacks with cellophane linings and package them for shipment. Then she had to put them on a midnight train."

Harland came up with a package he would sell to restaurants: the recipe (which included the spices), a pressure cooker, take-out cartons and advertising material. He also persuaded existing restaurant owners to add the KFC formula to their menus.

"Lots of nights I would sleep in the back of my car so I would have enough money to buy cookers the next day if someone took a franchise."

The hard work paid off, and the concept known as KFC took shape, quickly becoming a fast-food sensation. By 1963, the recipe was franchised to more than 600 outlets in America and Canada. Harland visited independent restaurants throughout the US, doing a spot of what he called Coloneling—ensuring that customers were happy. It marked a turning point in the business in more ways than one.

Expansion wasn't Harland's sole growth strategy, and he constantly sought to innovate the business. The first food offered "to go" was at a restaurant in Jacksonville, Florida, in 1957, inspired by an idea from Harland's daughter Margaret. Also in 1957, the chicken was sold in the now-famous buckets for the first time, under the equally well-known slogan "Finger lickin' good." In 1960, for the first time, Harland's vision of bringing the recipe to the people had paid off handsomely. He could now boast 190 franchisees running 600 franchise sites across the US and Canada.

Going global

Three years later, in 1963, the business was thriving with 17 employees, but it was getting too big for Harland to handle. In the previous year alone, he had traveled 200,000 miles to drum up new business and cater to existing franchisees, and he was not getting any younger. An attractive offer from an investment group headed by John Brown, Jack Massey and Pete Harman (the first person to buy into the franchise 12 years earlier) proved hard to refuse. Harland agreed to sell for what was then a substantial sum of $2 million ($14 million today) on the condition that he still keep a hand in the business as an ambassador for the company. He was in charge of quality control, and his image was used as the company trademark. Under the terms of the agreement, the investment group bought national and international franchise rights, excluding England, Florida, Utah and Montana. Harland retained ownership of the franchises in Canada.

The new owners pumped investment funds into the business and the company set its sights on expanding more, both within North America and globally.

Soon KFC outlets spanned all 50 states, and the business established a foothold in Puerto Rico, Mexico, Japan, Jamaica and the Bahamas. The first European site opened in Preston, England, in 1964. In the mid-1960s, KFC ranked sixth in volume among food-service companies, with 1,500 take-out stands and restaurants. Franchising remained the core of the business's expansion plans, and the now well-known red-and-white-striped buildings were developed to attract tourists and residents to the brand.

In 1966, the KFC Advertising Co-op was established, giving franchisees 10 votes and the company three when deciding advertising budgets and campaigns. Franchisees benefited from a share in company equipment and supply sales, and a National Franchisee Advisory Council was also established.

Franchising remained the core of the business's expansion plans, and the now well-known red-and-white-striped buildings were developed to attract tourists and residents to the brand.

Buoyed by the success of the business's rapid expansion, the company went public, listing on the New York Stock Exchange in 1969, with Harland buying the first 100 shares.

At this point the new owners were looking at ways to streamline the business. Plans to reduce overhead—in particular labor costs—were put into action, by transforming Harland's original idea of a sit-down eatery into a fast-food, stand-up concept, with emphasis on fast service. The business grew at a phenomenal rate, and some franchisees had already become millionaires. But KFC found that such growth was to come at a price. With franchisees making money at such a fast rate, there was very little incentive for them to stay with KFC long-term instead of turning to new ventures (at one point the management team had 21 millionaires reporting to it!). This meant that successful franchisees were only prepared to commit to the business for a year or two, resulting in a lack of strongly established, and experienced, franchisees.

At the same time, negative reports about the accounting practices of other franchise operations appeared in the media, and as a result—although the reports were not connected to KFC—the company's share price took a beating, dropping to $10 per share from a high of $55.50 in 1969. It signaled a worrying time for the business, and several key players, including Jack Massey, resigned following a series of disagreements. A new management team with a background in food and finance was swiftly appointed to revive financial fortunes. It signaled the end of the road for Harland's involvement with the company, and he resigned from the board of directors. At the grand old age of 80, even he knew his limits.

In an article in the *New York Times*, he said: "[I] realized that I was someplace I had no place being ... Everything that a board of a big corporation does is over my head, and I'm confused by the talk and high finance discussed at these meetings."

Changing hands

As part of the plan to revive KFC, the business merged with food and alcoholic beverage business Heublein Inc. in 1971, when sales stood at $700 million, and John Brown left the business following this deal. It seemed a wise move as Heublein's expertise was in marketing, an area in which the business received a much-needed boost. Introducing new products such as barbecued ribs was also the order of the day, and although the new lines proved popular, they masked the fact that sales of fried chicken were declining. After a while the sales boost waned, and the business once again began to falter.

By the early 1970s, relationships with existing US franchisees were at an all-time low, a problem that had been brewing since Brown and Massey bought the business. Franchisees were now selling more per store than company-owned units and resented paying royalty fees to what they perceived to be an ineffective brand owner.

Franchisees felt Heublein was too corporate for their liking, and a contract battle ensued. The management team was determined to rely on positive relationships built in the past, despite a number of disputes over contracts and a communication breakdown.

Consequently, the brand's image began to suffer in the public eye, and turnaround plans began in earnest for the physical identity of the business and for its core product, fried chicken. Efforts were made to revert to Harland's original cooking methods and the menu was scaled down to reduce costs. Sadly, Harland died in 1980 from leukemia and was unable to see the transformation take effect.

New horizons

Going back to basics helped lift the business's fortunes and culminated in an advertising campaign—"We do chicken right"—that proved so successful it ran for seven years. In 1982, parent company Heublein was acquired by R.J. Reynolds Industries, which provided a vital cash injection, a platform for further international expansion, and a new vision for the business. That year, sales reached an impressive $2.4 billion, largely credited to the fact that the business refused to imitate competitors and introduce a flurry of new products, concentrating instead on refining its existing proposition.

Going back to basics helped lift the business's fortunes and culminated in an advertising campaign—"We do chicken right"—that proved so successful it ran for seven years.

It was a turnaround that did not go unnoticed by food and beverage giant PepsiCo, and in 1986, keen to secure a large market for its own drinks, it acquired KFC for $840 million, impressed by the latter's increase in worldwide revenues. It seemed a natural fit, too, as PepsiCo already owned fellow fast-food chains Taco Bell and Pizza Hut.

The new owners wanted to continue to develop the business and therefore opened the Colonel Sanders Technical Center to foster product development. The business experimented with the concept of oven-roasted chicken and a home delivery model. It also set its sights on further global expansion, culminating with the opening of an outlet in the People's Republic of China in 1987—the first US fast-food chain to establish a presence in the country.

On the outside the business appeared to have gotten back on track, but relationships with US franchisees were still strained. Although they were impressed with their new owner's expertise and access to international markets, many American franchisees felt they did not have enough say in the business. Competitors were developing new product lines while KFC struggled to innovate the fried chicken concept, with Hot Wings and sandwich-style chicken its only new offerings.

It was a different story globally, however, as international markets continued to thrive, on both the financial and franchisee-relationship side, with pre-tax profits of $92 million in 1992, as opposed to $86 million in America. Sales in Asia and operations in Australia were particularly strong, and the company seized the opportunity to capitalize on this, with plans to open an outlet outside of the US every day. Innovations introduced in global operations were often used as a model for entering new markets.

Where are they now?

One of KFC's healthier options.

Amid growing concerns about the health risks associated with fried foods in 1991, the business changed its name to KFC. PepsiCo sold KFC to Yum! Restaurants International along with its other fast-food businesses in 2002. The business continues to thrive today, adjusting its product range as consumer demand shifts. For instance, the company has removed all trans fats from its products, and Kentucky Grilled Chicken was launched in 2009 in North America to great success.

In keeping with growing concerns regarding the environment, in 2011 KFC also launched its first eco-friendly restaurant in Indianapolis. The restaurant, designed "with the planet in mind," provides another example of how KFC will continually adapt to the times to ensure it remains a profitable business.

It may be over 30 years since Colonel Harland Sanders died, but his standards and belief in the product have lived on. His secret recipe is one that is guarded closely even today, locked away in a vault in Louisville, Kentucky. Only a handful of people know what goes into the recipe, and they are sworn to secrecy. Meanwhile, millions of people enjoy the Colonel's products every day, across the world.

Microsoft

A technology empire begins

Founders: **Bill Gates (shown) and Paul Allen**	
Age of founders: **20 and 22**	
Background: **Students of computing**	
Founded in: **1975**	
Headquarters: **Redmond, Washington**	
Business type: **Computer software**	

One of the world's richest people, Bill Gates hardly needs an introduction. Software made by the company he co-founded runs almost all personal computers (PCs) in the world today. Microsoft is one of the world's largest corporations, making over $23 billion in profit on revenue of almost $70 billion in 2011.

Yet, this company began in the same way as many others in this book, with two ambitious young people who had a dream. Back then, in 1975, there were no PCs on desks or in homes, and the few people who knew what a "computer" was knew them as substantial machines that took up a large room and needed specialists to operate them. Even so, Bill, a college student, and his co-founder, Paul Allen, a recent graduate, believed that software and computers were going to grow dramatically as a business, and they were determined to be part of it. Even with their foresight, they could not have dreamed back then of quite how far their vision would go.

Computer skills

Bill was born in Seattle in 1955 to an affluent family, with his father a prominent lawyer. He was gifted at math but was otherwise unremarkable. In 1968, his first year at private school, the school got its first computer—in fact, just a terminal linked into a PDP-10 computer made by Digital Equipment Corporation. The computer was owned by General Electric Corporation, which leased it by the hour to Bill's school. It was a very long way from today's computers, which meant it was popular with just a handful of boys who wrote programs on it using a programming language called BASIC (Beginner's All-purpose Symbolic Instruction Code). Bill's first programs were games: first tic-tac-toe, then *Lunar Lander*, a game about landing a space shuttle safely on the moon before it ran out of fuel.

Bill would spend hours in his school's computer lab using this machine, and it was here that he met Paul, a fellow school pupil two years older than Bill. They continued to develop their interest in computers at school, running up enormous bills way beyond anything the school had originally imagined. The school understandably set limits on the amount of time they could spend on the computer.

Bill and Paul literally breathed computers day and night, and when Bill was only 13 years old, they were tasked with their first "IT project" for the Computer Center Corporation ("C-Cubed"). The company, recently established in Seattle, owned a mainframe computer that Bill's school hooked up to using its terminal. A company director was impressed with Bill and the other students' skills and tasked them with finding software bugs in return for unlimited time on the computer after normal working hours; the boys were often there until midnight!

"It was when we got free time at C-Cubed that we really got into computers," Bill remembers. "I mean, then I became hard core. It was day and night." Through this the boys were able to ask the C-Cubed staff all sorts of questions, vastly expanding their computing knowledge. Bill and Paul stood out from their school friends because of their enthusiasm for computers.

Over the next few years, word spread about Bill's and Paul's abilities, and they were asked to develop a payroll system for a local company in return for receiving more computer time and some royalties on any sales of the system. After that, they came up with a program that could count city traffic which they sold to the city of Seattle, but they reportedly never made much profit from it.

Software adopter

In 1973, Bill enrolled at Harvard University, where he proved himself one of the most gifted students at math. Also at Harvard, he met fellow student Steve Ballmer, who was studying math and science and who would later play a significant role in Microsoft's history. Much like in high school, however, Bill found himself missing classes on a regular basis to indulge his passion for computers. He even considered quitting college to look for a job and had several interviews. While Bill was undecided about what the future would hold, the US economy, too, was looking unstable. By 1973, the US officially entered a period of economic recession.

Over the next two years, while the recession deepened, Bill continued to study at Harvard, but he also kept in close touch with Paul, who was now working for computing company Honeywell, based in Boston. The young men were convinced that there would be an enormous computing boom and were determined to be part of it. After their earlier forays into the business world, they knew they wanted to set up their own business and were on the lookout for the right time and opportunity to do so.

Chance sighting

In January 1975, on his way to visit Bill at college, Paul came across a trade magazine for the computer industry, *Popular Electronics*, featuring a new computer called the Altair 8080 on the cover. This machine was manufactured by Model Instrumentation and Telemetry System (MITS), a company based in Albuquerque, New Mexico, which claimed it would offer the world's first affordable computer for the general public. Thousands of people had already placed orders for one, eager to get their hands on what was then a revolutionary piece of technology. The Altair bore little resemblance to the computers we use today, lacking both keyboard and mouse. These computers had to be assembled from a kit and then programmed in binary code using switches on the front panel. Unsurprisingly, this limited their appeal to electronics enthusiasts.

Bill and Paul felt sure that this was the opportunity for which they had been waiting. They thought that they could write a version of BASIC for the Altair, which would be much easier to use than the binary code. MITS would be sure to sell lots of copies of it, earning good money for Bill and Paul.

Just a few days after the magazine had come out announcing the Altair, they phoned Ed Roberts, the head of MITS, to offer him a BASIC program for the Altair. This move demonstrated the pair's ambition and drive, for in reality, although they had talked about writing a version of BASIC, they had not actually developed anything yet; they wanted to gauge the company's reaction first. Roberts explained that he had received many such calls, and that the first people to deliver a program that worked would get the deal. "We realized that the revolution might happen without us," Bill said. "After we saw that article, there was no question of where our life would focus."

Risky business

The pair faced two serious challenges, however: neither of them had access to an Altair computer (or had even seen one with his own eyes—in fact the only one in the world was still at MITS at this stage), and they hadn't even begun to write the software. MITS asked Paul and Bill to fly out the following month to demonstrate their program, unknowingly giving them the time they needed to write it. Sensing their first real opportunity to start a computer business, Bill and Paul set about writing the software. Using Harvard University's computers, Paul worked on a program to imitate the Altair's system as closely as possible, working at night after his day job, while Bill worked both day and night writing reams upon reams of code for the BASIC language itself. Although BASIC had already been invented, nobody had ever made a version for a minicomputer, let alone something as small as the new Altair, and many experts declared that it could not be done.

As their deadline drew closer, Paul and Bill roped in fellow Harvard students to help complete the code. Eight weeks after the phone call to Ed Roberts, Paul flew out to Albuquerque to meet with MITS. None of the MITS executives believed that the program would work, and indeed just one bug could have stopped it. But against all the odds, Paul used BASIC to get the Altair to add 2 + 2, and the machine gave the crowd watching the answer: 4. The program worked!

Bill negotiated a deal whereby MITS agreed to buy the rights to the program, even though there were still quite a few bugs that needed to be fixed. The two young men celebrated what would turn out to be their new company's first deal by going out for ice cream and soft drinks.

Things moved quickly from there. In June 1975, both Paul and Bill moved to Albuquerque, with Paul working officially as director of software at Altair (having left Honeywell) while Bill took a leave of absence from Harvard and worked on perfecting the software code. They both signed a 10-year contract giving MITS exclusive rights to the Altair version of BASIC and the right to license it out to third parties. For their part, Bill and Paul received a royalty of between $30 and $60 for every copy sold, and MITS agreed to promote and market their software. When BASIC was sold together with an Altair it would typically cost around $50, whereas when sold separately, the price could be as much as 10 times more.

The two young men celebrated what would turn out to be their new company's first deal by going out for ice cream and soft drinks.

Paul and Bill also formalized their partnership at this point, with Bill initially owning 60 percent and Paul 40 percent, as Bill argued that he had done more of the initial programming. They later changed this split so that Bill ended up with 64 percent and Paul 36 percent. Despite being independently wealthy from a trust fund he had inherited, Bill was determined not to use that money for his business, so he and Paul kept their costs to a bare minimum, sharing a room in a dingy Albuquerque hotel to start.

They quickly hired two of their friends from the computer club at their school in Seattle to help them work on debugging BASIC and other programs for the Altair. The four shared an apartment and shared an obsessive work ethic, with all of them utterly committed to developing software as fast as they could, building up enormous team spirit between them. They worked at a small office next to MITS and would often fall asleep at work. One time a MITS executive was giving someone a tour of the office and came across Bill asleep on the floor.

Orders for Altairs flooded in and MITS could barely keep up with the demand. Strangely enough, though, sales of the software remained in the low hundreds, and Bill soon figured out why: his version of BASIC had been pirated and was being distributed freely among Altair users. While these users were happy to pay for the hardware and associated computer accessories, it became clear that they saw software as something to be shared freely.

It was not a view that Bill subscribed to, however. He already believed that software, more than anything else, would be the single most important force for the future of personal computing, and for this to happen, it had to be paid for. He was so passionate about this that he wrote a letter to a trade magazine, bemoaning the fact that people expected software to be free. If this were the case, how would developers be paid? Such was Bill's passion that his letter gained considerable support from business partners and led to paid-for, copyrighted software becoming the industry standard.

It was not only the letter that was significant, but the way Bill signed it: "Bill Gates, general partner, Micro-Soft." They had come up with this name during the summer by combining microcomputer with software. Bill and Paul soon dropped the hyphen.

Microsoft takes shape

While Paul worked at MITS, both he and Bill also developed their software company. They were enormously excited by the potential of the burgeoning PC market and were desperate to take advantage of it. MITS launched a floppy disk drive for the Altair and asked Paul and Bill to adapt their BASIC program to work with it.

The following year, in 1976, Paul quit MITS to concentrate on Microsoft full-time, and the business hired new programmers and moved into its first offices, on the eighth floor of a bank building in Albuquerque. In November of that year, they registered the name Microsoft as a trademark. Bill formally dropped out of Harvard at the end of 1976 to concentrate full-time on the business. His parents were not happy with his decision and tried to talk him out of it, but he was absolutely convinced that computers would eventually enable people and businesses to save time and money, thus creating an enormous business opportunity, and he was determined to be part of this impending growth.

MITS may have been the company that launched Bill and Paul toward fame, but less than two years later, it was holding back Microsoft's growth potential. MITS was still struggling to keep up with demand for Altairs and was facing some serious reliability issues with some key components. Meanwhile, dozens of new competitors wanted to license a version of Microsoft's BASIC. Bill negotiated deal after deal with these companies, but under the terms of Microsoft's agreement with MITS, MITS had to approve these deals. MITS felt the deals were too competitive and withheld its approval, enraging Bill, who felt deprived of enormous income.

Bill formally dropped out of Harvard. ... He was absolutely convinced that computers would eventually enable people and businesses to save time and money, thus creating an enormous business opportunity, and he was determined to be part of this impending growth.

Before long, MITS was in decline and struggling, and in 1977 it was sold to Pertec Computer Corporation. Pertec wanted MITS for its rights to BASIC. Bill and Paul knew they had to wrestle control of their program back somehow, as their original contract with MITS had set a limit on how much they could get paid. They now knew that the market potential for it was substantially larger.

They consulted Bill's father, the Seattle lawyer. A clause in their original contract stated that MITS had to use its "best efforts" to sub-license the BASIC program, and Microsoft was able to prove that by refusing to sign deals with other manufacturers, MITS was in breach of the contract.

Microsoft used this to get the rights to its program back, after a three-week-long hearing. Microsoft then set about selling versions of its BASIC program to manufacturers of other computers, such as Commodore's PET, Tandy's TRS80, and Apple's Apple II, which were all taking off. Bill, who was a voracious reader of business books, negotiated the deals, while Paul concentrated on programming.

In an astounding feat, Bill took the company to Japan when it was just two years old. He found a computer whiz kid there his own age, Kuzuhiko Nishi, and used him as an agent to build business with Japan's growing computer companies.

The bigger picture

At the time, Bill and Paul had what seemed extraordinarily ambitious goals for their company: they wanted a computer on every desk and envisioned a future with Microsoft on every computer. As these computers became more powerful, the demand for more powerful software grew. It was now possible, for example, to move words around documents in word-processing programs and to manipulate crude images at much faster speeds than previously possible.

Over the next three years the founders added new programs, mainly other programming languages. They continued to work long hours, with Bill getting involved with the programming as well as driving the sales efforts. He called several big corporations to persuade them to use his software and programming languages on their mainframe computers. This approach worked wonders: as more and more companies became interested in the company's software, the business grew. Bill hired programmers to help with this expansion, many of whom he knew from his high school and college days.

At the time, Bill and Paul had what seemed extraordinarily ambitious goals for their company: they wanted a computer on every desk and envisioned a future with Microsoft on every computer.

By 1978, Microsoft had around a dozen employees, but Bill was finding it harder and harder to persuade programmers to move to Albuquerque. Since Microsoft had no more links with MITS, it didn't seem to make sense to keep the business there. Subsequently, they decided to relocate the business, and although most technology companies at the time were located in California, they chose Seattle, close to where Bill was brought up and where his family still lived.

The move coincided with a rethink of the business. In keeping with the original vision, Bill knew that for Microsoft to thrive, he would need to come up with something bigger and more ambitious than BASIC software systems. He wanted to tap into the burgeoning market for operating system and word-processing software. Bill also needed to get more sales expertise on board, and he turned to his college friend Steve Ballmer. He joined Microsoft as business manager, and soon became an expert at promoting and marketing the business.

Golden opportunity

What would turn out to be one of the century's greatest business opportunities presented itself toward the end of 1979. Bill had found out that hardware manufacturer IBM, the world's leading manufacturer of mainframe computers, was looking for an operating system for a new PC that it was to launch shortly. This was IBM's first attempt to make a substantial impact in the PC market, which it could see was growing rapidly. As IBM wanted the product made in a short space of time, it decided not to build its own computer from scratch but to buy different elements from other companies.

Bill decided that Microsoft should be the company to create the operating system IBM needed. Microsoft bought an existing software system from a company called Seattle Computer for a hotly negotiated one-off fee of $50,000 (and a few other minor rights—spare a thought for the people who sold it for relative peanuts) and used this as the basis for a new operating system called MS-DOS (Microsoft Disk Operating System). Microsoft put nearly half of its programmers (there were around 60 by this time) to work on this system over the course of a year.

Microsoft then attempted to license this software to IBM. It was a very competitive battle, with other software companies also very keen to work with IBM on what they all thought would be an enormously successful new product launch. In the end, Microsoft won, and it negotiated to license its operating system to IBM on a royalty basis. (Having learned from its experience with MITS, Microsoft insisted that it retain the rights to the program.) Every time a copy of MS-DOS was sold, IBM would pay a fee to Microsoft. IBM agreed and signed the deal that was the making of Microsoft as we now know it.

Microsoft's ubiquitous software.

Just one year later, in 1981, MS-DOS became the industry standard and sales more than doubled at Microsoft, from $7 million in 1980 to $16 million a year later. Part of the reason for this rapid growth was that as IBM had used off-the-shelf parts to build its PCs, it was easy for other computer manufacturers to follow suit and build similar machines, all of which could run MS-DOS. Bill was quick to capitalize on this, supplying MS-DOS software to IBM competitors. By 1982, Microsoft's revenues had grown to $32 million and the company had grown to around 200 employees.

Every time a copy of MS-DOS was sold, IBM would pay a fee to Microsoft. IBM agreed and signed the deal that was the making of Microsoft as we now know it.

Just a year later, however, Paul made the decision to leave. Having been diagnosed with Hodgkin's disease, an illness that could be treated, he decided he wanted to focus on other interests.

Where are they now?

Throughout the 1980s, Bill concentrated on growing an international sales force for Microsoft and developing additional products, including Office and Windows, so named because of the separate frames that users could create on their computer screens. Microsoft launched the first version of Windows in 1985, though it would take several upgrades before it really began to take off.

Microsoft went public in 1986, listing its shares on the NASDAQ. The company's spectacular performance in the stock market made an estimated four billionaires and 12,000 millionaires out of Microsoft employees alone and cemented Microsoft's status as one of the largest tech companies in the world, with a net worth of $224 billion in 2011.

Bill stepped down as chief executive in 2000, with Steve Ballmer taking over. In 2008 Bill announced that he was focusing on a career in philanthropy; he remains chairman of the business.

Chapter authors

SPANX	Carol Tice
Electronic Arts	Carol Tice
Pixar	Carol Tice
Zipcar	Carol Tice
eBay	Kim Benjamin
Etsy	Carol Tice
Groupon	Carol Tice
LinkedIn	Kim Benjamin
Match.com	Ryan Platt
Twitter	Carol Tice
TripAdvisor	Jeff Meyer
Zynga	Carol Tice
Chipotle Mexican Grill	Carol Tice
Gatorade	Jeff Meyer
Jamba Juice	Carol Tice
Pinkberry	Carol Tice
Whole Foods Market	Jeff Meyer
Blackberry (RIM)	Stephanie Welstead
Dropbox	Jeff Meyer
Google	Stephanie Welstead
The Coca-Cola Company	Beth Bishop
IBM	Kim Benjamin
The Walt Disney Company	Sara Rizk
KFC	Kim Benjamin
Microsoft	Kim Benjamin